THE AGE
OF ARTHUR

THE AGE
OF ARTHUR

A History of
the British Isles from 350 to 650

JOHN MORRIS

Senior Lecturer in History
University College London

Volume One: Roman Britain
and the Empire of Arthur

PHILLIMORE

1977
Published by
PHILLIMORE & CO. LTD.
London and Chichester

Head Office: Shopwyke Hall,
Chichester, Sussex, England

First published by Weidenfeld and Nicolson
1973

ISBN 0 85033 289 3

Printed and bound in Great Britain by Biddles Ltd
www.biddles.co.uk

To
C.E. STEVENS
who inspired

CONTENTS

Table of Dates

Summary of Events

Abbreviations

Notes

Index

MAPS

INTRODUCTION

This book surveys the history of the British Isles between the end of Roman Britain and the birth of England and Wales. Its aim is to make that history manageable, like the history of other periods.

In the 420s, the government of Roman Britain enlisted Saxon, or English barbarians from Germany to strengthen their defences; but in the 440s the English rebelled. Half a century of bitter fighting destroyed the Roman economy and technology of Britain, but the British won the war, under the leadership of Arthur, who restored the forms of Roman imperial government. The empire of Arthur lasted for some twenty years and on his death fragmented into a large number of small independent successor states. The English were contained within substantial defined reservations until they rebelled for a second time, at the end of the sixth century. In a generation they subdued most of what is now England; thenceforth the independent native British were confined to the west, and were called Welsh, a word that in old English meant 'foreigners'.

The personality of Arthur is unknown and unknowable. But he was as real as Alfred the Great or William the Conqueror; and his impact upon future ages mattered as much, or more so. Enough evidence survives from the hundred years after his death to show that reality was remembered for three generations, before legend engulfed his memory. More is known of his achievement, of the causes of his sovereignty and of its consequences than of the man himself. His triumph was the last victory of western Rome; his short lived empire created the future nations of the English and the Welsh; and it was during his reign and under his authority that the Scots first came to Scotland. His victory and his defeat turned Roman Britain into Great Britain. His name overshadows his age.

Two centuries of war and of separate co-existence moulded a political society unlike that of Europe, where Roman and barbarian experience merged more easily. These centuries are a historical period in their own right, more than a transition or interlude between Rome and the Middle Ages. To be understood, a well-defined period needs a name, as clear in meaning as Roman, Norman or

Tudor. The fifth and sixth centuries in Britain are properly termed the Age of Arthur, for modern historical convention normally labels periods according to their principal rulers. In early medieval Europe it distinguishes Merovingian and Carolingian periods, so called after dynasties who took their names from individuals. The Carolingian age extends from the grandfather of Charles the Great to his grandchildren's time; but the substance of history does not turn upon the personal ancestry of rulers. Though he had no royal father and founded no dynasty, Arthur was the heir of the emperors before him, and the kings who followed knew themselves to be 'heirs of great Arthur'. He straddles two centuries, and names them as fitly as Charles the Great names the eighth and ninth centuries in Europe.

The Arthurian age is the starting point of future British history. Thereafter, Britain has comprised England, Wales and Scotland; previously, these three countries did not exist. Their later history is harder to understand if their formative years are overlooked; for nations, like people, tend to form habits in infancy that their adult years harden and modify. But the early history must be seen in its own context; if its evidence is superficially raked over in a search for the origins of later institutions, then it is as uninformative as an archaeological site plundered by treasure hunters.

These centuries have often been termed the 'Dark Ages'. They are not dark for lack of evidence. The quantity of evidence is immense and unusually complex, hard to understand. Therefore it has been neglected, abandoned to a small number of specialists, who have often been obliged to limit their studies to their own particular patch. The specialist in pagan English pottery or brooches is rarely conversant with the literature of early Ireland, with late Roman administration, with Welsh or Germanic law, with Italian theology or old Welsh poems, with the techniques of the farmer and the shipbuilder, or with a dozen other disciplines that must be brought together, and related to the history of Europe, if the age is to be understood.

No one can be master of all these trades. The historian must be content to be the pupil and interpreter of many of them. But he must do his best to bring them together, for the evidence seems obscure only because its modern study is inadequate and fragmented. The significance of excavated objects cannot be perceived until they can be related to the written record of the people who used them. Yet most of the texts are made up of half truths, for they are abstracts derived from lost originals, distorted by the ignorance or interest of their compilers. They await the kind of critical scrutiny that centuries of scholarship have lavished upon the texts of other periods. Because that work has not yet been undertaken the historian of the fifth and sixth centuries has special problems. He has no main 'reliable' narrative witness, like Tacitus or Bede, to justify him in dismissing other evidence as 'unreliable' or 'forged'. He must borrow from the techniques of the archaeologist, and must uncover a mass of separate detail, most of it encrusted and corroded by the distortion of later ages. He must clean off as much of the distortion as he can, try to discover what the original sources said and then relate their statements to one another, and to the rest of the evidence.

The aim is modest, and has been well expressed by Professor Ludwig Bieler.

> according to a widely accepted view, it is the historian's task to find out 'what actually happened'. . . . This, I believe, is impossible. The historian cannot do more than collect, assess and interpret evidence.

He has to sum up like a judge, and decide like a jury. He may not blankly refuse to decide, but he cannot proclaim certainty. He must give an informed opinion on what is probable and improbable, and return an open verdict when the balance of evidence suggests no probability. He may not insinuate like an advocate, whose plea that evidence falls short of absolute proof covertly invites his hearers to disbelieve the evidence. It is irrelevant for him to assert his personal belief or disbelief. There is a reason for every statement in every text, and for the place where every archaeological object was found. His business is to ferret out the reasons. He may conclude that an author lied or misunderstood; but falsehood must be demonstrated as carefully as accuracy, and may not be casually implied by labelling a statement 'dubious', without argument. But, unlike the verdict of the jury, his conclusion is constantly subject to appeal, and he must therefore clearly distinguish between what his evidence says and what he deduces from it, that others may easily correct his inferences in the light of new evidence and deeper understanding. If he fails to offer clear conclusions from the evidence he knows, he infects his readers with false beliefs and woolly notions; if he leaves no conclusion to correct, the importance of new evidence is easily missed. He must acknowledge his own sympathies as openly as a Tacitus or a Bede, for the historian who rashly pretends to be free of bias unconsciously surrenders to the superficial assumptions of his own day; and is therefore always misleading, and usually dull.

The evidence must first be collected. Most of the main texts are printed, but many are to be found only in large or specialist libraries. They cannot be studied unless they are assembled for constant reference and comparison; and this book could not have been written without the exceptional facilities generously provided by librarians, especially of University College London, and of the London Library, who permitted rare volumes to be retained on loan for years at a time. The difficulty of getting at the sources is one of the main reasons why the period is so poorly understood; for any historical study is lamed if it can only be undertaken by a few experts, whose judgement their readers cannot easily criticise. If the Arthurian period is to be studied seriously in the future, the first need is to make the sources accessible, no longer the secret lore of the learned. The first steps have been taken. The most important single texts, *Gildas*, *Nennius* and *Patrick*, will shortly be easily available, in text and translation, with comment; the rest of the main evidence is collected in my *Arthurian Sources* (forthcoming), where the separate texts of Annals, Genealogies, Saints' Lives and other sources are collated, and the scattered information about people, places and problems is assembled and assessed in detail. The study of this collected evidence prompts the conclusions here expressed, some of which are bound to seem abrupt and dogmatic until these publications appear.

The Age of Arthur interprets this evidence. It places most weight on contemporary statements, for in any age the contemporary cannot outrageously falsify the knowledge that he shares with his readers; for the same reason, texts written within living oral memory of the events they relate command respect. A modern writer may distort the actions and motives of contemporary individuals or distant peoples, but he could not assert that modern Britain is immune from war or ignorant of electric power; he might bamboozle an illiterate audience with a story that Napoleon fought Marlborough at Minden, but he could not pretend that Gladstone lived in the eighteenth century, for many men are still alive who know that Gladstone lived in their fathers' time. So when Gildas told his readers that theirs was an age of civil war and external peace, and that Vortigern and Ambrosius Aurelianus had lived in their fathers' time, he could not have done so if these matters of public knowledge were wholly untrue. But once the threshold of living memory is passed, after about a hundred years, the antiquity of a text is of small moment; many that were written a thousand years later follow their sources more closely than others written two or three hundred years after the event.

Interpretation rests upon bringing the evidence together, once the superficial deposit of later fancy has been removed, for it is no use discussing the meaning of the sources, until we know what they do and do not say, as exactly as we can. The history is narrated and described by bringing their separate statements together. Not much faith can be placed on a single statement by a single source; confidence grows when a number of independent sources each tell something of the same story. The proof of the pudding is in the eating. The evidence hangs together, and tells its own story. Innumerable separate details combine into a plain and credible tale, more coherent than any that an ingenious later historian could devise.

The tale is plain. But any account that is built up from a mass of small items of evidence seems complex at first sight. It is doubly difficult to explain the age of Arthur simply, for most of the names are unfamiliar. The historians of later periods, whose kings are conveniently numbered, may assume that their readers know that Henry VII reigned before Henry VIII; and many well known tales make it clear that Elizabeth ruled after and not before the Henries. But in the fifth and sixth centuries even the names of persons of comparable importance are known only to specialists, and their relation to each other in time and place is often clouded, compelling examination of the evidence. In order that the unfamiliar names, dates and events may be more easily understood, a short Summary of Events and a Table of Dates is provided.

The story that the sources tell raised a difficulty that was not at first foreseen. It had been intended to start from the relatively firm ground of the late Roman Empire, and to end in the middle of the seventh century, whose events Bede recorded within living memory. But it soon became apparent that much that has been written in modern times about the seventh and eighth centuries jars awkwardly against the earlier evidence. The reason is evident. Many of those who studied the early English were well acquainted with later medieval history, and looked back from the standpoint of Norman or Plantagenet England. But the processes of history move forward in time; men are influenced by the experience of their forebears, but they know nothing of their descendants' problems; and history looks different when viewed the right way up. It has therefore been necessary to discuss some later problems, where misconceptions about the Arthurian period and its immediate sequel have caused misunderstanding. This discussion does not set out to contradict what others have written; rather, it deals with different questions, for much that looked puzzling from an eleventh-century standpoint seems no problem at all in the context of the sixth century, while some of the assumptions that seemed natural to historians of the middle ages prove alien to thinking of earlier ages. It has also been necessary to discuss some aspects of barbarian and medieval European history that have not been systematically explored; and therefore to disregard some modern notions entertained about them. Such differences of approach do not assert greater wisdom or understanding; they are the result of fortunate chances that have given me the opportunity to read and sift more varied sources than most other individuals.

It has only recently become possible to attempt an overall history of the Arthurian age, thanks to a number of important publications that have pulled together several sections of the evidence. They rest upon much detailed work, whose conclusions cannot always be discussed within the limits of this book. It has proved necessary to stick to the principle expressed by H.M. and N.K.Chadwick in the preface to their *Growth of Literature*:

> if we had read more widely, we would not have completed this book . . . which might have been the better course. The amount of time at our disposal is limited; we have preferred to give as much of it as possible to the primary authorities.

It is therefore necessary to apologise to the very many scholars whose work is not here acknowledged, and has often not been adequately assessed. It is also impossible to acknowledge the many scholars whose kind advice has been freely offered on many details; my expressed gratitude must be limited to those whose unfailing patience my many queries have most heartily exploited, notably Professor Kenneth Jackson and Professor Idris Foster; Mr J.M.Dodgson and Professor D.M.Wilson; and Professor Christopher Hawkes; to Michael Gullick, who drew the maps to my specification, with limitless patience; and to Dr John

Wilkes, Dr Ann Ward and Miss Vivienne Menkes, who have kindly read and commented upon the typescript. None of them of course bear any responsibility for the way in which their advice has been treated. I am also grateful to the indulgence of the publisher, since the mass of unfamiliar names and concepts has made it necessary to use capitals, figures and punctuation for clarity and emphasis, in disregard of convention; and I am particularly indebted to the advice and help of Julian Shuckburgh and Sue Phillpott.

The interpretation here given of the Arthurian Age can be no more than a preliminary attempt to open up questions, and to make it easier for future specialist studies to relate their conclusions to a wider context. The book is therefore published in the confident expectation that many of its conclusions will soon be modified or corrected. It will have served its purpose if it makes such correction possible. It would be kind if readers who detect figure mistakes or errors of fact, in the text or the notes, would notify the author, via the publisher.

This reprint includes some corrections of substance. It has not yet been possible to correct minor misprints, spelling and punctuation which do not mislead.

John Morris

This is a heavy book, not easily absorbed at one reading. For the sake of the reader's staying power, purpose and pocket, the limp edition has therefore been divided into three volumes, sold separately, covering the events of the fifth century; of the sixth and seventh; and an analysis of the changing society.

I have avoided the current fashion of chopping history into little boxes, mis-leadingly labelled 'social', 'economic', 'political' or the like. History is simply the study of the interaction of men with one another and with their environment. 'Economic forces' and 'social pressures' mean nothing more than the overall effect of a lot of people of varied strengths pushing and being pushed in different directions; the actions of these people are 'political'. But you cannot make sense of men's struggles or passivity until you have got the events in the right order. Until you know which events and which people came first, and where, you cannot know who put what idea into whose head when. Until you know that, you cannot begin to guess why some forces and pressures were acceptable and changed men's lives, why others were damp failures.

The order of these three volumes is, therefore, a narrative of who did what when, followed by an analysis of who they were, why they did it, and to what effect. The ultimate effect is the society in which we live to-day.

John Morris

CHAPTER ONE

BRITAIN IN 350

In 350 Britain had been Roman for more than three hundred years. The lives and thoughts of her people were shaped and bounded by an economy common to the whole Roman empire; their public events were determined by imperial politics, their administration was controlled by men appointed in Italy. The empire still seemed eternal, an unquestioned guarantee of lasting peace. War was virtually confined to the frontiers, while behind them men knew of it only by hearsay. Within the Roman peace Britain had been particularly fortunate; barbarians might assault the northern forts or raid the coasts, but in the interior only one armed conflict is recorded in ten generations.

Much had changed in centuries of peace. Long ago, in the forgotten past, the British had been resentful natives ruled by foreign Romans. But for one hundred and forty years all freeborn provincials had been full Roman citizens, and five generations had made a reality of citizenship. Social difference divided the gentleman from the labourer, but each was as Roman as his counterpart in Italy or Africa or elsewhere. Apart from a handful of visitors, official or private, from other provinces, all the Romans in Britain were British, all the British Roman. The fourth-century Londoner was as much a Roman as the modern Londoner is English; to contrast 'Britons' with 'Romans' in the fourth century is as meaningless as to contrast modern Kentishmen with Englishmen.

Yet one immense difference distinguishes Roman and modern concepts of statehood. The Englishman confronts a German, a Frenchman, a Russian, who shares his civilisation, but obeys a separate national government. No comparable foreign state inflamed the patriotic sentiments of the Roman. Except in distant Persia, the frontier was the limit of civilisation, and the only foreigners were bloodthirsty savages whose law was the custom of their kin, or the command of warrior chiefs who drank deep in timber halls. The enemies of Britain, the Picts across the Forth and Clyde, the Scots of Ireland, the Franks and Saxons of the Low Countries, were barbarians like other foreigners, eager to burst upon the tempting wealth of Rome, plundering and killing poor and rich alike. In the face of the enemy, the common bond that linked Roman to Roman mattered more than the tensions which sundered one class or region from another. Half a century later, the poet Claudian sang of Rome who

Took the conquered to her bosom,
Made mankind a single family,
Mother, not mistress, of the nations,
Turning her subjects to citizens,
Conquering far-off lands a second time
By the bond of affection.

His orthodox enthusiasm was more than the propaganda of a government apologist. The event justified him, for, as the empire collapsed, none of its subject peoples took the opportunity to proclaim freedom from Rome; on the contrary, even the most radical rebels strove for a government better able to prolong its protective authority.

The common bond of Rome united unlike worlds, now separately ruled by two sons of the great Constantine. From his father's new city of Constantinople, Constantius reigned over the Greek-speaking provinces of the eastern mediterranean, whose magnates controlled three-quarters of the wealth of the empire and whose literate urban civilisation was older than Rome. The poorer western provinces obeyed his brother Constans. There, Roman conquest had first brought civilisation and towns, whose self-evident superiority had wiped out all but the haziest memories of the illiterate barbarian past.

In Britain and northern Gaul, urban civilisation had matured slowly. At first, government initiative had prompted the foundation of a few large towns, at once the symbol and the means of alien rule, each of them the capital of a native *civitas*, a people organised as a state. Each was the seat of a native administration, chosen by and from the native aristocracy, governing their fellow citizens under the remote but powerful supervision of the imperial governor. Recently, the word *civitas*, state, had shifted its meaning, to denote the physical city, the master and the natural head of all the urban and rural districts within its territory, termed *vici* and *pagi*. But the concentration of political authority matched a devolution of the economy. In the early empire, the roads between the towns had been furnished with small post-stations, each equipped with horses, carriages and waggons for the service of the government; but by the fourth century the majority of these stations had developed into thriving market towns, civil *vici* within their *civitas*.

In the early empire Britain had been polarised between a handful of imposing towns and a mass of farms and hamlets. Their pre-Roman economy was modified by the acquisition of commercial pottery, and presumably of more perishable manufactures; by a sprinkle of silver and copper coins, signs of produce sold on the market; and by corn-drying ovens, evidently constructed to service the same market. A few fortunate farmers, for the most part living within a mile or two of a town and a few hundred yards of a main road, prospered enough to build themselves solid, oblong stone-footed houses, with six or eight rooms on the ground floor; but they are rare exceptions beside the multitude of homesteads whose only archaeological trace is a trayful of potsherds, a few coins, or the post-holes of a timber cottage, often surrounded by tiny subdivided fields, the witness of peasant holdings still partitioned among the farmer's children.

In the fourth century, the solid farms are more numerous, the older ones enlarged and better appointed, save in a few coastal areas exposed to pirate raids, notably in Norfolk and the west Sussex plain. But the startling innovation is the sudden appearance, from about the beginning of the century, of great country mansions, normally enclosing three sides of a square some 150 feet to 200 feet long, containing anything from thirty to seventy ground-floor rooms, elaborately furnished with patterned mosaics, wall-paintings, heated rooms. Commonest in the Cotswold country, these houses are as commodious as their modern equivalents, Compton Wynyates, Hatfield House and the like, and one or two challenge comparison with Blenheim Palace. They are the homes of a nobility who lived more amply than any of their successors before the days of the Tudors, if not of the Georges.

Great men lived splendidly throughout the empire, but the scale and speed of recent prosperity was peculiar to Britain. Ninety years before, about the 260s, the continental frontiers had suddenly disintegrated, weakened by internal discord and assailed by barbarians grown more confident. Goths and Persians, Nubians and Moors had overrun the provinces they bordered, and the most terrible of all German invasions across the Rhine had destroyed the unwalled cities of Gaul. Only Italy and Britain escaped prolonged devastation. But the enemy were raiders who sought plunder to carry home; they were not yet invaders intent on settlement, and they therefore withdrew before a succession of strong military governments. The old frontiers were restored; but the wasted lands of northern Gaul recovered slowly, if at all. Henceforth the armies of the Rhine, whose needs they had hitherto supplied, were compelled to look to the cornlands and pastures of Britain for a substantial part of their supplies. The new-found prosperity of British agriculture is due, at least in part, to the sufferings of Gaul.

The fourth-century noblemen of Britain are voiceless and nameless. Whatever they wrote or did or said is unremembered. No document survives to illustrate their tastes and attitudes or to record their actions. Even their names are unknown. Nothing remains but the excavated ruins of their villas, set beside the archaeological traces of their peasants and their towns. Yet these material fragments describe a secure and comfortable aristocracy little different from their peers in Gaul. The nobility of Gaul lived in similar houses in the same economy, and something of their writing, their thinking and their action, described in their own words, has survived. The texture of their lives is plainly set forth in the easy verses of Ausonius, a fourth-century gentleman of Bordeaux upon whom chance thrust high office and great wealth. His favourite residence remained his ancestral estate of 1,000 acres, situated a few miles upstream from the city, whither

> The clear river's tidal flow
> Takes me by boat from home,
> And brings me home again. . . .
> Not far from town I live,
> Yet not hard by. . . .
> I change about,
> And get the best of town
> And country, turn by turn.

He was not only a landed gentleman, passing a part of the season in town; he was Professor of Latin in the University of Bordeaux, like his uncle before him. His father studied medicine and practised as a doctor, attending the poor without fee; he growled that though he sat on the local council, as befitted his rank, he never ran for public office, since he could not abide 'political agitation, party intrigue, lawsuits and scandal'. These were men whose code enjoined a paternal responsibility towards their social inferiors, and a duty of public service to the city of their birth and to the empire.

The rise of Ausonius and the proliferation of country mansions in Britain were symptoms of a general trend, the concentration of property in the hands of fewer and mightier magnates, at the expense of the poor and middling freeholders. Ausonius managed the numerous estates on which he did not live through his inefficient agent Philo,

> The image of his class,
> Grey, shockhaired, unkempt,
> A blustering bully . . .
> Visiting peasants, farms, towns and villages.

Increasingly, the great men passed the crippling burden of taxation on to the poor, and the Treasury found it cheaper to acquiesce. The law kept pace with economic change, reinforcing the authority of the *dominus*, master, over his dependents, distinguishing between *honestiores*, gentlemen, whom it condemned to fines, exile or execution by the sword, and *humiliores*, small freeholders, tenants, peasants, who expiated the same offences by torture, mutilation or burning at the stake. Starved by excessive taxation, bullied by blustering agents, denied justice in a landlord's court, the poor of farm, town and village were impelled to standing discontent and occasional rebellion.

The territorial magnates of the fourth century were powerful masters in their own districts, but they no longer dominated the central government. The old empire had been governed by the aristocracy of Italy, and of the Latin provinces of the western mediterranean coasts; and they had maintained a thinly spread frontier army on a shoestring budget. It was a necessary evil, but its costs were kept down because it was a static army largely financed by local supply. The new army was larger; the disasters of the mid-third century compelled it to maintain considerable mobile reserves, whose supply cost more. The new government was dominated by military men, who looked upon civilian landowners as the army's paymasters, and resented their selfish reluctance to pay for the army that protected their wealth. To constrain them to pay adequate taxes the government developed its bureaucracy, ill-paid, corrupt and ever-expanding. Its operations engulfed most of the finances and much of the jurisdiction that local landowners had once controlled through city councils. Fourth-century taxation assessed estates by the *caput*, head, and the *iugum*, yoke, that commonly measured the capacity of land; but the demands of revenue officials were more easily evaded by magnates than by modest landowners or town councillors.

The political administration was streamlined into an ordered hierarchy of small provinces, subject to four Praetorian Prefects, whose vice-prefects, or Vicars, each headed a *diocese* of several provinces. The four provinces of Britain, their capitals probably Cirencester, London, Lincoln and York, together constituted a single diocese within the prefecture of the Gauls. But the Vicars and the Provincial Governors were usually modest gentlemen whose tenure lasted one or two years; and they were exposed to the threats and bribes of provincial notables, who were often men of higher standing and greater political influence. Military commanders were as vulnerable. The *Magister Militum*, commander-in-chief, in control of a large field army and a variety of static frontier garrisons, was himself a man of might, high enough in rank to fear none but the emperor; but his subordinate officers were normally no more eminent than the civilian governors. In Britain, they were the Count of the Coast, later termed the Saxon Shore, who commanded a series of forts from Portsmouth to the Wash, and the *Dux Britanniarum*, responsible at York for the garrisons that held the northern frontier and policed the Pennines.

The geography of Britain gave the chance of somewhat greater independence to some of the governors and generals, for the towns, the great houses and the prosperous farms were virtually confined to the lowland south and east. Geologically, Britain is divided by a belt of limestone that snakes northwards from Lyme Regis by way of the Cotswolds, to the east of the Avon, the Trent and the Vale of York, to meet the sea again above Scarborough. It separates the fertile open lowland to the south and east from the heavier soils beyond. The north-west midlands are also low lying; and though all the lowland is interspersed with areas of heavy clay, that were often not broken to the plough before the later middle ages, it is free from natural obstacles, save for forests through which roads might easily be driven. It is therefore easily conquered, and as easily absorbs the civilisation of the conqueror. Beyond lie the rougher and poorer highland masses, the Pennines, the Welsh mountains, and the south-western moorlands of Exmoor, Dartmoor and Bodmin Moor. These three highland regions are separated from one another by the low-lying but less rewarding soils of Staffordshire and Cheshire, and by the rich lands of the Severn estuary.

These two gaps constitute the military keys to Britain in all ages. There the Roman armies constructed the fortresses of Chester and Wroxeter, of Gloucester and Caerleon; there were fought the decisive battles of the later English conquest, at Chester, and at Dyrham in Gloucestershire; there the Norman kings placed their marcher earldoms, and learnt from experience that the charge of Gloucester and Chester was most wisely entrusted to the king or his brother. Once these regions were secured, the sundered highlands found it hard to co-ordinate attack upon the lowlands, more natural to fight their battles on their own, easy to fight one another; for their hills enclose a multitude of valleys, whose population readily finds cause of dispute with its nearest neighbours. Control of the Severn and Dee estuaries has always secured the mastery of Britain. The Belgae and the Scandinavians failed to hold them or Britain; the armies of Parliament retained them in 1643 and 1644 and split the king's forces; and if Spanish, French or German armies had made good their landing, Chester and Gloucester would have become their necessary objectives, for the geography of Britain at all times concentrates political power in the lowlands, if the lowlands can hold their borders.

The geography of Britain also sharply separated the military from the civil power. Towns and villas, noblemen and their dependants were confined to the lowlands and the Severn shores. The backward conservative valleys of the Pennines, the Welsh mountains and the western moors supported no powerful landed nobility, and their only towns were those that grew around the army's forts. These differences also affected the social structure of Roman Britain. Throughout the empire the peasantry bore the double burden of rent and taxation that maintained the armies, the landowners and the administration. In the fourth century government and defence cost more, and the larger share of the burden fell upon the peasant. In many provinces much of the rural population was almost literally starved, paying up to five sixths of its produce in rent

---

Map 1

⌗	OLD ROCKS Palaeozoic and earlier
≡	SANDSTONES Triassic
∴	LIASSIC AND RHAETIC Jurassic
⌒∫	OOLITIC LIMESTONE Jurassic
⋮⋮	OXFORD AND KIMMERIDGE CLAYS
◈	WEALDEN BEDS
▭	CHALK with greensand and gault
⦚	TERTIARY BEDS
⼳	SCATTERED DRIFT DEPOSITS ON CHALK

MAP I THE SHAPE AND SOILS OF BRITAIN

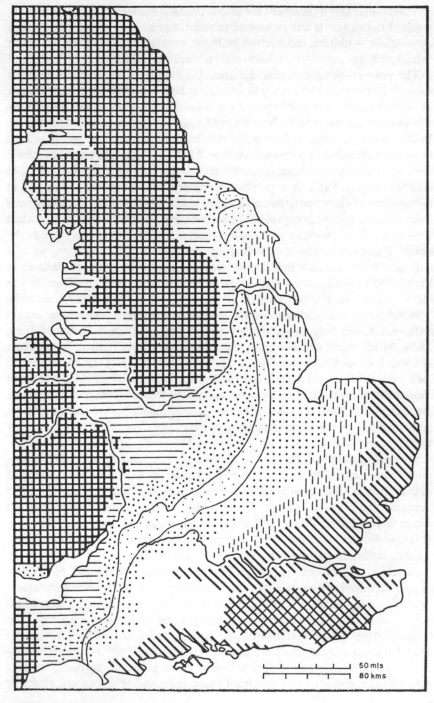

50 mls
80 kms

and tax, dwindling in numbers because it could not afford to rear children. In much of the empire it was too cowed to resist, but in parts of Gaul and Spain, above all in Armorica, the modern Brittany, peasant discontent was confident enough to break into the sustained revolt termed *Bacauda*.

The peasants of Britain may not have been quite so badly off as those of Europe. The evidence is not easy to assess, for the economy of the continent must be studied mainly through written documents, the economy of Britain principally through archaeological discovery, and unlike evidence is hard to compare. In the excavated towns of Britain the standard of physical comfort is not low; money was abundant and isolated farms could afford plenty of pottery. Some old farmsteads equipped themselves in the fourth century with window glass and doorkeys, evidence at least of property worth stealing. A two-roomed cottage in the grounds of the country house of Hambleden, near Henley, was plainly the residence of a quite poor dependant of the mansion, but one room was furnished with a tiled floor, the other with central heating. Several other sites suggest the homes of cultivators who lived well above subsistence level.

It also seems possible that society was more integrated in Britain than in Europe. The fourth century was an age of massive concentration of property in the ownership of a small number of great magnates. The Church and the Treasury, cities and individuals owned many different estates; one senator owned a dozen villas in Italy alone, another owned estates in various parts of Italy, Sicily, Africa, Spain and Britain. They were in the main sustained by the rents of tenants, whose labour also contributed to the cultivation of the home farm on each estate; agricultural slaves were few, but the pressure of famine and taxation constrained many small proprietors to become the tenants of magnates. When an estate changed hands, the rents of its tenants continued, but the owner of many estates needed only a few country houses; many lapsed into disrepair when they passed to absentee owners. A few were turned to productive use; but in Britain, in the great majority of the large rural houses, the splendidly appointed living-rooms remained in the occupation of well-to-do owners until the last age of Roman Britain. Those whose living-rooms were adapted to a more modest living standard, suitable to a bailiff, or were converted to agricultural or industrial use, as at Darenth in Kent or at Totternhoe by Dunstable, are a small minority. It is therefore possible that property was less concentrated, the proportion of resident landowners somewhat higher than in Europe.

Several considerations suggest possible explanations of the difference. The sharply increased prosperity of the fourth-century lowlands must to some extent have offset the pressure of rent and tax; there was less need for landowners to sell out to greater men, and some of the new riches are likely to have filtered down to some of the poorer cultivators. The geography of Britain also encouraged among them a sturdier outlook. The poorer highlands did not know the institutions of the great landlord, rich enough to build a villa. By reason of their poverty the highlands lived somewhat more independently than the exploited tenants of most of the empire. It is unlikely that their outlook was wholly bounded by the hills; possible that it enabled the lowlanders as well to withstand some of the grosser extortions that peasants elsewhere could not escape.

Fourth-century Britain differed from Europe and from its own past. In contrast to the polarised economy of the early empire, mid fourth-century Britain was an integrated community, graded from village and market town to local capital, from peasant croft through considerable farm to palatial mansion; it was dominated by a small aristocracy, based on the land, but still controlling the towns, its leaders the social equals or superiors of the governors and generals appointed by the imperial government. It was an orderly, secure society, where each man kept his place as clearly as in eighteenth-century England. The great men of Roman York or Cirencester would have been content to accept with little change the idealised panegyric that Ausonius of Bordeaux addressed to the citizens of Trier, the chief city of Belgic Gaul,

> Let me recall your peaceful farmers,
> Your skilful lawyers and your compelling orators,
> High champions of the accused.
>
> Let me recall the men your Council honoured,
> Your chief citizens, your own senators,
> The men your schools have trained in eloquence
> To match Quintilian himself;
>
> The men who rule their own towns,
> And keep the Bench unstained
> By the executioner's axe;
>
> The Vicars you have sent to govern Italy
> Or the British of the north,
> Or Rome itself, the world's capital,
> Its senate and its people.

CHAPTER TWO

THE ENDING OF THE WESTERN EMPIRE

Rebellion 350–353

In January 350, a military conspiracy in Gaul proclaimed Magnentius emperor. He was a senior officer, probably of British birth, son of a German settled in the empire by Constantine. Gaul, Italy, Africa, Spain and Britain quickly accepted his authority, and the high aristocracy welcomed him in Rome, where he married a daughter of one of the great senatorial families, Justina. Constans, the young emperor of the west, was soon killed, and his brother Constantius instigated the Germans of the Rhineland to attack and delay Magnentius while he assembled his own forces. The Germans were disastrously successful. For several years the Alamanni 'destroyed many wealthy cities and . . . overran the Gauls at will without serious opposition'; Strassburg, Wurms and Mainz fell, while enemy forces sporadically besieged Sens, Autun and other towns. Magnentius enlisted Frank and Saxon allies, but the main body of the Franks took the opportunity to seize Cologne and establish permanent homes on the left bank of the lower Rhine; Lyon itself, the chief town of central and northern Gaul, was attacked by *Laeti* and *Gentiles*, mixed German peoples who had been settled a generation or two earlier within the empire, in the double capacity of tied peasants and local militia. Constantius advanced slowly, carefully ensuring the loyalty of the Danube armies, and defeated Magnentius at Mursa, in the northern Balkans, by the Danube. The casualties were rated at something like a tenth of the whole Roman army. Constantius recovered Gaul in 353, but the whole of the Roman Rhineland was in the occupation of unsubdued barbarians for several years more.

The character of the new ruler of the west was depressing. Numerous contemporaries outline the same mournful portrait of a timorous bigot. Magnentius was a forceful commander, but Constantius at Mursa

> stayed away in a church outside the town. . . . The bishop, Valens . . . was the first to tell the frightened emperor that the enemy had fled. When Constantius enquired for the messenger, Valens replied that he was an angel. The credulous emperor believed him, attributing his victory to the merit of the bishop rather than to the valour of his troops.

The rational historian Sulpicius Severus despised the superstitious emperor;

but rationality was passing into eclipse, for Constantius' credulity foreshadowed the beliefs of the centuries ahead, to whom divine intervention was the natural explanation of human success and human failure.

Constantius' first concern was with precautionary vengeance, especially concentrated upon the nobility of Britain. Their sufferings are related by the contemporary historian Ammian, a serving army officer, whose disconsolate narrative is our principal source for the history of the next twenty-five years. The surviving portion of his work begins with the year 353, and his opening words on the west describe Constantius' inquisition, whose first named victim was a count Gerontius. The emperor's

> weak and narrow mind concluded that everything was directed against his safety. . . . The bloody flattery of courtiers enflamed the emperor's vain and angry suspicions. . . .
>
> Chief among the flatterers was the Secretary Paul. . . . This viper . . . was sent to Britain to arrest some officers who had dared to conspire with Magnentius. Arbitrarily extending his commission, he flooded over the fortunes of many men, . . . framing accusations in contempt of truth.
>
> Martinus, then Vicar of the Britains . . . repeatedly requested the release of the innocent . . . When . . . Paul . . . threatened to arrest him and his staff . . . Martinus, in alarm, drew his own sword on Paul, . . . but failed to kill him, and therefore drove it into his own side. By that disgraceful death died a most just ruler.
>
> The bloody Paul returned to Constantius with a train of wretched filthy prisoners, for whom the racks, the hooks and other instruments of torture were made ready. Many lost their property, others were exiled, some executed. It is not easy to recollect an occasion under Constantius when a man was acquitted, though the accusation against him was but a whisper.

The punishment of Britain was exceptional; a convenient nursery of earlier and later rebellions, the island had doubtless sheltered the nucleus of the conspiracy. The victims have left some slight archaeological trace. An unusual number of coin hoards of this date are distributed all over the lowlands, often near villas. They look like the property of men deprived by the Secretary Paul of lands and liberty, who never came home to recover their money or disclose its whereabouts. Much of the confiscated property, whether retained by the crown, or sold, or granted to the favoured, passed to absentee owners. The revolt of Magnentius had decimated the Roman army and wasted Gaul; it also wounded the expanding aristocracy of Britain. The conspirators had intended to replace a weak and silly prince with an able general; their costly failure was a prelude to the disasters of the next half-century, that led public sentiment to a hopeless contempt for the enfeebled state.

Christian Dissent 350–361

As men began to lose respect for the state, they transferred their hopes to religion; and for the rest of the century, religious conflict mattered more and more in the political life of the Roman world. In the end, Christianity was to carry all before it, but its permanent triumph was by no means assured in 350. The Christian religion was rooted in the Greek east, and was strongest among the urban poor. Early experience left an imprint upon Christian thought that later theology was never able to eradicate; orthodox teaching long emphasised that salvation is the easy prerogative of the poor and lowly, that wealth and property are by definition evil, that the rich man is a prisoner of sin. Early in the second century, accepted apostolic teaching forbade the Christian to live like those who do not earn their sustenance 'by their own toil and sweat, but live by the unrighteous exploitation of other men's labour'; a generation later, a Christian leader in Rome, where rich converts were most numerous, pleaded that the rich man, though admittedly evil and unprofitable, might nonetheless be of some service to the virtuous Christian poor, just as the barren elm supports the useful vine. Even at the end of the century, Irenaeus, then the acknowledged spokesman of orthodoxy, asked '*Unde possessio?*' 'What is the origin of property?', and replied that it stemmed from the Mammon of Iniquity and was always the product of avarice and injustice.

From about the year 200 Christianity had begun to attract men of wealth and substance and to make its first impact upon natives of the Latin west, in Italy and Africa; but in Gaul and Britain, Christians remained few and insignificant. Government persecution, from 250 onward, failed to break the Christians, and its failure made them stronger in lands where they were already known; in a world demoralised by submission to authority, a faith that men held dearer than life commanded respect, and the Christians rightly claimed that every martyr made ten converts. Yet the Christians were ill-prepared for premature success. In 312 civil war made Constantine emperor of the west. As men realised that the new ruler was a devout Christian, bishops were bewildered by sudden promotion from the status of furtive sectaries to that of influential government advisers, and veteran confessors mistrusted the mass of new converts who embraced the emperor's religion. The body of simple Christians was confused, for the rival partisans of innumerable discords within the empire, social, regional and political, all learned to argue in a Christian idiom, and to discover that some older trend in Christian thought served their interest.

Confusion was worst in the east, where Christians were strongest. In the west, Christians were by now numerous in Africa and parts of Italy; the major cities of Provence had their bishops, as had the Rhineland towns, where government offices and field army units were plentiful. But in the rest of Gaul, no more than nine Christian communities are known to have existed before Constantine. The new faith first appeared in the west as a government religion, attractive to men of substance who sought government favour; but it was still weak in ordinary towns, non-existent in the countryside. It did not win the hearts of the people until later, when religious controversy united the Gauls against alien government and turned the church into a champion of the subject against unjust authority.

The controversy that overshadowed all others took its name from Arius, a priest of Alexandria who revived an ancient heresy in a new form. Plebeian Christians had for centuries clung to their faith in the God who died the death of a common criminal, the 'stumbling block to the Gentiles'. Arianism held that God the Father was of a similar, not the same, substance to God the Son, who died, and was by implication superior. The dispute deeply divided the churches when Constantine mastered the eastern provinces in 324. Like his predecessors, he believed that to escape the anger of heaven the Roman people must achieve unity in belief; unlike them, he sought unity under the Christian God. When the Christians divided, he strove for unity, and his first important initiative as emperor of the east, in 325, was to convene the first world conference of Christians at Nicaea, near the future Constantinople, where Europe and Asia meet.

In practice, the Arians proved somewhat more tractable than their orthodox opponents, and found a firm champion in the new eastern emperor, Constantius, in 337. His brother Constans therefore championed the orthodox, and when Constantius exiled the recalcitrant catholic leader Athanasius, Constans threatened war if he were not reinstated. Constantius yielded, but when he conquered the west in 353, he resolved to enforce unity behind the Arian creed. The weaker Latin Christians seemed to have little chance against the all-powerful emperor; but they withstood him, and thereby began to earn public sympathy, for their resistance voiced the resentment of the west against a Greek tyrant. At first, the emperor's energy won ground; the pliant were rewarded, and the obstinate were exiled, so that prudent men, though they might respect the integrity of the victims, learned to avoid their fate. In 359 the emperor was ready for a general assault.

The sequel is described by the contemporary Gallic historian Sulpicius Severus. The emperor summoned the western bishops to meet at Rimini, and promised the consulate to the prefect Taurus if he engineered unanimous agreement. Four hundred bishops assembled, and the emperor ordered that their expenses should be defrayed by the Treasury. The bishops of Gaul and Britain rejected the offer. But

> three of the British bishops, whose means were small, accepted the state allowance, rejecting the collections made for them, arguing that it was more Christian to be a burden upon the state than upon individuals. . . . Our bishop Gavidius called them pig-headed, but my own view is quite the opposite.

At first the Arians numbered no more than eighty, one-fifth of the whole. But the orthodox were induced to send a delegation to Constantinople, who brought back a statement 'couched in dubious wording, that expressed the catholic discipline with a heretical undertone'. The Congress was 'dismayed and confused', for 'protracted sessions had overcome their resolution'. The weaker gave in, and 'when the tide turned it became a torrent'. The prefect warned that they had been cooped up seven months in the city, and that once winter set in in earnest, they had no hope of getting home across the Alps. In the end, all but fifteen yielded, and the obstinate minority were exiled and deposed, so that formal unanimity was achieved. The minority seem to have included the bishop of London, Augurius.

Within a year, the resolution that had been secured by so much degrading government intrigue was a dead letter. Under the leadership of Bishop Hilary of Poitiers the Christian communities of Gaul refused to endorse it, and excommunicated the few determined Arians in their midst. Their temerity was vindicated when Constantius ceased to rule Gaul soon after. Non-Christians looked with distasteful wonder upon the obscure and sordid wrangles of the Christians; but the churches of Gaul for the first time appeared in a new light, as a force that was independent of government, and able to defy it with impunity. From its early years the church of Gaul and Britain was able to voice and organise the protest of the resentful subject.

Imperial Recovery 361–375

The strength of the Christians did not mature overnight. The wretched dispute of Rimini made few converts; but it brought no benefit to the government. An emperor who was at pains to manipulate conference votes in order to win the nominal approval of small conventicles of his humbler subjects earned the contempt of nobleman and plebeian, pagan and Christian; and seemed to mock the memory of bygone rulers, whose edicts men had accepted without question. Constantius' timid tyranny, the ferocity of his vengeance, and the upstart power of his low-born Greek administrators, aroused angry resentment. It soon found a leader. When he returned to the east, Constantius installed his young nephew Julian as ruler of Gaul. The inexperienced university student proved himself a brilliant and inspiring general; a couple of vigorous campaigns subdued the Franks and Alamanni, who had overrun the Roman Rhineland with the connivance of Constantius, and Julian restored the old frontier. At home, his drastic reform of the corrupt revenue departments delighted the commons and offended the bureaucracy.

Julian won golden opinions, but Constantius rightly saw his dazzling victories and soaring popularity as a threat, and sought to forestall it by posting his crack regiments to the east, early in 360. The troops feared to leave their homes exposed to German invaders, and proclaimed the unwilling Julian emperor. The armies of east and west again left their frontiers to fight each other, threatening a repetition of the disaster of Mursa. It was averted by the timely death of Constantius, which enabled his army to accept the rule of Julian.

The new emperor was an intellectual sickened by the sordid Arian dispute; he sought to rival both Christian factions with an esoteric pagan priesthood, hastily erected in pale imitation of the Christian hierarchy. In the west, and particularly in Britain, governors and loyal towns repaired derelict temples and founded new ones; but the sickness of the old Gods was mortal, and the revival, unconvincing even to its pagan supporters, disappeared on the death of its author, who was cut down by an unknown hand in Mesopotamia in 363. In his stead, the Army Council elevated a senior officer of unobtrusive Catholic orthodoxy, and on his speedy death replaced him with a like-minded colleague.

Valentinian let religion alone; resigning the theological east to his undistinguished brother Valens, he campaigned energetically in the west, and covered his European frontier with massive defences, reinforced by heavy fortifications of the interior towns. In the course of his operations, a serious incursion on the frontiers of Britain was reported; it was an irritant distraction, repeating similar raids in 360 and 364 when the emperor detached a senior general with four of the field army's crack regiments to spend some months in Britain. In 367

> a barbarian alliance brought Britain to her knees; Nectaridus, Count of the Coastal Defence, was killed, the general Fullofaudes ambushed . . . the Picts plundered at will, as did the warlike Attacotti and the Irish. . . . The Franks, and their Saxon neighbours, raided the Gallic coast, breaking in where they could.

Valentinian despatched Count Theodosius with a scratch force, soon reinforced, as in 360, with four crack regiments. He marched from Richborough to 'London, an old town later called Augusta', splitting his force into small detachments to round up bands of enemy plunderers. Next spring, he

> bravely and energetically set out from Augusta, anciently styled London, with an army raised by his skilful diligence, bringing maximum help to the beaten and discomfited British. Dispersing various peoples whom an insolence bred of impunity had emboldened to attack the Romans, he thoroughly restored the damaged towns and forts, founded long ago to keep the peace.

The invasion of 367 seems a problem; the considerable space that Ammian allots it would seem to argue an exceptionally heavy blow, that should have shown clear archaeological trace. Earlier and later disasters have left a grim trail of burnt buildings, unburied skeletons, unreclaimed coin hoards; but, though generations of excavators have tried to relate their discoveries to Ammian's story, there is very little evidence of any widespread destruction in lowland Britain in the 360s. One or two country houses seem to have been abandoned at about this time, but hundreds lived on intact, often for many years more; much of the London region declined in the later fourth century, but the cause is more likely to have been flood than fire, the work of nature rather than of barbarians. The prominence that Ammian gives to the exploits of Count Theodosius has a simpler explanation; Theodosius' son was emperor when Ammian wrote. The dead-pan flattery that monarchy commands in any age prompted the historian to devote many paragraphs to the triumph of the emperor's father, but the crisis that made Julian detach an equal force in 360 might be dismissed in a couple of lines, for its commander had less illustrious children.

Obligation to a patron might distort Ammian's emphasis, but not his facts; for he is a sober and scrupulous reporter, second only to Tacitus in the canon of Roman historians. The field army that Valentinian detached arrived in time to save the south; for, though the Count of the Coast was killed, the enemy broke in only 'where they could', in numbers few enough to be rounded up by 'small detachments'. Franks and Saxons were not mentioned in the invasion of 360, and their effort in Britain in 367 was modest, a minor enterprise when compared with the 'multitude of Saxons' whom Valentinian with difficulty repulsed on the lower Rhine in 370. The nature of their intervention is to be inferred from Ammian's incidental mention of a 'barbarian alliance'. The alliance is echoed in the historical tradition of the Irish, who held that about this time their High King married a Saxon wife, mother to the great Niall of the Nine Hostages, ancestress of almost all future High Kings. The condition of an alliance, sealed by a royal marriage, was evidently a diversionary raid; some Saxons undertook to pin down the armies of the south-east, while the Irish and Picts assailed the north and west.

The northern assault was far more serious; it was only after Count Theodosius marched out from London that he encountered 'various peoples' in arms, and it was in the north that he had work to do when they were beaten; for he

> protected the frontier with look-outs and garrisons, recovering a province that had yielded to enemy control, so restoring it that, as his report advised, it should have a legitimate governor, and be henceforth styled Valentia. Meanwhile, the *Areani*, instituted in times gone by . . . had gradually become corrupt; he disbanded them, for they were convicted of taking bribes to betray our army to the enemy. . . . Their duty was to penetrate deep into enemy territory and give our commanders warning of the movements of border peoples.

Archaeological discovery and native historical record make ample comment on Theodosius' northern settlement, in contrast to their reticence about his southern skirmishes. The 'look-outs' are evidently the signal-stations, wooden towers resting on four splayed feet, which lined the north Yorkshire coast from the estuary of the Tees to Bridlington Bay; they are served by roads that radiate from Malton, whither a coastal defence unit named the 'Anticipators' was transferred from Brough-on-Humber. New defences are commonly erected because experience has shown their need; the towers were a novel form of defence, upon a coast previously unfortified. Their siting indicates the danger they were meant to meet. They were able to warn the garrison at Malton of enemy vessels approaching the rich lands of the East Riding from the north; but their siting pays no attention to any threat from the Germanic raiders to the south-east. The Pictish fleet had evidently learnt to turn the flank of Hadrian's Wall.

Picts and Saxons were still raiders, whose object was to sail home speedily with plunder; but the Irish had larger ambitions. Substantial numbers settled in western Britain, and Irish tradition extends the authority of Crimthann, the mid fourth-century High King, over 'Britain as far as the Channel'. Irish colonies are abundantly attested in Wales and the south-west, but evidence is weaker for the north-west. The probable reason is the recovery of the territory that became the new province of Valentia; the Roman texts suggest that it lay in and about Lancashire.

On the northern frontier, Theodosius devised a new policy, whose impact was felt for a thousand years. Hitherto, Hadrian's Wall had been protected by a screen of forts, slanting the Cheviots from the neighbourhood of Carlisle towards Tweedmouth; they had served as the headquarters of the long-range reconnaissance patrol units, who were suspected of collusion with the enemy. Ammian reports that the units were then disbanded, and excavation has shown that the forts were then abandoned. The nature of the defence system that replaced them is outlined by the genealogists of the early middle ages. Their business was to trace the descent of the princes they served from well-known heroes of the late Roman period; as with most genealogists, the links in their chain are often dubious, but both ends are stronger, for living potentates seek connection with remembered rulers, not with invented names.

The northern lists concern four dynasties established north of Hadrian's Wall, a few generations before the emergence of the fifth-century kingdoms south of the Wall. The texts are obscured by their copyists' lack of understanding, but the originals appear to have recorded the establishment, about the period 370 to 380, of Quintilius Clemens on the Clyde, of Paternus, son of Tacitus, over the Votadini of the north-east coast, and of Antonius Donatus in south-west Scotland, and perhaps also in Selkirk. The fourth list is the most corrupt; it seems to mean that Catellius Decianus was imposed upon the northern Votadini, the Lothians beyond the Tweed, perhaps as far as the lower Forth about Stirling, in the territory that was later called the Manau of Gododdin. The date may also be about the 370s, or a little later.

The lists are independent of each other. But each says something of each ruler's origin; Clemens seems to have come from the mediterranean, Tacitus from Kent, Decianus from an island whose name is corrupted out of recognition. Donatus, but not the others, is said to have derived his authority from the emperor Maximus (381–388). All have Roman names. All the names are given in the old-fashioned form of *nomen* and *cognomen*, family and personal name, that in the later fourth century remained principally in vogue among the local nobility of the western *civitates*. Men so named were not native kings to whom Rome granted recognition, but Roman officers placed over border barbarians.

The policy that the medieval lists suggest is that which Theodosius is known to have devised. He applied it to the African frontier a few years later. There Ammian reports that in 371 he subdued border peoples 'by a mixture of intimidation and bribery', and then 'put reliable *praefecti* in charge of the peoples he encountered'. Subsequently the great African churchman, St Augustine of Hippo approved his policy, commenting that

> a few years ago a small number of barbarian peoples were pacified and attached to the Roman frontier, so that they no longer had their own kings, but were ruled by prefects appointed by the Roman Empire,

and adding that they soon after began to accept Christianity. It is evident that Theodosius applied to the British frontier in 368 the same policy that he carried through in Africa in 371, appointing Roman *praefecti gentium* as rulers of the border barbarians.

The installation of *praefecti* was one among several forms of government; circumstances decided the choice between alternatives. Valentia became a province, but Ammian's carefully chosen words stress that 'in his report' Theodosius advised that it be given a *legitimum rectorem*, a regular governor; the phrase implies that alternatives had been considered and rejected. The appointment of a prefect was one of several possibilities; Valentinian chose a different alternative a few years later. A deposed king of the Alamanni of the upper Rhine, named Fraomar, was transferred to Britain, his title changed to Tribune of a unit of Alamanni within the Roman army; though an army officer in law, his force was enough to make him the effective master of the district in which it was stationed; but its location is not known.

As the authority of the central government disintegrated in the next century, practice ironed out the differences, preferring to name the substance of power rather than its formal title. In northern Britain, as in Europe, officers clung to their authority, and bequeathed it to their sons, founding hereditary dynasties. Fraomar is not known to have left heirs, but the commanders appointed in a later age to Demetia, south-west Wales, also used officially the Roman military titles of Tribune and Protector, though contemporaries called them kings. The double usage lasted for several generations; when Patrick denounced the depradations of the Clydesiders under Clemens' grandson Coroticus, about the 450s, he protested that their behaviour made them

> not citizens of the holy Romans, but of the devil, living in the enemy ways of the barbarians.

The Damnonii of the Clyde had never themselves been Roman citizens; to Patrick, the prefect's grandson and his men were still Romans appointed to rule barbarians, but they had succumbed to his subjects' way of life. Coroticus was in practice a king; and the dynasties that Theodosius established in the name of Valentinian span the gulf between Rome and the middle ages. The dynasty of

Clemens of the Clyde endured until the Norman conquest; the dynasty of Paternus, transferred to Wales, expired in the thirteenth century, in the person of Llewellyn the Great, and its sovereign authority is perpetuated in the modern title of Prince of Wales.

Huns and Goths 375-400

Count Theodosius' expedition to Britain was an incident in Valentinian's western wars, soon to be eclipsed by portentous troubles that drew him to the Danube, where he died in 375. The western provinces and the Rhine armies acknowledged his adult son Gratian, but the Danubian officers proclaimed and controlled his infant son Valentinian II, child of Magnentius' turbulent widow, the aristocratic Justina, whom Valentinian had found it politic to marry. Gratian endured the rebuff, but broke with his father's military government. His tutor, the poet Ausonius of Bordeaux, became Prefect of Italy, guiding the administration of the west, while the influence of the empress Justina prevailed in the Balkan provinces. For the last time the high aristocracy of Rome had a government they liked; their spokesman Symmachus, patron of the conservative paganism now fashionable among them, sighed gratefully, 'Now the emperors do what the nobility want.'

Novel and more frightful dangers from beyond the Danube soon overshadowed domestic politics. Just before Valentinian's death, the Huns had crossed the Volga. Ferocious nomads, seen always on their tough desert ponies, like some fearful Scythian reincarnation of the ancient centaurs, their frightfulness fell little short of their reputation. A primitive people, ignorant of fields and farms, had no use for live prisoners, save as concubines; without fixed homes to defend, they could be defeated only by total annihilation. Their first onslaught destroyed the empire of the eastern Goths, and they remained the terrible masters of central Europe for eighty years. The western Visigoths sought safety on the Roman bank of the broad Danube. The government of Valens admitted the Visigothic refugees, but corruption let them keep their arms, and at the same time assured that they were fed only at outrageous famine prices. Life was intolerable for a people unprovided with coin, whose only marketable commodities were their children. When the scared Roman general tried to assassinate their leaders, and bungled his treachery, the starved and indignant Goths rebelled, destroying the army and the emperor of the east at Adrianople in 378.

In place of Valens, Gratian enthroned Theodosius, son of the general who had rescued Britain in 367. The energy of the emperor Theodosius in the long run preserved the eastern provinces; the Balkans were cleared by individual bands of Goths, hired to contain and subdue their fellow-countrymen. But this immediate solution begot new and bitter long term tensions. The sentiments of the Goths were divided; chieftains saw the prospect of power, wealth and the status within the superior civilisation of Rome with other eyes than the rank and file, whose continuing poverty perpetuated their patriotic hatred of the Roman name.

Roman opinion was equally torn; though Germans had long been frequent in the regular units of the Roman army, especially among the field officers, whole-sale reliance on mercenary captains was suspect and unpopular. The federate allies were bound to the Roman society they guarded only by a personal contract with its sovereign, that dimly anticipated the patterns of medieval military rule. Federates were not admitted into the western provinces until the 5th century, but wherever they settled, landlord and peasant alike suffered from the boorish arrogance of the ubiquitous Germans; conservative opinion resented the in-decent political prominence of their leaders, and sighed nostalgically for the days when Romans were masters of their own empire. Yet governments justly pleaded the compulsions of political realism, for they learnt that political and military success accrued to those with cash enough to hire the most barbarians, and tact enough to flatter the barbarian leaders' yearning for social and political acceptance.

The first crisis came quickly, and came in Britain. The miscellaneous grievances of Gratian's subjects found a focus in the army's dislike of his privileged bar-barian bodyguard; for the young prince's gentle manners inspired no counter-balancing respect. One critic drily called him 'more pious than was good for the state', while his tutor Ausonius found but two virtues to praise; his excellence at running, wrestling and jumping; and his modest dress, daily church-going, abstemious table and chaste bed. The virtues of the athlete and the choirboy were fatal to the emperor, and a few years after Adrianople the diocese of Britain proclaimed Magnus Maximus, a Spaniard who had served under the elder Theodosius, and who now repelled a renewed Pict and Irish invasion. In 383 Gaul abandoned Gratian without a struggle, and soon after Spain, Africa and Italy acknowledged Maximus as emperor. Theodosius, heavily committed in his own territories, accepted the rebel for a while, but in 388 defeated and killed him in another bloody Balkan battle. Native tradition believed that the British units of his army settled in Armorica, the future Brittany.

The costly adventures of Magnentius and Julian were repeated, for the Franks again plundered Cologne, and extended their settlements about the lower Rhine. Yet Theodosius' success failed to tame the disaffected west; four years later the barbarian commander of the Rhine armies deposed young Valentinian, and Theodosius was again obliged to reconquer the west by force. Both armies en-gaged alien allies. Though Theodosius was reinforced by substantial forces of Arabs, Georgians and Goths, his victory was achieved only by the timely pur-chase of a considerable body of his rival's German allies. He died four months later, in January 395. He was the last sole ruler of the Roman world, the last to dominate his own government. Thereafter, the manner of political struggle changed. The docile sons and grandsons of Theodosius submitted to the direction of ambitious ministers, who learnt that power was more cheaply bought by palace intrigue and by assassination than by armed rebellion. Laymen and churchmen henceforth agreed to support the existing sovereign, however contemptible, in preference to the ablest rebel; for the victory or defeat of a rebel equally entailed disastrous civil war.

The principle of legitimacy triumphed too late to save the western provinces. The general Stilicho, son of a Roman officer of Vandal birth, controlled Honorius, the new emperor of the west, and sought a like authority over his brother Arcadius, emperor in Constantinople. The successive ministers of Arcadius, despite their mutual hostility, shared a common fear of Stilicho; and both courts were agitated by the struggle between those who sought to curtail the political power of German ministers and soldiers, and those who tried to assimilate and baptise the barbarians.

The multiple divisions of the Roman government emboldened the independent barbarians to renewed attacks. But at first Stilicho was brilliantly successful. Between 395 and 400 he won two resounding victories. An African border prince named Gildo, placed in command of the Roman armies, transferred his nominal allegiance to Arcadius, starving Rome of corn. But, with the support of magnates of the province, Stilicho swiftly subdued the rebel. Immediately thereafter he gained his second frontier victory, by the repulse of another concerted attack upon Britain by the Picts, the Irish and the Saxons. His victories demonstrated that a strong and able ruler could still hold the frontiers of the west.

The Fall of the West 400–410

In 400, the empire still seemed to be more than holding its own. Civil war was at a discount, separatism was checked, the frontiers were intact. Official policy and private judgment might reasonably anticipate the indefinite continuance of the familiar Roman world. Yet ten years later, western Rome had disintegrated beyond repair.

The decade of disaster opened with a crisis in the east. When a Gothic general seized Constantinople, his men were massacred in a fury of anti-German resentment. At the time, the recovery of Constantinople seemed a hopeful sign of reviving Roman strength, matching the western triumphs of Stilicho. Thenceforth, though individual Germans might hold high command, the eastern empire was permanently free of turbulent barbarian federate allies. It proved able to finance a native government and a native army; and when necessary to pay barbarians to go elsewhere.

But the salvation of the richer east proved to be the ruin of the impoverished west. The restless nation of the Visigoths, long quartered in the eastern Balkan provinces, deemed it easier to attack Italy. Stilicho twice held their able ruler Alaric, but in 403 he had to strip the western frontiers of

> the units that defended Rhaetia (Bavaria) . . . of the legion deployed
> in far-off Britain, that curbs the savage Irish and reads the marks
> tattooed upon the bodies of dying Picts, the regiments set against the
> blonde Sigambri (the Franks of the lower Rhine).

The legion was probably the Twentieth from Chester.

The temporary rescue of Italy entailed the permanent ruin of Gaul. A vast host of Vandals, Suebi and Alans, escaping from the central European dominion of the Huns, crossed the ill-defended Rhine, and fanned out across the interior provinces, threatening to invade Britain. Italy was powerless to help, and the British proclaimed a native emperor, Constantine III. He crossed to Gaul, and expelled the invaders; but they withdrew the wrong way, not back across the Rhine, but across the Pyrenees into Spain. There most of them stayed. The Suebi destroyed their Alan allies, and their descendants still inhabit north-western Spain; the Vandals passed on, to leave their name in Andalusia, and ultimately to found a stable kingdom in what had been Roman Africa.

The disaster cost Stilicho his life. He was arrested and executed in 408. The government of Honorius, insecure in Rome, had withdrawn to the shelter of the malarial marshes of Ravenna; and the anti-German party now sought to imitate Constantinople, by massacring the barbarian garrisons. But the aristocracy of Italy lacked the strength that had preserved the east. Without men or money or political resolution, the government of Ravenna was blown rudderless by changing winds. It attacked Constantine in Gaul, and killed his generals; their successors, 'Ediovinchus a Frank, and Gerontius a Briton', counter-attacked with vigour. Renewed civil war turned confusion into chaos. The *Bacauda*, the peasant rebels of the *maquis*, joined in against Ravenna; the Spanish relatives of the imperial family rose against Constantine's son, Constans, and Gerontius replaced him with an emperor of his own making. The armies of the Rhine elevated local emperors, and in Italy Alaric enthroned his own puppet emperor. While half a dozen feeble western governments disputed the majestic title of Roman emperor, Britain was subjected to continuing Irish assaults, and an exceptionally heavy Saxon raid. The failing Constantine was no longer able to help, and the states of Britain were impelled to restore their allegiance, too late, to the legitimate emperor in Italy.

The western empire reeled; its provinces had faced blows as heavy in the past, but never in such rapid succession. The end came on 24 August 410, when slaves or plebeian malcontents opened the gates of Rome to Alaric. He withdrew in less than a week, with a huge waggon train of loot and captives, including the emperor's sister, Galla Placidia, whom his successor married. A few years later, in 418, when the debris of rival emperors had been tidied away, the government of Honorius granted federate status to the unconquerable Visigoths. They were settled in Aquitaine, under the ordinary billeting laws, that had been designed long ago to provide temporary maintenance for troops on the move. They were allocated the use of a third of the lands and houses of their civilian hosts, exempted from the jurisdiction of magistrates, subjected only to the military discipline of their commanding officer. But old laws carry new meanings in a changed society. Since their settlement was permanent, and their commander was their national king, they in fact established the first medieval kingdom, owing only corporate and nominal allegiance to the emperor. Burgundians and others soon established comparable kingdoms, and these new nations smashed the fragile shell of imperial authority when they grew to maturity a few decades later.

The fall of the city shattered men's illusions, and a fearsome unknown future could no longer be denied. From Bethlehem, St. Jerome wept

> The Roman empire is beheaded; in the one City, the whole world dies. . . . All things born are doomed to die . . . every work of man is destroyed by age; . . . but who would have believed that Rome would crumble, at once the mother and the tomb of her children? She who enslaved the east . . . is herself a slave.

Old men mourned; but younger men were capable of looking to the future with confidence, even welcoming escape from a dead past. One young Briton wrote home from Sicily:

> you tell me that everyone is saying that the world is coming to an end. So what? It happened before. Remember Noah's time. . . . But after the Flood, men were holier.

The continuous history of a thousand years of Greek and Roman civilisation had suddenly snapped, leaving men nakedly aware, at the time, that the end had come. Those who could look beyond the deluge with assurance had already written off the headless corpse of the Roman empire. They were the conscious architects of Christendom, impatient to clear away the debris of the past that they might build upon its ruins a new society, that which in retrospect we call the 'middle ages'.

Christian Reform 361–400

Western Rome was mortally wounded in 410, though its death agonies were to last two generations more. As the state decayed, men looked elsewhere for protection and salvation. They found a Christian church, reformed and strengthened, that had learned from the disgrace of Rimini and the warning of Julian's abortive pagan revival. The leaders of western reform were three outstanding contemporaries, Damasus, Ambrose and Martin. They differed greatly in their work and outlook; but in a single generation, between 365 and 395, their combined endeavours transformed the structure, the morality and the composition of Latin Christianity.

Damasus secured the bishopric of Rome in 366, after bloody election riots. A masterful organiser, he induced the pious emperor Gratian to surrender to him the title of *Pontifex Maximus*, the ancient chief priesthood of the city of Rome, held by Julius Caesar and all the emperors after him. The title, and the magisterial authority it conveyed, make Damasus the first bishop of Rome to whom the modern term 'Pope' may fitly be applied. His contemporary Ammian was impressed by his novel and deliberate ostentation,

> riding in a carriage, wearing conspicuous clothes, keeping a table
> better than the emperor's;

and Ammian contrasted his magnificence with

> some of the provincial bishops, whose moderation in food and
> drink, whose plain apparel and downcast eyes commend their
> modest purity to the eternal deity.

The contrast between the splendour of a Roman prelate and the humility proper to a priest of Christ has provoked comment in most later ages. But Damasus took a political decision attuned to his times. Rome was still in men's minds the head and mistress of the civilised world, though it was no longer the residence of the emperor. The secular government was headed by the city prefect, but the Christian church needed a head whose authority extended over the empire. Praetextatus, the prefect of the City, the grand old man of aristocratic paganism, sensed the power of his rival, and protested with a jibe, 'Make me Bishop of Rome, and I will turn Christian'. The jest recognised reality, for Damasus had erected a Christian magistracy as powerful as the prefecture, and destined to outlive it for many centuries.

Damasus gave Latin Christendom a visible and efficient head. He also strengthened the sinews that bound it together. He commissioned the prolific scholar Jerome to prepare a single authoritative translation of the scriptures; and Jerome's Latin text, called the Vulgate, is still the canonical bible of the Latin church. Damasus also asserted the conscious independence of the Christian community by cleaning out the catacombs, and opening them as permanent exhibitions, in honour of Christians whose conscience had defied the unjust authority of secular government. The veneration of martyrs in small local shrines was not new; Damasus' innovation was to elevate the whole body of martyrs to a status in heaven and to make them a focus of worship on earth, whose observance emphasised that the Christian church was the independent equal of the political state.

The power of Damasus demonstrated the strength of the Christians; but it did not inspire personal affection. Ambrose of Milan combined the authority of the prelate with the humility of the priest. The son of a former praetorian prefect, he was himself governor of north-eastern Italy in 373, when a contested episcopal election threatened riots in Milan as violent as those in Rome in 366. A voice in the crowd, traditionally a child's, cried, 'Ambrose for Bishop!', and the crowd assented. Baptised, ordained and consecrated within a week, the former governor lived austerely with his brother and sister, dividing his considerable fortune between the church and the poor. To instil a like austerity into his clergy, he adapted to the urban Latin church the eastern phenomenon of the monk.

The solitary ascetic of the desert was older than Christianity; but monasticism did not become an important element in Christianity until the early fourth century, when tens of thousands of Egyptians migrated to the desert, during and after the persecution of Diocletian, rejecting the stresses of their civil society, to live in new communities, in direct personal relationship with God, without marriage or children. Though the example of Egypt spread to the deserts of Syria and Cappadocia, in western eyes the monks long remained another nasty oriental excess, slovenly drop-outs from decent society.

It was during the Arian controversy that Latin Christians observed that the monks were their steadfast allies against the heretics; and a number of wealthy nobles, men and women, adopted a personal monastic vow, living abstemiously in their own houses. Majority opinion in Rome condemned the novelty, and Jerome, the fiercest champion of the monks, withdrew to Bethlehem. But some provincial bishops responded to the new ideal. It was bishop Eusebius of Vercelli in northern Italy, who in the 350s

> first established monks who were also clergy, combining the ab-
> stinence of the monk with the discipline of the priest . . . though
> living in the town.

Ambrose praised, imitated and extended the practice of Eusebius, so that ordained monks, *in turba commorantes*, living among men, set a visible example of a more perfect life within ordinary society. In the next generation, numerous bishops induced all or part of their clergy to accept monastic vows, so that the cathedral monastery became a symbol of reform.

Damasus founded an independent Christian authority. Ambrose tested the strength of the church in conflict with the state. To the emperor Theodosius he stated the principle:

> In matters of finance you consult your departmental advisers; it is
> even more necessary that in matters of religion you should consult
> the priests of the Lord.

His warning to the usurper Maximus was sterner, that

> in the Old Testament, kingdoms were bestowed by priests, not
> usurped.

Words were put into practice when the empress Justina impounded one of the Milan churches for the use of Arian courtiers. Ambrose and his congregation occupied the church, cheering each other and intimidating the police cordon at the doors by singing songs, adapting the practice of the Greek east. Ambrose' defiant songs are the first Latin hymns; and the greatest of them, the *Te Deum*, belongs to this context and this generation, but not to this occasion. After three days, the police broke ranks and joined the besieged, thereby compelling the government to surrender.

The decisive conflict came in 390. When Theodosius massacred 3,000 citizens of Thessalonica, after a local rising, Ambrose refused to admit him to communion. After a few months of ineffectual resistance, the emperor yielded, performed penance, and consented to sign the ultimate decree, making non-Christian worship a civil crime. Theodosius' penance lies nearer to the experience of medieval princes who reigned a thousand years later than to the conduct of the emperors who had ruled in his own youth.

Italy learned that a well-loved bishop was stronger than the strongest emperor. Gaul learned a similar lesson from a very different man. Martin was a soldier, who won a discharge from Julian's army as a conscientious objector. He settled as a hermit near Poitiers, and an individual who practised in rural Gaul the fabulous asceticism of the east excited universal wonder, and was soon credited with the power to recall the dead to life. His biography was written in his lifetime by his friend and disciple, Sulpicius Severus. Against his will he was lured to Tours in 372, during another disputed election, and was acclaimed bishop by an 'incredibly large crowd of voters'. But he was opposed by

> a few ... including several of the bishops summoned for the consecration ... who ... described him ... as a lowborn person, of disgusting appearance, shabbily dressed, with untidy hair.

Martin resumed his hermit's life in a cave two miles from the city, gathering around him a monastic cathedral school of eighty pupils, including some sons of local notables, who shared his single wineless meal, and divided their time between prayer, the study of the classics, and the transcription of texts sacred and profane. The school, the *scriptorium* and the library were novelties, but they were an essential part of Martin's work, for

> many of his pupils became bishops; for what city or church was there, but longed for a bishop trained in the school of Martin?

The best-known of these pupils were Amator, later bishop of Auxerre, who is said to have ordained Patrick, and Victricius, later bishop of Rouen, who was to propagate Martin's teaching in Britain with considerable success.

Martin pioneered rural preaching, founding village churches in a land where Christianity was recent, hitherto virtually confined to the towns. His plebeian simplicity won the affection of peasants and of the urban poor, but it aroused opposition among his colleagues. His biographer Severus protested, 'It is the clergy alone, the bishops alone, who refuse to acknowledge him.' To Severus, they were men who 'degrade their dignity by subservience to royal hangers-on', whereas Martin compelled the choleric Valentinian to receive and heed him. He rebuked the usurper Maximus, intent on trying a case of heresy, in words as vigorous as those of Ambrose;

> for a lay judge to decide upon an ecclesiastical case would be a savage unheard-of crime;

and he long refused the emperor's invitation

to sit at table with a man who has killed one emperor and expelled another.

Maximus swallowed the insult, and at last induced Martin to come to court where he had to endure the company he most detested of 'bishops and women'. He sat beside the emperor at a public banquet, and

> the delighted king . . . ordered the cup to be offered first to the holy bishop, expecting and hoping that he would pass it back to him. . . . But, after drinking, Martin handed the cup to his own priest. . . . It made an impression . . . that Martin treated the emperor as no other bishop treated the minor officials.

Incidents like these made Martin a living legend; and made Sulpicius Severus' biography an immediate best seller, that became a model for an immense flood of 'Saints' Lives', popular literature published in Gaul and Britain during the next several centuries. The examples of Damasus, Ambrose and Martin showed that the Christians were champions of the underdog, strong enough to prevail. That example inspired millions outside their own sees, whose pressure impelled other bishops to respect the new morality. In one generation the success of the reformers turned the church of Gaul from a minority sect to a universal religion, so that by the end of the century 'the whole world became Christian', acquiescing without resistance in the new faith.

But conversion to Christianity did not mean that the convert ceased to be a pagan. As among many modern peoples, the same mind could accommodate several different religions at the same time; the church fathers might proclaim that 'the same mouth cannot praise Christ and Jupiter', but the poet Ausonius, consul and prefect, gave them the lie by composing hymns to Christ and also to Jupiter; and for centuries church councils found it necessary to disapprove of families who attended mass on Sunday morning, and sacrificed to their household gods on Sunday afternoon. What matters is that as late as 370, a majority of the population of the three Gauls still rejected the name of Christian, but that by 400 almost the entire population admitted Christianity. With Christianity, they accepted a new institution capable of binding their society together, as the old political fabric of the empire rotted away.

The triumph of Christianity came just in time, barely a decade before the capture of Rome, in 410, destroyed the emperor's hold upon the obedience of his subjects. Honorius lived thirteen years more, and his sister's son, Valentinian III, survived till 455. The prestige of the dynasty lent an authority that still mattered greatly in Gaul and Italy to those ministers who acted in its name; but Valentinian's successors, creatures of the successive German generals who dominated Italy, commanded little obedience beyond the Alps. Their feeble sovereignty persisted until Odovacer discontinued the nomination of western emperors, about 476, and transferred his nominal allegiance to Constantinople;

his administrative decision changed nothing of the realities of political power. Odovacer buried the western empire, but it had died twenty years before. The wistful comment of the chronicler Count Marcellinus accurately summarised its end:

> then fell the Empire of the West, nor had it ever strength to rise again.

CHAPTER THREE

INDEPENDENT BRITAIN:
THE EVIDENCE

The loss of Britain was a detail in the dissolution of the Empire. In the year when Rome itself fell to the Goths, it passed almost unnoticed; one historian gave it half a sentence, reporting that

> Honorius dealt with the states of Britain by letter, telling them to look to their own defence . . . and remained inactive.

There was little else that he could do. In the catastrophe of 410, the imperial government could take no initiative in Britain; it turned down a British request, for it was then unable to spare men or money for the defence of the island.

The letter reveals something of events in Britain. It was plainly sent in answer to a letter from Britain that had asked for men and money to defend the frontiers and coasts. The diocese had proclaimed the rival emperor Constantine III; but in 410, Constantine was visibly failing, and the British returned their allegiance to Honorius. They could not have done so without first renouncing the authority of Constantine's prefects, vicars and governors. But they did not themselves appoint others in their place; that was the business of the emperor. The address of the letter is altogether unusual. Contrary to normal precedent, it is not directed to government officers in the province, but to the 'cities', the *civitates* or states; it was evidently sent to a provincial council of delegates from the separate states, who had decided to renounce Constantine and to turn to Honorius for help. In refusing help, the imperial government legalised in advance whatever administration the British chose to set up; but it thereby created a novel problem that proved insoluble. For four hundred years, the separate states had run their own internal affairs, supervised and controlled by governors appointed by the emperor, to whose universally acknowledged authority the army also owed obedience. Now they were obliged to choose an agreed sovereign on their own. The history of the next two centuries is the story of their failure to agree upon a stable central government, capable of enforcing general obedience.

The break with Rome in 410 was purely governmental and administrative. No one deliberately decided to abandon Britain for ever; the imperial government confessed its inability to help at the moment. There was no 'Roman evacuation of Britain', no 'withdrawal of the legions'. Such troops as could be induced to cross the Channel had already been withdrawn, by Maximus and Theodosius, by Stilicho and Constantine III; the letter did not and could not try to remove those who remained. They were doubtless under strength; Honorius' rescript meant that henceforth their numbers could be maintained and increased only by a British government acting on its own, without outside help. The internal machinery of government was not changed, and the Roman civilisation of Britain lasted some thirty years more, its towns and villas, its agriculture, trade and industry little affected by political independence.

The Sources: Archaeology

The break seems sharper than it was because one of its incidental consequences was a total change in our sources of information. The written record was transformed, and archaeological evidence lost its bearings; the sources must be assessed before they can be used, to see what can and cannot be expected of them.

The archaeological remains of the Romans and of their successors differ greatly. The Romans of Britain are chiefly known from their buildings, and from the things they used while alive. But the pagan English are known mainly from their graves, distinguished by the gear which their relatives buried with them for their use after death, for, as yet, their homes and halls are little known; and the Christian descendants of both peoples left little behind them that an archaeologist can yet recognise.

The contrast is sharp. The Romans built in brick and stone, and used many pots and coins that excavation easily discovers. The jewellery, the funeral vessels, and the rusted iron weapons of the pagan English also remain. But their Christian successors, British and English, buried bare bones. The materials that they used in life have rarely survived. The old craft skills died with the civilisation of Rome, and for many centuries men relied mainly upon perishable materials, wood, leather and other substances that have not withstood the corrosive action of the seasons. The archaeology of Rome and of pagan English burial shouts loud; but, from the 5th century onward, archaeology whispers. Even the evidence of pottery is scant. Some sections of society in some parts of the country used some vessels, for the most part in the larger towns, in monasteries and halls; but pottery did not return to plentiful use on ordinary open-country farming sites until the 12th century or later.

After the Romans, there is much less archaeological evidence; and what there is is harder to assess. All historical evidence speaks clearly only when it is well dated; and in literate ages, archaeology is ultimately dated by texts. Most of what we know of Roman Britain is learnt from the close study of a vast mass of excavated coins and pots that tell the date of the buildings in which they are found. We know the dates from Roman writers, who record the reigns of the emperors whose names are stamped upon the coins, report the dates when particular sites were built or destroyed, or identify the men honoured in inscriptions. But from the fifth century to the seventh, there are no coins and hardly any inscriptions to connect the people with the pots and give them dates, and it is rarely possible to discover when individual sites began and ended.

The familiar methods of the archaeologist fail. Until the last age of Roman Britain, his dating rests upon the contrast between what he finds and what is not there; a site that has plenty of first-century material, but nothing of the second century, is rightly deemed to have been deserted, because the second-century material is plentiful elsewhere, and must have been there if the site were then in use. But from the fifth century onwards such assumptions are no longer justified. The evidence of coins dries up, for the western mints issued very little small change after 403, and hardly any of it reached Britain. So long as men used money at all, the only coins that they could use were those that circulated about 400.

These coins, and the pots and other objects that are commonly found with them, have much to tell of how and where the latest Romans lived; but they say little of when their society ended. The meaning of the evidence has long been muddied by the rash guesses of earlier archaeologists, who pretended that sites were deserted soon after the minting of the latest coin found on them. Recent work teaches a more sober judgment. In the later 4th century the circulation of money was restricted, so that the latest coins are plentiful only on some kinds of sites in some areas; and among them most of the bronze pieces in use about 400 were already twenty or thirty years old, so that on many sites a bronze coin of Gratian is the latest that is likely to have been used in 400 or in 450.

Future research may give a more certain guide. But at present the discovery of the latest Roman material can only argue that the site was used after about 370. By itself, archaeological evidence cannot show when a site ceased to be inhabited. The end of Roman civilisation in Britain is dated by texts; they describe its violent overthrow in and after the 440s, but it is rarely possible to assign a particular date to a particular site. It can only be said that the latest Roman buildings were built and used between about 370 and about 450. The evidence cannot normally give a closer date; and to the vast mass of older archaeological reports which confidently assert the desertion or destruction of a site 'in the late fourth century' must be added the cautious warning 'or early fifth'. Within this period, the evidence of archaeology is competent to describe the manner of men's lives, but not to date them.

The archaeology of the British is a new study. After the disappearance of Roman technology, the descendants of the last Romans in Britain used few objects that excavation can recognise. The work of the last twenty years has just begun to learn to detect their traces; some imported mediterranean pottery reached the shores of the Irish Sea, including south-western Britain, and here and there in Britain home-made wares are observed; some Roman towns and farms remained long in use, outliving the fifth century; a few cemeteries and one or two fortifications and halls of the sixth or seventh centuries are known.

But the number of sites is still small and the quantity of objects found in them is minute. The researches of the next few decades are likely to disclose much more, but at present the evidence of archaeology is too weak to add more than a few random comments to the recorded history of the British heirs of Rome.

By contrast, the remains of the pagan English are abundant. Upwards of 50,000 burials are known, from some fifteen hundred burial grounds, with tens of thousands of grave goods; some scores of houses and one or two villages have also been excavated, though few have yet been adequately published. Much of this extensive material can be dated quite closely, for it is richly ornamented. The study of changing ornament and form is commonly termed typology. It gives dates that are valid if other evidence provides check-points to anchor the stages of its evolution, and thereby to show their pace and direction. The art of the early English has secure anchors, over a period of nearly five centuries. Its recognisable forms begin in Germany, in graves of the third century that contain numerous Roman coins, many of them perhaps looted in the great raids of the 250s. These forms steadily develop until they come to an abrupt end in Germany about the end of the fifth century; but in their last few generations, the grave goods of Germany are matched in Britain, brooch for brooch and pot for pot, and the steady evolution of their styles continued in Britain long after it ended in Germany. The basis of their dating is and always has been the written record of the English settlement of Britain, whose beginnings were rightly placed early in the fifth century by Plettke, the German scholar who grounded the scientific study of these grave goods in 1914. In principle, that which is found in both Germany and Britain belongs to the fifth century; objects found in Germany, but not in Britain, belong to the fourth century or earlier; those found in Britain, but not in Germany, to the sixth or seventh century.

Within this general framework, there are several intermediate checkpoints. Many late Roman graves in Gaul contain a mixture of Germanic and datable Roman objects. Frankish and English pots and ornaments are sometimes buried in the same grave, in Europe and in Britain; and the archaeology of the Franks is fixed by the known dates of their first arrival in northern and in south-western Gaul, and in Bohemia, as well as by the burial of a king who died in 481. Some of the latest burials in Britain contain 7th century coins, and one in Yorkshire bears the name of the thane Lilla, killed in 625.

These and other simple indications tie down two main stages in the evolution of pagan English grave goods, before and after the end of the 5th century. But within the main stages a mass of detail is intricately related, for an immense variety of objects were buried, and each has its own history. Their dates cannot easily be determined by the random study of particular objects on their own. The material remains of any society need to be surveyed as a whole, and they cannot be sensibly assessed until they are measured against a yardstick, a class of object found often over wide areas through a long period of time, whose changing forms are relatively easy to comprehend. In the earlier Roman centuries the red pottery called Samian provides such a yardstick; it is found in great quantities on sites dated by texts, coins and inscriptions, and it gives dates to the local pottery types and other objects found with it. In pagan English graves there are two such yardsticks, the brooches termed 'cruciform' and 'saucer'. Both are found in large numbers over a period of nearly two centuries; both evolve rapidly and recognisably from small brooches with simple designs to large brooches with complex ornament. The simplest forms of both are found in north-western Germany as well as Britain, and were therefore in use in the 5th century. Later forms are not. These brooches give dates to other grave goods commonly found with them, and they in turn date others.

The time when these brooches first came into fashion is clearly marked. The immediate models from which the earliest cruciforms evolved are securely dated in the mixed Roman and Germanic burials of Europe to the decades on either side of 400. In the Elbe lands the first cruciforms are often found in pots that are virtually indistinguishable from others that contained the latest examples of the Germanic brooch termed the *Armbrustfibel*, or 'crossbow'; no 'crossbow' brooch has yet been reported in Britain, though doubtless one or two may some day be discovered. The conclusion is clear. The prototypes of the cruciform brooches came into use about the 390s, the earliest of those commonly called cruciforms a decade or two after 400; they were first buried at about the time when the earliest English burial grounds in Britain were opened; and they indicate the approximate date of a wide range of grave goods, including pottery vessels, that in turn date other vessels, and objects found in those vessels.

The evidence of the saucer brooch is slightly different. On present evidence, it won widespread popularity a little later than the cruciform, though some individual brooches may be earlier. Its main 5th century forms derive from the chip-carved decoration of the late Roman army and represent either five running scrolls or an equal armed cross with scroll ends; and these alone are frequent in the German homeland of the English. Both forms of decoration extended to Scandinavia as well as to Britain; the cruciform brooch there evolved on diverging lines, and though the saucer brooch itself did not spread in Scandinavia, its ornamental motifs were reproduced on other objects, especially on early forms of the brooches termed 'squareheaded'. The evolution of Scandinavian ornament provides a useful check upon parallel developments in Germany and Britain, but in Scandinavia there is little independent means of dating grave goods; successive attempts to found a dating system upon typology have failed to find firm ground, since for practical purposes 5th century Scandinavian dates depend upon the evidence of Britain and Germany, and have no valid means of correcting or challenging them.

Fashions changed quite quickly in the three generations between the first burials in English cemeteries in Britain and the end of the main German cemeteries, about 500; and change is still faster in the 6th century, between the end of the German cemeteries and the last generations of the pagan cemeteries in

Britain. Changing fashion indicates half a dozen overlapping periods in the two centuries of pagan burial in Britain. At present they cannot be examined in depth, and only certain kinds of objects can be dated, for no comprehensive catalogue of the material exists, and no overall survey on the scale of Plettke's work in Germany has been undertaken. Understanding is therefore easily obscured by a maze of false trails and facile assumptions, about coins or weapons, unchecked typology or 'animal' ornament and much else, whose illusory conclusions are difficult to assess.

It is not easy to distinguish conclusions that rest upon a quantity of weighty evidence from those whose base is slighter; and the facile habit of citing a particular conclusion as though it were itself evidence, without indication of the argument behind it, is therefore difficult to avoid. Bewilderment spreads when piecemeal conclusions are found to contradict each other. The resulting confusion tends to deter students from exploring these uncharted and undermanned regions of study, and to divert their energies into easier areas whose need for basic work is less. Nevertheless a few recent wider studies have made it possible to investigate some of the more important evidence comprehensively.

When dating sticks closely to a few sure witnesses, notably to the presence or absence of objects in Germany, and to the evidence of the cruciform and saucer brooches and grave goods found with them, then it becomes possible to observe some regional characteristics and to establish approximate dates for their beginning, change and end. But it is rarely wise to date an object or a grave more closely than to within a generation, for a fashion commonly lasts through the working life of a craftsman, and through the adult years of his customers; and older fashions linger after the novelties that replace them have begun to be made.

The evidence never justifies an assertion that such and such an object dates to 'about 400', or 'about 525' or any other specific time. The height of each fashion may be placed within a date bracket of about 30 or 40 years, but no closer. Moreover, any individual object may have been buried when it was a novelty, or when it was already antique. It is therefore rarely wise to date a single object or a single grave. Historical conclusions must rest upon the survey of large numbers of burials and burial grounds. In practice, the several regions of Britain show common characteristics, and marked differences, with grave goods that are found time and again in some districts in some periods, but are absent elsewhere; it is the regional study of all the evidence, not the study of particular objects or particular graveyards, that outlines the history of English expansion in Britain. That study permits some objects to be placed in overlapping generations of 30 or 40 years; within the half dozen periods so determined, it is possible to note the kind of objects that are present or absent, frequent or rare, and to learn from them something of the changing nature of early English society. The evidence is unevenly balanced; living Romans and dead Englishmen left ample material remains with few texts to explain them; the archaeology of the British is negligible, but many documents describe important aspects of their lives in some periods.

Texts

Written evidence is also uneven. The Romans of Britain are mute and anonymous. Not a word survives of their own literature. Mediterranean writers mentioned Britain when an important personage crossed the Channel, but most such visitors were soldiers, so that these notices outline the frontier wars, and say little of civilian life; and very few such persons came to Britain after 410. But in the last years of the western empire, the British found their own voice. The extant works written by British authors of the early fifth century fill a fair-sized bookshelf. Most, but not all of them wrote abroad, and most wrote theology. But theology was in their day the stuff of social and political controversy, so that these writings have much to say of the manner of life of the British, of their disputes, and of the ideas that moved them. Most of these writers were educated gentlemen, brought up in comfortable mansions; their books trace their cultivated Roman society down to about the year 440, but no further.

Its annihilation is described by their descendants, men barbarised in speech and understanding by the force of the explosion. Many of them try to report what happened; but the Roman past had been so savagely uprooted that they misconceived its nature, misunderstood the events they described, and the context in which they happened. Other writers were story-tellers, who were no more expected to conform to historical truth than a modern novelist. Their business was to edify and to entertain. In successive generations, new editions left out what offended the taste of their own day, or had no meaning, and added stories taken from other times and places, combining and distorting different originals.

Most of these texts are full of half-truths, seen out of focus. They cannot be interpreted until the date and purpose of each has been determined, the original separated from the additions, the contemporary report distinguished from the recollections of the next century, when living memory was still green, and both from the imagination of later ages. Even then, a single statement in a single text carries little weight; confidence comes only when independent texts from different peoples and different standpoints combine to record the same event or to outline the same situation. Their evidence is scantiest in the late fifth century; but from the beginning of the sixth century, its volume and its detail continually increase.

Gildas' Narrative

Only one work outlines a connected narrative of fifth-century British history. About 540, the priest Gildas published a forthright attack on the princes and bishops of his day, and began with a historical preface, tracing the origins of the evils he denounced. One statement, first set down within his own lifetime, and copied by a much later writer, reports that he was born beyond the Roman frontier, in the kingdom of the Clyde; but he was brought south in childhood, to be schooled in a fully Roman educational tradition by the shores of the Severn Sea. He was a man in his middle years when he wrote. His theme is that the disasters of the fifth century had been God's punishment of the sins of past generations; and that if their children, in his own day, do not quickly cease from evil, then God will destroy them, like the Israelites of old. His historical introduction refers to events broadly familiar to his readers, and selects those that prove his argument, illustrating the inborn wickedness of the British nation, the awfulness of divine vengeance, and God's favour to the endeavours of the virtuous and valiant few. The book is a sermon, not a history. Gildas set down so much of the past as he thought fit for his purpose, and left out what he held to be irrelevant thereto.

Gildas knew his Bible thoroughly; he also knew some classical authors, and the ecclesiastical literature of the late Empire; but he had almost no written sources for the history of Britain. He was dependent upon the memories of men who were old when he was young, and was grotesquely ignorant of earlier generations. From 'the time of the Roman emperors', he cites only two events, the rebellion of the 'unclean lioness', Boudicca, in 60, and of Maximus in 388, and uses them to show that the British had always been stubborn rebels against the laws of God and man. He knew nothing of the three hundred years between these revolts, and nothing of what followed. He knew the visible defences of the Roman frontier, the northern walls and the Saxon Shore forts of the south-east, but explained them as constructions of the early fifth century, due to two Roman expeditions, sent in response to appeals by the feckless British for help against the barbarians. Wholly ignorant of the events of 410, he supposed that the

> Romans told our country that they could not go on being worried
> by such troublesome expeditions, and that the Roman standards,
> her great and splendid army, could not be worn out for the sake of
> such unwarlike wandering thieves.

So they taught the British how to defend themselves, advising them to build the northern wall and southern coastal forts, and then

> said farewell, intending never to return.

When the British made a third appeal, further help was refused.

Gildas, like his readers, knew little and understood less of the Roman past. He had no conception that there had ever been a standing Roman army in Britain. His expeditions returned 'to Rome' or 'to Italy' when their work was done; the British were held down

> by whips rather than by military force . . . so that the island was
> regarded as Romania rather than Britannia.

He took Maximus for a native Briton, and when he went to Gaul, Britain lost her armed forces, her governors, brutal as they were, and the bulk of her youth

who went away, 'never to return'. He knew nothing of Theodosius, Stilicho or Constantine III; the 'Roman name' ended with Maximus; thenceforth Britain was Britannia, and 'Romania' meant the continent of Europe.

Gildas' narrative does not become real until he reaches the threshold of living memory, about a hundred years before his own time. The raids and expeditions were followed by a long period of peace and prosperity, so rich that 'no earlier age remembered the like'. Prosperity bred luxury and vice, manifested in repeated rebellion against legitimate rulers. Then came a rumour that the Picts threatened renewed invasion, this time aimed at settlement. The foolish councillors and the 'proud tyrant', the government of Britain, invited three shiploads of the 'unspeakable Saxons' to defend them against the Picts, and settled them in the east of the island. The Saxons thereafter increased their numbers, rebelled, and physically destroyed the civilisation of the island, so that a large part of the survivors emigrated overseas, taking with them such written records as remained. But in Britain a 'miserable remnant' rallied under the leadership of Ambrosius Aurelianus, son of an emperor who had been killed in the troubles, whose degenerate descendants survived in Gildas' own time. Ambrosius initiated a long war of alternating victory and defeat, that ended soon after a decisive British victory at Badon Hill, fought more than 43 years before Gildas wrote.

Nennius

Gildas' outline narrative is amplified by a mass of later documents. The fullest and earliest of them are contained in a collection of historical records first put together in the 8th century, known by the name of Nennius. The compiler did not try to write a history from his sources; he says with truth, 'I have made a heap of all I found,' and his editorship is confined to arranging his texts in what he considered to be their historical order. These documents are independent of each other, and need to be assessed individually. Some are fanciful legends, some concern the sixth and later centuries, but two are of major importance for the history of the fifth century; a *Kentish Chronicle* concerned with events between 425 and 460, and the work of a *Chronographer*, who strove to find exact dates for early fifth-century British events. Both documents were probably first written not much later than the sixth century. They are supplemented by a great quantity of later British and Irish material, and a little contemporary evidence.

Dates

None of these documents touches more than a part of the story that Gildas outlines. They have no context and their meaning is obscure until that story is dated. Just enough is recorded to outline the context. For more than a century after the break with Rome in 410, no event can be dated to a precise year; but three of the main events in Gildas' narrative are dated to within a year or two by contemporaries, two of them by European writers, who relate them to the known chronology of Europe. These three dates give a time scale to Gildas' story, and a context for the rest of the evidence.

The revolt of the English, or Saxons, is reported by a Gaulish chronicler who wrote in 452; he placed it ten years earlier, in or about the year 442, when

> Britain, which had hitherto suffered a variety of disasters, passed into the control of the Saxons.

The statement is terse, but it is clear, definite and decisive; it explains another vaguer contemporary allusion. It is the chronicler's only reference to Britain in his own day, and is therefore an event that seemed to him of first importance. Writing ten years after the event, he understood it to mean that the Saxons had mastered Britain, as Visigoths and Burgundians had mastered parts of Gaul; and that their rule had come to stay. In 452, it could not be known that Germanic supremacy was to be overthrown in Britain, that its ultimate victory was to be postponed for more than a hundred years.

The English came to Britain some time before they rebelled. Both Gildas and the Nennius texts say that a small force was first recruited, and later swelled its numbers until it was strong enough to revolt. The length of that period can hardly have been less than ten years. But it cannot have been much longer, for contemporaries had remarked upon resounding British victories in the first years of independence, about 411 or 412; thereafter followed a long period of peace, and several rulers rose and fell before the English came. The renewed danger that prompted the British government to invite their aid cannot have occurred much before 420 or 425; the first English arrived somewhere in or about the 420s, probably nearer to 430 than to 420. Very many texts call their leader Hengest, and give the name Vortigern to the British ruler who invited them, Gildas' 'proud tyrant'. The *Kentish Chronicle* and Nennius' Chronographer calculate exact dates by a variety of reckonings, putting Vortigern's accession to power in 425, the arrival of the English in his fourth year, 428. The date cannot be pressed to the exact year; but it cannot be more than a year or two wrong.

The second date is the migration. Several contemporary Gauls give reports of the British immigrants, whose fighting force they reckoned at 12,000; with wives and children, old folk and servants, the total must have been four or five times as large. The migration was complete before 461, when a 'Bishop of the British' took his place beside the territorial bishops of the northern Gallic cities in a church council; the British were then recently arrived, for a few years later they had been absorbed into the settled sees of Gaul, and no longer had their separate bishop. The migration dates to the end of the 450s, fifteen or more years after the English rebellion.

Gildas himself supplies the third date. Writing about 540, or a year or two earlier, he complained that orderly government survived during the lifetime of those who had witnessed the wars, but

> when they died, and their place was taken by a generation that had
> not experienced the troubles, and knew only our present security,
> all the controls of truth and justice were shaken and overthrown.

The men he denounced were not rebellious youth, but the rulers of his own time, men mature in years; the wars had ended before their time. This is the kind of statement that a man cannot make about his own lifetime unless it is substantially true; if it were not, all his readers would know that he was lying. The troubles ended with Badon, and they ended a generation or more before Gildas wrote. He adds a more precise date. The battle had been fought forty-three years and one month before. The date is not far from 495.

Three dates in a century are not many; but they are enough to tie down Gildas' timeless narrative, and to relate it to the rest of the evidence. But though they are clear, they have been obscured by an unhappy mistake of Gildas. His narrative rests on the oral tradition of living memory that knew no dates, and was hazy about the interval between events. He knew a single dated document, an appeal for help against unnamed barbarians, sent by 'the British' to the Roman commander in Gaul, 'Aëtius, consul for the third time'. The date is between 446 and 454, but Gildas did not know it. He had to guess the place at which he should insert the letter in his narrative, and he guessed wrong. He knew only a tradition of appeals to Rome for help against the Picts, in the years after 410, and so he cited the letter in connection with these appeals. But the date of Aëtius makes it clear that the enemy were Saxons, the cause of the appeal the revolt of about 442.

Bede

The earliest and best-known edition of Gildas' introductory chapters was published by the English historian Bede in 731. Bede's *History of the English Church* begins with the landing of St Augustine in Kent in 597. It is prefaced by a historical introduction surveying the Roman and pre-Roman past, taken chiefly from continental writers; and when they failed him, after 410, his account of the fifth century is a word-for-word transcript of Gildas, leaving out some of his more exuberant language, with a little added from other sources; and when Gildas failed him, at the end of the fifth century, he jumped straight into his main narrative at 597, with no account at all of the sixth century.

Before 597, Bede is a secondary writer; all the sources that he knew are extant, known to us independently; and many other texts are known which were not available to Bede. Though his readers may admire the skill with which he used his sources, they can learn nothing from his introductory chapters that they could not also learn elsewhere. But Bede, and his readers, were bedevilled by Gildas' mistake. Bede's problem was to link Gildas' dateless story with datable continental events; he did not know the Chronicle of 452, and the only date he had was the Aëtius letter. He wrestled with it in vain. In his own Chronicle, published in 725, he placed the letter among the events of the 430s. Six years later, in the History, he had discovered its date, and entered it at 446; but he had no evidence that could help him to correct Gildas' mistake; he had to preserve Gildas' order of events, although the intervals were plainly wrong, giving a very few years where Gildas had written 'a long time', and placing many years between events that Gildas made consecutive. Bede therefore allowed as much time as he could for Gildas' long interval between the letter and the coming of the Saxons, and dated their arrival to the reign of the emperors Marcian and Valentinian, in his reckoning, which was one year out, between 449 and 456; later still, the 9th century editors of the Saxon Chronicle, to suit the form of their annals, left out Bede's date bracket, and entered the arrival of Hengest under the year 449.

Bede's error was unavoidable; he inherited Gildas' mistake, and had no means of righting it. But it entailed lasting confusion. Bede is one of the world's great historians, widely read by millions of men over the centuries; but Gildas is a little-known preacher, read only by a few scholars. The date 449 or 450, that Bede gave as an approximation, was repeated as an exact year by the Saxon Chronicle, and was universally accepted by English historians for centuries; it has only recently succumbed to the pressure of contrary evidence. It has hamstrung the study of pagan English archaeology; for it was long maintained, on the supposed authority of Bede, that the cemeteries in Britain could not be earlier than 450. But German scholars paid no attention to Bede; relying upon the Chronicle of 452, they placed the first Saxon pots and brooches in Britain in the early fifth century, almost 50 years earlier than the date assigned to the same objects by their English colleagues. Few archaeologists now maintain the date of 450, but the litter of mistaken judgments founded upon that error is by no means yet cleared up. Students of the Saxon Chronicle have been similarly handicapped; its text began with a list of events, and a note of the approximate interval between them, to which later editors added years in AD dates. The sequence of these inserted dates begins with 449; it is approximately 20 years too late, so that all the events to which the early editors assigned AD dates in the fifth century, or the first years of the sixth century, are misdated; twenty years needs to be subtracted from each date, in order to recover the time scale of the earliest version. But printed texts still give only the dates inserted in the manuscripts, without editorial correction.

This long-lived confusion is an instance of the problems that have caused the Arthurian centuries to be regarded as dark, obscure and difficult. Darkness is not deeply embedded in the evidence itself; mistakes like Gildas' misunderstanding of the Aëtius letter are common to most early writers, in Europe as in Britain. They are the ordinary stuff of historical criticism; and over the centuries modern scholarship has sorted out most such confusions in European texts. Obscurity is not to be blamed upon the sources, but upon modern scholarship; it is the fault of the workmen, not of their tools. Yet the fault does not lie in the quality of the workmanship; it arises simply because the work has not been done; the labourers are too few.

Words

Confusion is made worse because the words that describe peoples and nations altered their meaning in an age of rapid change. The stable society of the Roman British before 410 is easily recognised, altogether different from the barbarians in Ireland and beyond the Forth and Clyde. From the seventh century onward the political geography of the British Isles is also readily intelligible; four main nations, the English, the Welsh, the Irish and the peoples of the future Scotland, shared the same religion and a similar culture, though each was still divided into a number of small states. But in the centuries between, new names and old jostle each other. The British were no longer Roman, but were still British. They coined an additional name for themselves, the 'fellow-countrymen', *cives* in Latin, *combrogi* in their own language, whose modern forms are *Cymry* in Welsh, *Cumber* in English. The English knew them by both names, and added a third, calling them 'foreigners', *wealh* or *wylisc* in Old English, *Welsh* in modern English. All these words are alternative descriptions of the same people.

The various names of the Welsh are real and ancient, but made-up modern names still obscure the identity of the English. The newcomers from Germany were drawn from many different nations, but in Britain they adopted a general collective name, 'Engle', or 'Englisc', which Latin writers wrote as *Angli*, and evidently did so before the middle of the 6th century. The form 'Angle' is an invention of recent antiquarians, a simple transliteration of the ordinary Latin word for 'English'. It was not restricted to the territories of the East, Middle and Northern 'Angles', but also comprehended the West, East, South and Middle 'Saxons'; for in their oldest written record, the laws of the 7th century, king Ine styled himself 'king of the West Saxons', but described his subjects as 'Englishmen' or 'Welshmen', not as 'Saxons'. Saxon became a collective national term, but no individual in Britain is known to have been called a 'Saxon' in his own language. 'Saxon' was the term which foreigners applied to the entire nation, and still do; *Saesnaeg* and *Sasanach* are the modern Welsh and Irish words for 'English', and in the elegant Latin of the 7th and 8th centuries *Saxonia* was used as freely of the Northumbrian 'Angles' as of the 'Saxons' of Wessex. Frisians and Jutes, 'Angles' and Saxons, Alamanni and Scandinavians all called themselves English when they settled in Britain, and were all described as 'Saxons' by their British neighbours. In time, custom fixed upon their southern territories the national name used of them by their British neighbours, Saxons, western and southern, eastern and middle, and restricted their own national name, English, 'Angle', to their northern and midland territories. The words do not mean that the south country was settled by immigrants from lower Saxony, the north and midlands by men from Angel in Schleswig. Saxon and Angle are valid terms for regions of Britain, but not for the continental origin of their inhabitants.

Later accident increased the confusion. Eighth-century continental writers devised the term *Angli Saxones*, English Saxons, to distinguish the Saxons of Britain from those of Germany. Early in the ninth century, when the Wessex kings mastered all the English, they took over the term to demonstrate that they were as English as their Mercian predecessors; and sometimes varied it to 'Angul-' or 'Anglo-Saxones', or distinguished the West Saxons with the more honourable title of 'West Angli', and encouraged new words like 'Angligena' or 'Angelcyn'. The usage was short-lived, and was confined to official documents, chiefly in Latin. It was occasionally employed thereafter by those who copied such Latin documents, but it was not revived in the English language until the 18th century, and was employed to link the English colonists in America with their cousins at home, as well as to denote their remote ancestors. Its usage spread slowly, and the terms 'Old English' or 'Saxon' long remained in use; it was not until the 20th century that the unhappy hybrid 'Anglo-Saxon' altogether prevailed, under the influence of historians who pretended that English history begins with the Norman Conquest, and welcomed a word that divorced the pre-Conquest English from their descendants. It is already beginning to pass from use, for many archaeologists are discovering that the terms pagan, middle and late Saxon convey a clearer meaning.

Other peoples were known by different names in different languages, but their usage is simpler. 'Scot' is the Latin name for the Irish, and 'Pict', painted, is the Latin name for the British beyond the Forth, whom Rome never subdued; the Irish called them 'Cruithni', British, and knew their country as Alba, or Albania, Albany, from Albion, the earliest name of Britain, that was known to the ancient Greek travellers. It was not until the 9th century that an Irish Scot dynasty secured the throne of Pictland, and ultimately gave their dynastic name to all northern Britain, thenceforth called Scotland. These terms confuse the unwary, but none are in conflict; British and Welsh, English and Saxon, Scot and Irish are interchangeable terms, naming the same nations in different languages.

Personal names also have their problems. It is not always obvious whether the same name refers to different people, or the same person. As in all ages, common sense is the only guide. Some names are rare, others frequent; some are restricted to particular times, regions or social levels. Some, like Caswallon, Edward or Caradog remain in use, others, like Edbert or Fernvael, passed from fashion; others again, like Hengest or Maelgwn, were used by one person only, and were rarely given to others, if at all. But sometimes a great man's eminence prompted parents to name their children after him; as in modern times, Florence Nightingale, named uniquely after the city in which she was born, made her strange name so common for three generations in southern England that it became almost a synonym for servant-girl; and therefore passed from use. In recognising persons, it is obvious that a common name like Ceredic does not by itself help to identify the people who bore it, unless further detail links them; but to suppose that two separate persons of the same date and status bore the unique names of Hengest or Maelgwn would be as idle as to suggest that two different persons called Marlborough commanded the armies of early 18th century England.

The roots of confusion are names hazily understood and dates apparently contradictory. Gildas' narrative, and the contemporary evidence that dates it, divide the history of fifth-century Britain into three main periods. The generation from the break with Rome in 410 to the outbreak of the first Saxon revolt about 442 is the last age of Roman Britain. Then followed nearly twenty years of conflict between the Roman British and the Saxons, or English, that ended when the bulk of the organised southern British forces accepted defeat and sent their emigrants to Gaul, shortly before 461. The third period, a generation of about 35 years, from about 460 to 495, witnessed the successful resistance of the British. That resistance was begun by Ambrosius; some time before the final victory of Badon, its captaincy passed to Arthur.

The outline of the next century is simpler. British and English traditions both prolong the peace of Badon for three-quarters of a century. A second Saxon revolt won decisive victories in the 570s, and by the early 7th century had permanently mastered most of what is now England. Gildas' narrative is supplemented by a good deal of detail until about 460; from then until the 530s, evidence is meagre; thereafter, information rapidly becomes fuller, and increasing contemporary and continental evidence gives growing confirmation and precision.

CHAPTER FOUR

INDEPENDENT BRITAIN: VORTIGERN

Civil Government

Britain was still Roman in 410, and remained Roman for a generation. Political independence did not disrupt the settled Roman economy. In 429 Germanus of Auxerre encountered opulent bishops and normal civil life, and at about the same date Patrick found his family secure in their property; in the 440s Patrick was concerned with cultured bishops who still exercised normal ecclesiastical authority, while Germanus met a civil government that still ruled its region effectively in southern Britain. But since the imperial government no longer gave protection, the British had to fight to keep their civilisation. Roman writers were impressed when

> the British people took up arms, bore the brunt of the attack, and freed their cities from the barbarian threat.

Various sources name their enemies. The Gallic Chronicle of 452 reports a dreadful Saxon raid upon the Channel coasts in 411. The Irish Annals put the death of the high king Niall in the Channel a few years earlier, and Gildas recounts victories in colourful detail, that may repeat a story told in his native north-west.

> Hordes of Picts and Irish . . . swarmed from their coracles . . . and seized the whole of the far north, as far as the Wall. . . . Our countrymen abandoned their cities and high walls . . . and the disasters from abroad were aggravated by internal disorders, for repeated incursions had emptied the whole land of food.

However, when the Romans refused to help, the British rallied and

> went on fighting back, basing themselves on hills and caves, moorland and woods, . . . trusting not in man, but in God; they then defeated the enemy raiders for the first time. . . . The enemy withdrew.

A bare Irish record of a battle, or a ravaging, of the Clyde, in the time of Niall's successor, Nath-I, may remember the same attack.

Gildas and the continental contemporaries agree on the essential fact of British success against the barbarians. The Gallic writer names Saxon enemies,

Gildas names the Irish and the Picts; the Irish allege their own presence in the Channel and in the far north, and have left scattered traces of a considerable settlement in western Britain.

Military victory was achieved by the armies of Britain. Raising and maintaining armies requires a political government, and one contemporary says something of how it came to power. A homily addressed to a young widow, published in or about the year 411, bears the name of a British bishop named Fastidius. One passage concerns contemporary political events. The author consoled the widow for the seeming injustice of God, who had taken her virtuous husband, though so many evil-doers were left alive, and referred her to what was happening in the world about them at the time, when

> we see before us many instances of wicked men, the sum of their sins complete, who are being judged at this present moment, and denied this present life no less than the life to come. This is not hard to understand, for in changing times we expect the deaths of magistrates who have lived criminally; for the greater their power, the bolder their sins. . . . Those who have freely shed the blood of others are now forced to shed their own. . . . Some lie unburied, food for the beasts and birds of the air. Others have been individually torn limb from limb. Their judgements killed many husbands, widowed many women, orphaned many children, leaving them bare and beggared . . . for they plundered the property of the men they killed. But now it is their wives who are widowed, their sons who are orphans, begging their daily bread from strangers.

A government had recently been overthrown by violence; rough justice killed some and lynched some, but others received a formal trial. It was not simply a peasant or plebeian rising, for victors and vanquished were both men of property. But the language is remarkable. Governments in plenty were overthrown in the fourth and fifth centuries. But they were personal governments; their enemies uniformly abuse the 'satellites' of an 'unspeakable tyrant' or 'wicked minister'. Fastidius' account is unique because the fallen rulers are not described as the agents of any tyrant or minister; they are magistrates, treated as equals of each other. His language suits the exceptional situation in Britain in 410 or 411. It may be that the government which had seized power in order to secure help from Italy was itself overthrown when that help was not forthcoming. If it had tried and executed Constantine's leading supporters as rebels against Honorius, it could not expect mercy from their friends when its promise came to nothing.

The political events of the next dozen years are not recorded. But the political forces, the pressures and the institutions which decided them are known. In Britain, as in Gaul and Italy, there were two main native political forces, the landed nobility and the army. In Europe, there was a third force that had as yet no equivalent in Britain, the power of large barbarian peoples headed by their kings. But Britain may have had one political pressure that was negligible in Europe. In and about the year 410 British writers abroad, notably the unnamed author known as the Sicilian Briton, developed an astonishingly advanced egalitarian political philosophy, exalting the Christian virtues of the poor against the sin of riches, and urging the abolition of the rich. Their views had a brief influence, sufficient to provoke popular disturbances in Rome and alarm the imperial government for a few months in 418. Their tracts refer to individual outspoken plebeians who dared to lift their voices and argue politics with men of substance, demanding social justice. One at least of their writings still circulated in Britain more than a century later, and is cited by Gildas. An egalitarian peasant commune subsisted for a short while in Armorica, but there is little sign of such peasant rebellion in Britain, and the writings of the Sicilian Briton and his fellows agitated the urban rather than rural poor in Italy. In Britain, Fastidius condemns the old government and approves the new, and urges with unusual force the view that in a stable society governments and men of property must use their wealth to care for the poor.

> Do you think yourself Christian if you oppress the poor? . . . If you enrich yourself by making many others poor? If you wring your food from others' tears? . . . If, when you are bidden to distribute your own property, you seize other people's . . . ?
> A Christian is a man who . . . never allows a poor man to be oppressed when he is by . . . whose doors are open to all, whose table every poor man knows, whose food is offered to all.

The sentiments of Christian charity are not novel, but such insistence in the fifth century is exceptional; so is its context, related to a government which Fastidius regards, or pretends to regard, as committed to practise them. These writings do not suggest that the urban or rural poor constituted an independent organised political movement with a social programme of its own. They do suggest that the pressure of the poor for social justice was somewhat more effective in Britain than in Europe.

Europe resolved these conflicting pressures by continuing the government in

---

Peoples and Places　　　　　　　　　　　　　　　　**Map 2**

● Capitals of *Civitates*

■ Coloniae; legionary fortresses; and London

○ Other major military centres

MAP 2 ROMAN BRITAIN

Atecotti?

Northern Picts

Southern Picts

Damnonii Votadini

Selgovae

Novantae

Carlisle   Corbridge

Brigantes

Aldborough
York

Ribchester   Parisii

Brough

Chester   Lincoln

Ordovices Decangi

Wroxeter   Coritani

Leicester

Caistor

Iceni

Cornovii

Catuvellauni Trinovantes

Demetae

Carmarthen   Dobunni

Gloucester   Colchester

Silures   St Albans

Caerleon   Cirencester   London

Caerwent   Cantium

Atrebates   Silchester

Winchester   Canterbury

Belgae   Chichester

Dumnonii   Durotriges

Exeter

Dorchester

50 mls
80 kms

the name of the infant and feeble heirs of legitimate emperors. Britain had no such legitimate heirs. Yet the long-established constitution of the Empire was the only possible form of government. An emperor ruled through civilian prefects, military *magistri*, and lesser departmental heads, appointed consuls to name the year and to discharge the ancient formal functions of the Roman state. Aristocratic tradition had in the past tried to run the empire by a council of appointed noblemen, and had failed. It was impossible to revive such governmental forms in the fifth century, in Europe or in Britain; the army, and the plebs, had for centuries rejected aristocratic government in favour of a monarchy able to curb senators and to reduce the risk of civil war. The governments of 410 and 411 were necessarily created by the *civitates* meeting in council to get rid of the emperor Constantine and to find a successor. When their natural choice, Honorius, failed them, they had to seek another. They could not themselves endure, without an emperor. But it was not easy to agree upon an emperor whose government all would accept. Any stable ruler must command the obedience both of the aristocracy and of the army; and must prove tolerable to the plebs. An emperor, whatever his origin, must heed the whole of the pressures within the empire; but his subjects pressed chiefly the interests of their own group and class. Noblemen naturally distrusted a military emperor, generals distrusted a civilian. Any magnate appointed to rule must encounter the resistance of his fellow noblemen, who knew that his origins and claims were no better than theirs, so soon as other pressures forced him into policies they resented. An army officer crowned emperor risked both the jealousy of his colleagues and their resentment at concessions to the civilian taxpayer. Civil conflict was as inevitable in Britain as in Europe, when once there was no clear succession.

A few notices assert the obvious, that such emperors were appointed, and faced civil war. Procopius, writing in Constantinople in about 550, says that after the end of Roman rule, Britain was governed by 'tyrants', illegitimate emperors. Gildas, writing ten years earlier in Britain, says that in the early fifth century, after the repulse of the barbarians and during the period of prosperity,

> kings were anointed ... and soon after slain ... by those who had anointed them.

From the late 4th century on, the word 'king', *rex*, was used colloquially of emperors, though never officially; and the letter of Honorius legitimised emperors who ruled in Britain alone. One of them is known. The parents of Ambrosius Aurelianus, who headed the resistance of the 460s, had 'worn the purple'; the words mean that his father was emperor, for no subject 'wore the purple'. He is perhaps the Ambrosius who is reported to have been Vortigern's rival in the 430s.

The government of an emperor required imperial officers and institutions, prefects, masters of the soldiers, consuls, senators. One of them is attested; the Sicilian Briton, writing home to a wealthy relative who sat in judgement on a tribunal, and therefore held office, politely wished him an 'everlasting consulate'.

The probable meaning is that he was a consul, recognised in Britain alone. But the institution that looms largest in the narratives of Gildas and Nennius is the Council. The Council of the province or diocese, composed of magnates from the separate *civitates*, was a normal institution. It was usually weak in the face of the imperial government; but when the magnates of Britain could make and unmake their own emperors, the Council clearly mattered more, and may well have taken the place of the Senate.

The Army

Vortigern is said to have come to power about 425. He is described as king or tyrant; as such, he held the power, and probably the title, of an emperor. Nothing is reported of the persons or the circumstances that brought him to power, but the principal political interests that pressed upon his government are known. They were rooted in different regions. Throughout the lowlands, territorial magnates were still powerful, especially rich and numerous in the Cotswold country. Beyond them lay the poorer states of Dumnonia, Devon and Cornwall, of Demetia, Pembroke and Carmarthen, and of central and northern Wales; there landowners were humbler men, nearer to their tenants in interest and outlook, in language and culture, with less Latinity in their speech and thought; and it is probable that more of the land was farmed directly by its owners.

The third main region of Roman Britain, the north, was the domain of the army; and the army had the means to make and unmake governments. There is plenty of archaeological evidence for the late Roman army in Britain, and a precise contemporary description survives. But the evidence is difficult to assess and interpret. The *Notitia Dignitatum*, or List of Offices, is a comprehensive schedule of all senior civilian departments, and of the army units, throughout the Roman Empire; its western lists were kept up to date until the early 420s, about the time of Vortigern's accession. They were maintained by the imperial government in Italy; but it had not ruled Britain since the enthronement of Constantine III in 406, and it is unlikely that the British lists had been revised thereafter. They were retained because the separation of Britain from the rest of the empire was the result of an emergency, and might be ended.

Three distinct commands are recorded in Britain. A small mobile field army force, of three infantry and six cavalry units, under a *comes*, or count, had no fixed stations; and might have followed Constantine to Gaul. The names and stations of two static frontier commands are also entered, the coastal garrisons of the Saxon Shore, under their own *comes*, from Southampton Water to the Wash, and the army of the north, under its *dux*, or general, whose headquarters were at York. The static units were hard to move, for their wives and children were exposed to enemy attack if they were absent. Stilicho managed to withdraw a legion in 403, and perhaps some Saxon Shore forces, and Constantine III may have persuaded some at least of the younger men to follow him abroad; but it is unlikely that the bulk of the garrisons could have been induced to leave.

Elsewhere in the empire, most garrisons stayed where they were until they were overwhelmed.

In most of the empire, garrison units of the 'major schedule', normally those raised in the fourth century, and the legions, are listed first in the *Notitia*, followed by the 'lesser schedule' of the auxiliary units that survived from the early Roman army, the *alae* and *cohortes*, wings or squadrons of cavalry and regiments or battalions of infantry; where a military command extends over more than one civil province, the units in each province are listed separately. The northern British list follows the normal pattern. After the legion at York, and fourth-century units in the Pennine forts, follows the 'lesser schedule', with a cross heading 'Also on the Line of the Wall', naming the auxiliaries from Wallsend to Westmorland. It is followed by a new list, of one unit of the major schedule and two of the lesser, in Lancashire and the West Riding; the second list clearly relates to a different province, perhaps Valentia.

Throughout the empire, the units of the major schedule were still effective fighting units, wherever evidence is available to show their history; but those of the lesser schedule were not. Some were wholly absorbed in civil administration; some existed only in name; and ultimately many of their personnel spent much of their time earning a civilian livelihood. At best they could defend their homes against attack; for they were armed. A commander might commonly deploy his major units, or move their station, at least within their own region; but he would be fortunate if he could persuade the lesser units to operate beyond the next neighbouring fort. So long as he retained the allegiance of his men, the *dux* at York might rely upon his major units to secure the Pennines against a lowland government, in case of dispute; and might in times of crisis induce detachments to aid the south against an enemy, or to challenge its authority. But essentially his armies, and those of the *comes* on the south-eastern coast, were regional forces, not readily available for the defence of the rest of the country, or for interference in its government.

No adequate commentary on the *Notitia* has yet been published; its absence has permitted strange speculations, based chiefly on considerations of the British lists on their own. In particular, it is often asserted that the Wall list was fifty or a hundred years out of date by the 420s, and that the units named had long ceased to exist, chiefly because the Wall was badly battered in the disaster of 367, and was restored by makeshift repairs, to which labourers from the civilian south contributed. The text does not justify such inferences; nowhere else does it preserve lists so long obsolete, and in Britain it notes the changes introduced in 368, omitting the forts north of the Wall that were then abandoned; it places upon the Wall lesser schedule units whose engineering standards are likely to have been as poor as those that excavation has revealed. It is likely that, as in Egypt and on the Danube, units maimed by invasion were left under strength, perhaps paid in kind rather than in cash, and allowed to dwindle to the calibre of an ineffectual local militia.

The names of the units are however of secondary importance. Though late coins are rare upon the Wall, late pottery abounds, and lasts as long as Roman pottery was manufactured in Britain. Some of it was made locally, but the bulk of it was imported from far away, chiefly from the kilns of the East Riding; and these imports argue that the Wall forts were still supplied by the army command at York. The date when these kilns ceased production is not known, but it is unlikely to have been much later than the Saxon revolt of the 440s. The disappearance of the pottery is evidence of the closure of the kilns, but has no bearing on the ultimate fate of the Wall forts; when their population could no longer import, it had to do without imports. No evidence is available for most forts; but some rebuilding is very late, and burials of the later 5th century, and of the 6th, some of them British, some Germanic, have been reported from a dozen forts; and some elaborate rebuilding looks as late. The burials are evidence that some men continued to live in some of the forts, whether or not they constituted the fading relics of the units named in the *Notitia*.

One section of the northern command seems to have perished early. The watch towers of the Yorkshire coast, unlike the forts of the Saxon Shore, the Pennines and the Wall, were violently destroyed; the skeletons of armed men and dogs, who rotted where they fell, are lurid witness of a final disaster. The skeletons give no date; but at one poor farming site near the Scarborough tower, the British population was replaced by an English settlement as poor, probably during the fifth century. It may be that the population fled when the tower was stormed, and that thereafter the English were installed in their place.

Excavation has shown other fortifications, not named in the *Notitia*. The four corners of Wales, Chester and Caernarvon, Cardiff and Carmarthen, are left out of the lists, perhaps because much of the Welsh coast was in the hands of Irish settlers. No fortifications are known in Dumnonia; but a few late Roman coins on coastal sites from Barnstaple to Plymouth, in regions where coins of all periods are rare, may be the consequence of government payments to local militia, in districts also open to the Irish. In the interior, there is no record of military forces, other than the small field army that may or may not have remained. But the massive fortifications of late Roman towns point to a huge gap in our knowledge; there is nothing to show who manned their walls and bastions, though the walls were built for armed men to hold. Their defence necessarily fell to the local population, ill-equipped, ill-trained and inexperienced, perhaps sometimes reinforced by army units. Excavation hints at local officers; the ceremonial symbol of military rank was the belt, *cingulum*, worn by military and civil officers, splendidly adorned for higher ranks. Many such belts have been discovered; the more elaborate are decorated in the style termed *Kerbschnitt*, or 'chip-carving'. The ornament imitates in bronze the technique of wood-carving, and is probably of Germanic inspiration, though it was the fashion for officers of any nationality all along the western frontiers from about 380 to about 430.

These belts are sometimes found in graves, and a man who was buried with military equipment was usually a barbarian, who followed barbarian burial customs. There were many German officers in the late Roman army; most of them commanded native Romans, and were themselves assimilated to Roman and Christian ways, but there were also a few units of Germans, officered by Germans. Few remained permanently German, for many of those that were maintained for more than twenty or thirty years commonly drew their recruits from the frontier where they were stationed, and became Roman, retaining only the name of their original nationality. But two or three newly raised barbarian units are known to have served in Britain, and there were doubtless others that have left no trace.

There were also humbler German forces in the western empire, termed *gentiles*, perhaps also in Britain. The *Notitia* lists among them *Laeti*, mostly Frankish, in Gaul, and *Sarmatae* in Gaul and Italy. The Gallic *Laeti* were the descendants of prisoners surrendered by treaty at the end of the third century, who were settled in or near the towns of the interior, with the double purpose of agricultural labour on landlords' estates and of local defence. The last page of the list is missing; it may have included *gentiles* settled in Britain, though they may not have been called either *Laeti* or *Sarmatae*. Recent archaeological observation suggests that such communities existed. Some men were buried in Roman cemeteries, with ordinary 4th-century pots, but also with Germanic spears, as at Colchester. But from the end of the third century onward, a number of commercial Roman potteries in Britain manufactured for sale a variety of wheel-made wares, whose shapes and decoration imitated the hand-made vessels of the Saxons and English of the lower Elbe lands of Germany. They are found chiefly in the eastern and midland counties, between the Bedfordshire Ouse and the Thames estuary, most of them in or near Roman towns and country houses, occasionally also in Saxon Shore forts. They were made for customers who liked and bought Saxon styles; and it is likely that such customers were of Saxon origin, *gentiles* settled in Britain, at much the same time, and on much the same terms, as the *Laeti* of Gaul. They have nothing to do with the later pagan English immigrants of the fifth century; they used normal Roman cemeteries and their wares were not buried in pagan English graves. By the time of Hengest, four or five generations after their settlement in Britain, they can have had no common cause with their distant kinsmen; for Germans beyond the frontier had little love for those among them who took service with the empire. The interest and affection of the *gentiles* tied them to the economy of Britain, and numbered them among the allies and defenders of Rome.

The military forces of the south are likely to have consisted of local residents, prepared to defend only their own walls; of a few German army units; of *gentiles*; and of such field army units as Constantine III and his successors had been able to raise and maintain in Britain. Unless the armed forces of the north and south agreed to obey a British emperor, each must follow its own fate. What little is known of the disintegration of the Roman army elsewhere indicates the possibilities that lay before them. In northern Gaul, the last Roman commander-in-chief, Aegidius, refused allegiance to the puppet emperors of later fifth-century Italy. His independent command became a kingdom, that he bequeathed to his son Syagrius, who maintained it until he was overwhelmed by the Franks in 486. Another general established a similar kingdom in Dalmatia, and left it to his nephew.

Similar possibilities were open to the *dux* at York, whose major units still provided combatant units. Detailed information on the fate of auxiliary army units of the lesser schedule comes from the Danube. In the province of *Noricum Ripense*, roughly the territory of modern Austria, a monk named Severinus stiffened the resistance of the still Roman towns again the barbarians, who dominated the countryside. His biographer, writing in 511, about events forty or fifty years earlier, naively remarked

> While the Roman Empire still existed, they used to maintain soldiers in many towns at the public expense. . . . When this custom lapsed, . . . the unit at Passau continued it. Some soldiers from this unit were sent to Italy to fetch the last pay due to their comrades. . . .

They were murdered by barbarians. But if they had reached Rome, the *Notitia* proved their entitlement. It names their unit, the 9th Batavians, which had been stationed for 400 years at Passau, on the Inn, now the frontier between Austria and Germany, and had given the place its Roman name, *Batavis*. Here, one unit long outlived the collapse of the frontier. The defence of different towns along that frontier greatly varied. In one of them, 'the tribune Mamertinus, later a bishop' commanded a few frightened soldiers who dared take the field only when Severinus inspired them with a rousing speech and a blessing. Another town was burdened with a barbarian garrison, apparently of federate allies of Rome; another, once the fortress of a legion, was now packed with refugees from abandoned towns, but there is no sign of troops; the citizens themselves mounted guard on the walls.

Lesser units were as feeble, and as long-lived, in Egypt, where no barbarians overawed the countryside. Some of the units named in the *Notitia* continued to raise local recruits in the 580s; and their grandchildren served in the same units when the Moslems overran Egypt in 640. But though the recruits became regular soldiers, they were part-timers, boatmen, bakers, basket-makers, who worked at their trade in the morning, and paraded for drill in the afternoon.

These reports from the Danube and the Nile match the evidence excavated in Britain. When civilians and soldiers sheltered together inside the walls of forts, the distinction between them was blurred, as in Egypt. The northern British frontier was not stormed, like the Danube; but in much of the south, during and after the Saxon revolt, conditions were similar. Barbarians roamed at will in the open country. Some towns were abandoned, others were not; the uneven scatter of military equipment suggests that some towns were defended by military units, of Roman or barbarian origin, whose morale and discipline is likely to have been as varied as on the Danube. It is unwise to look for a definite time when the male population of a town or fort ceased to be a military unit, or to suppose that each place was abandoned at the same date. The frontier garrisons dwindled and disintegrated, the fate of each of them separately determined by local accidents. In Britain, as elsewhere, the Roman army did not die; like the proverbial old soldier, it faded away.

In Britain, there is no sign that the frontier was ever stormed or evacuated. On the contrary, it held, and barred the Picts from attacking south by land. Its central authority remained, to develop like that of Aegidius in Gaul. The future political organisation of the north is outlined in the genealogies, whose later names are celebrated in the old Welsh poems, at the end of the sixth century. The several dynasties of the Pennines and the Wall trace their common origin to Coel Hen, whom they place early in the fifth century. One of the greater dynasties ends with Eleuther of the Great Army, and his son Peredur of York. The kings named might all have been actual descendants of Coel; but the genealogy would take the same form, and treat them as descendants, if they were subordinate commanders who rejected the sovereignty of York, but founded their authority thereon. The early tradition is that Coel ruled the whole of the north, south of the Wall, the territory that the *Notitia* assigned to the *dux*; but that in later generations it split into a number of independent kingdoms. It suggests that, like Aegidius, he was the last Roman commander, who turned his command to a kingdom. But his kingdom lasted longer than that of Aegidius. So did his name; for medieval fantasy turned him into Old King Cole, and on the strength of the name transferred him to Colchester.

In the early fifth century, the *dux* was not yet a king; but his army made him an independent ruler who need not bow to a government he did not respect. His power was limited by the difficulty of moving his forces out of their own territory, and by the sudden cessation of his normal resources. His predecessors had looked to Italy for men and money. He could look only to Britain, and the wealth that must maintain the army was concentrated in the hands of wealthy southern magnates. Therein lay the basis of agreement between the military and the civil power; or of disagreement. In the years immediately after 410, there was evidently concord. The British repelled their enemies with outstanding success; and could hardly have done so unless the *dux*, the *comes* and the civil government worked together; and unless some effective forces were recruited and maintained in the south.

Concord did not endure. Gildas complained that

> the island grew affluent. The abundance of commodities out-
> stripped the memory of any earlier age. But with prosperity grew
> luxury . . . and all the vices natural to man . . . hatred of truth . . .
> and love of lies. . . . Kings were anointed . . . and soon after slain.

Throughout the late empire, landowners had no love of armies; the imperia, government found continuing difficulty in raising recruits, for landowners pulled every excuse to avoid surrendering their tenants and labourers, and to avoid payment of taxation. The magnates of Italy and Gaul resisted the demands of a legitimate long-established government for men and money, even when danger was acute; their peers in Britain are unlikely to have met their obligations willingly in times of peace and prosperity. Britain cannot have escaped the consequences that followed in Europe; the government was forced to walk the tight-rope between the needs of the army and the interest of the landowners; its officers, in search of money, squeezed the peasant and the poorer landowner, who lacked the strength to defy or cheat the tax-collector. The root conflicts between the rich and the poor, the army and the civilians, were sharpened by personal antagon-isms between individual generals, individual magnates and individual states. Secular conflict inflamed religious dispute, and rival theological ideologies surfaced into bitter clashes in times of political crisis. In Europe, the universal fear of civil war attached public opinion to the legitimate dynasty, so that conflict might be resolved by the intrigues of ministers, who ruled in the name of inoffensive nonentities. But Britain had no legitimate dynasty; a change of government still required the overthrow of an emperor, and therefore 'kings were anointed and soon after slain'.

Vortigern

Out of these conflicts came Vortigern. The genealogists make him a notable of Gloucester, one of the four known *coloniae* of Britain, the only one of them situa-ted among the great mansions of the Cotswolds. Tradition sets him among the wealthiest of the landed aristocracy. Other rulers are credited with a like origin; Ambrosius Aurelianus was a 'gentleman', a *vir modestus*; and his father had been emperor before him. It is not easy to see that persons elevated by the *civitates* of Britain could have had any other origin, unless it were military.

Vortigern excelled among his fellows, for he managed to preserve his authority for a generation, despite disastrous reverses, where his predecessors had been quickly overthrown. His success betokens a wide support, and his name suggests its origin. It cannot have been his normal and original name. The other known notables of early fifth-century Britain all bore ordinary Roman names, even if they also had British names. Several did. Patrick, of a fifth-century landed family, was also called 'Maun'; the Cornovian Marcus in the sixth century was also named Conomorus; and the original text of the genealogies may have read 'Vortigern, that is Vitalis' (or Vitalinus), later misinterpreted as 'Vortigern, son of Vitalinus'.

But Vortigern is not a name. It is a description. It means 'Overking'. It was not a title, and did not become so; but it is a description that fitted one person only, as surely as in the 1940s 'the Old Man' meant Churchill and no one else, or as a century before 'the Duke' meant Wellington and no other duke. The widespread use of the word implies that it was popularised by people who spoke British rather than Latin; and that they liked him. He seems to have appealed to their affections, for two of his three sons were known by their native names, and are among the earliest late Roman notables known to have used such rustic native names in preference to polished Roman names. It is therefore possible that one of the reasons that enabled him to maintain a longer and stronger authority is that he was able to call upon support from the poorer areas of Wales and the south-west, as well as from the Cotswold magnates; and that he may have appeared as the champion of the peasant, the urban poor and the underdog, echoing the radical sentiments of Fastidius. Such support, and such sentiments, must have offended some amongst his fellow magnates; but it was a support that gave strength, as popular support had once strengthened Caesar against Pompey, and was in a later age to strengthen the Tudor kings against the great lords. Vortigern's name was perhaps Vitalinus; his formal title is not known. It was quite possibly emperor, 'Imperator Caesar Augustus'; and he would have followed precedent if he named Hengest his *Magister Militum*, commander-in-chief.

Picts and Saxons

Whatever the forces that brought him to power, Vortigern faced a serious external crisis on his accession.

> The feathered flight of a not unfamiliar rumour reached the keen ears of everyone, that their old enemies were come again, bent as was their wont on destruction and on inhabiting the country from end to end. Yet they took no profit from the news . . . but rather . . . rushed down the broad way that leads to death . . . until . . . a deadly plague struck down so many in a short space, with no sword, that the living could not bury all the dead.

The danger was new and severe. The enemies were not merely raiders; they now aimed at conquest and settlement. Goth, Burgundian and Vandal had shown that barbarians might settle within the empire, and had warned Romans of the consequence. The faint native traditions of the Picts emphasise their own rising ambition; after a list of bare unmeaning names, the first of their kings to whom their records give a date or ascribe an action was Drust son of Erp, who 'fought a hundred battles' and is said to have reigned from 414 to 458, in Vortigern's time. Gildas' 'old enemies' were the northerners. The Picts, as well as the Irish, were to him, *transmarini*, from overseas; both sailed to Britain 'in their coracles' and both had carried their booty home 'across the sea'. Gildas is not composing an academic study of British geography; he describes the means by which the enemy reached the Roman diocese. The Irish came by sea because they lived in an island; the Picts came by sea because the northern frontier armies withstood them by land, and because even without armies, many hundreds of miles of poor country separated them from the riches of the south. These riches were vulnerable. The Cotswolds lay open to Irish landings by the Severn Sea, and were also less than a week's march down the Icknield Way from the flat beaches of the east coast.

The 'rumour' reached the British well in advance of the invasion. Evidently some fresh initiative had advertised the enemy intention before their armada was ready. This event may have been the destruction of the Yorkshire signal towers, a necessary preliminary to any Pictish offensive. Their end was sudden and final. All that can be said of its date is that it was probably before the first English settlement in the East Riding, in the earlier 5th century. One scrap of evidence suggests the possibility that Pictish raiders may have penetrated as far as Norfolk.

The British took no immediate action. But events moved fast.

> The time drew nigh, when the iniquities of Britain should be fulfilled, as with the Amorites of old. A Council was convened, to decide upon the best and soundest means of withstanding the frequent brutal invasions and raids of the aforesaid peoples.
>
> All the members of the council, and the proud tyrant, were struck blind. . . . To hold back the northern peoples, they introduced into the island the vile unspeakable Saxons, hated of God and man alike. . . . Nothing more frightful had ever happened to this island, nothing more bitter. The utter blindness of their wits! What raw hopeless stupidity! Of their own free will, they invited in under the same roof the enemy they feared worse than death. . . . So the brood of cubs burst from the lair of the barbarian lioness, in three 'keels', as they call warships in their language. . . . At the orders of the ill-fated tyrant, they first fixed their fearful claws upon the eastern part of the island, as though to defend it. . . . Their dam, learning of the success of the first contingent, sent over a larger draft of satellite dogs. . . . Thus were the barbarians introduced . . . in the guise of soldiers running great risk for their kind 'hosts', as the liars asserted. They demanded 'supplies' which were granted and for a long time 'shut the dog's mouth'.

Nennius' Kentish Chronicle is shorter, but more detailed.

> Then came three 'keels', driven into exile from Germany. In them were the brothers Hors and Hengest. . . . Vortigern welcomed them then, and handed over to them the island that in their language is called Thanet, in ours Ruoihm.

The Nennius Chronographer dates their coming to the year 428, the fourth year of Vortigern.

Gildas' retrospective fury is understandable; but, at the time, the Council's decision was not so silly. Governments before and after successfully set a thief to catch a thief, and it was plain sense to hire Saxons, the greatest seamen of the age, against seaborne invaders. Hengest was an outstanding freebooter, a Dane allied with Jutes in Frisia, whose fame in German saga outlived his contemporaries. The Saxons were settled, like the Goths of Gaul and other barbarians, under the normal billeting laws, whose technical terms, 'hosts' (*hospites*) and 'supplies' (*annona*), Gildas accurately repeats.

Such federate settlement was a novelty in the western empire, first permitted some ten years before, when the Visigoths were established in Aquitaine in 418. The Visigoths were a large and dangerous people, united by powerful national kings. Hengest's men were few, a scratch force recruited by an adventurer for the occasion. The first small contingent is said to have been conveyed in three 'keels', that could have carried no more than a few hundred men; even if tradition exaggerated, it amounted to no more than the addition of one barbarian unit to the army of Britain; the newcomers did not amount to an independent power, capable of acting on their own initiative, until later events had much increased their numbers. In the 420s they were innocently few, tucked away on a remote offshore island, no threat to the security of Britain.

Vortigern's councillors would have found it hard to make a rational case against the employment of a tiny force under a capable captain, though men already knew the dangers of barbarian allies, and were soon to learn the almost limitless opportunities open to a resolute commander. In a society that had relied for centuries upon professional soldiers, a few armed men might terrify thousands

---

Map 3

	Inhumation		Cremation		Mixed rite	Uncertain rite
	alone	with a little Cremation	alone	with a little Inhumation		
Large cemeteries	▮	▮-	▬	▬	✚	
Cemeteries	▯	▯-	▭	▭	⊕	
A few burials	‖		=			//
Single or family burials						/

House or houses	△
Uncertain date	?
Roman roads	---

58

MAP 3 PAGAN ENGLISH SETTLEMENT I
THE EARLIER 5th CENTURY

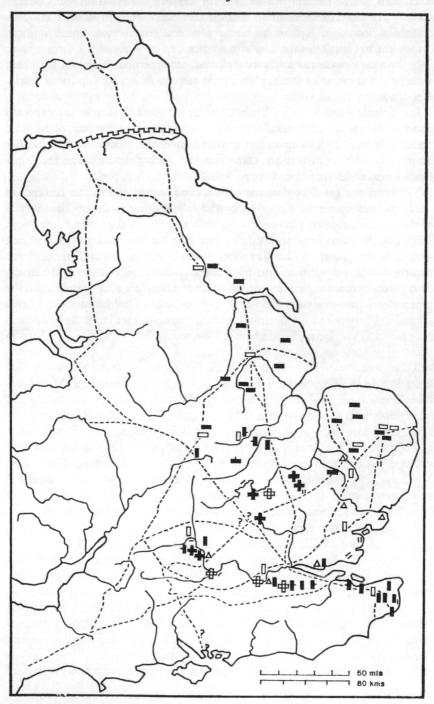

50 mls

80 kms

of civilians, whose instinct was to fly from weapons, unless town walls offered shelter. Yet the enlistment of so small a contingent seemed to offer effective defence at low cost. Roman landlords who grudged recruits found it more convenient to contribute the cost of a soldier than to surrender a farmworker; and, since cash payments might be deferred, each member of the Council that authorised the hiring of the English might reasonably hope to dodge at least a part of the imposts he voted.

But a single small force on Thanet was no adequate answer to the expected invasion. It was speedily reinforced by 'a larger draft of satellite dogs', who 'fixed their fearful claws upon the eastern part of the island'. Excavation has pinpointed the places where the claws fastened. Map 3 distinguishes the pagan English cemeteries that contain grave goods of the earliest period.

The excavated evidence does not permit close dating; and cannot distinguish the first comers from the larger drafts who followed, up to the middle decades of the century; save that an unusually large number of the earliest urns from Caistor-by-Norwich suggests that the city may be included among the first settlement areas; and very early brooches from Luton and Abingdon also argue that their owners were among the first comers. But throughout the fifth century, each group of new immigrants tended to settle near their fellows, and even the cemeteries whose earliest burials date from the end of the century are located around and between earlier burial grounds. The map cannot locate the individual sites to which Vortigern's first federates were posted, but it indicates the districts that they protected against the Pictish threat.

These forces were stationed far from the enemy, near to the lands they defended. It is an axiom of military science that a commander's dispositions reveal the nature of the attack he anticipates, or intends to launch himself. Vortigern's allies lined the north road from York to Stamford, with outposts near the Lincolnshire coast, but were most numerous in Norfolk. A few sites in north-east Kent and in the Colchester area closed the estuary of the Thames, and a few guarded the southern approaches to London. Inland, forces by Cambridge, Dunstable and Dorchester-on-Thames, with northward protection at Sandy and Kempston by Bedford, secured the major intersections of the Icknield Way. These dispositions are an intelligible answer to a seaborne invasion threatened from the north, aimed at the riches of the Cotswolds, whose most likely landfall was foreseen on the north Norfolk coast, at the head of the Icknield Way. Relatively strong forces also took precautions against the most obvious alternative, a landing on the Humber, to be followed by a march down the north road or the Fosse Way. A much lighter force forestalled the less likely alternative, that the enemy might by-pass the main defences and sail all the way to the Thames; and Portsmouth harbour was perhaps also protected. The reserves by the Icknield Way formed a last resort, in case the enemy succeeded in piercing the coastal screen. Vortigern and Hengest knew their business.

These dispositions also reveal something of the political situation; their wide distribution demonstrates that the greater part of the lowlands acknowledged the authority of Vortigern and the Council, while the presence of federates at York and the East Riding shows that the northern armies concurred. It is also evident that the northern armies were still regarded as an effective force. No foreigners were yet established north of York; since they were not needed, the army clearly felt able to hold the land frontier on its own. In the east and south, Germanic troops were accepted almost everywhere. Within the area of their settlement, most of the major towns and many smaller places have fifth-century Saxon cemeteries just outside their walls, positioned like the Roman burial grounds. They are clearly the cemeteries of forces billeted in or near the towns. The outstanding exception is Verulamium, where extensive excavation has so far shown no sign of English burials earlier than the 7th century. The government of the Catuvellauni evidently declined to receive a garrison in their capital; they might reasonably have regarded the forces stationed in their territory about Dunstable, thirteen miles to the north, as sufficient protection.

Either the Picts attempted invasion and suffered defeat, or they abandoned the project in face of the massive defences. No invasion succeeded, and the sequel was a British counter-attack. The initial plan showed a boldness of conception foreign to the static defence that had dogged Roman military thought in the fourth century; it provided not only an elastic net to trap an invader, but a means of going out to meet him. The core of the heavy concentration in Norfolk was a group of sites close to the navigable waters of the Yare; and Yarmouth offers the most northerly adequate base whence a large flotilla of beached vessels might quickly reach the open sea. The Saxons were above all seamen, the Picts landsmen who travelled by sea; experienced sailors needed no manual of strategy to teach them that enemy transports were best sunk at sea, or attacked in a night-time anchorage. But whether or not these convenient opportunities were then used, the Saxon seamen are said to have counter-attacked a few years later. The Kentish Chronicle reports that

> Hengest said to Vortigern . . . 'Take my advice, and you will never fear conquest by any man or any people, for my people are strong. I will invite my son and his cousin, fine warriors, to fight against the Irish. Give them the lands of the north, next to the Wall. . . . He invited Octha and Ebissa with forty keels; when they had sailed round against the Picts and plundered the Orkneys, they came and occupied several districts beyond the 'Frenessican Sea', as far as the borders of the Picts.

Gildas records recent enemy penetration as far as the Wall, and though the original purpose of the northern expedition is said to have been to restrain the Irish, Octha was established upon the Pictish border, after attacking their coasts and the islands beyond. He and his men may well be those who first used a group of dateless cemeteries in northern Northumberland, whose dead were interred with no grave goods, save an occasional Saxon knife to prove their nationality; and who left a few place names in south-western Scotland, notably Dumfries, the fortress of the Frisians.

Vortigern's decision brought notable and immediate success. The menace of the highlanders, which for centuries had bogged down upon the British frontier the largest army of the Roman empire, was for ever stilled. Not until 1745 did the south country again have cause to fear invasion from the lands beyond the Forth. Though in the long run the invitation to the barbarians of the lower Elbe was to turn southern Britain into England, immediately it saved Britain from becoming Pictland. Two of the three ancient enemies had been quieted, by pitting one against the other.

The Irish

The danger from the Irish was met by other and subtler means. Though Hengest is said to have offered to fight the Irish, Gildas and the Kentish Chronicler emphasise that the main weight of the English forces was directed against the Picts. The archaeological evidence concurs. Saxon cemeteries are found in the east, not in the west. Their distribution is a result of the decision of Vortigern and his council; if they had decided to use the English against the Irish, the cemeteries would be found in Cumberland, Wales and the south-west. They did not so decide. Nevertheless, the Irish were ancient enemies of the British, repeatedly and recently allies of the Picts, and already had numerous colonies in western Britain. The Picts might reasonably expect their Irish allies to join them against the British.

One incident shows that there was danger in the west. In 429 the bishops of Gaul, with papal approval, sent bishop Germanus of Auxerre to combat the Pelagian heresy in Britain; the date is given by Prosper of Aquitaine, a well-informed contemporary. But since the date given for Hengest's arrival, 428, is much less precise, it cannot be known whether Germanus came before or after Hengest. During the bishop's visit, 'the Saxons and the Picts made a joint campaign against the British', at Easter time. Germanus, who had commanded armies before he took orders,

> offered himself as commander. His light troops thoroughly explored the country through which the enemy's advance was expected; choosing a valley set among high hills, he drew up his army ... in ambush. As the enemy approached, he ordered the whole force to respond with a great shout when he cried out. The bishops cried out thrice together 'Alleluia'; the whole army replied with a single voice, and the great cry rebounded, shut in by the surrounding hills. The enemy column was terrified; the very frame of heaven and the rocks around seemed to threaten them. ... They fled in all directions ... many drowning in the river they had to cross. ... The bishops won a bloodless victory, gained by faith, not by the might of men.

The biographer who tells the tale, Constantius, was probably well acquainted with Bishop Lupus, who was with Germanus at the battle, and it is his first-hand account that he reproduces. The rocky valley and the broad river are real features of the British countryside, most obviously to be sought in Wales; there, in and near the Vale of Llangollen, a number of early traditions honour Germanus. At first sight, Picts and Saxons seem out of place in Wales, where the normal enemies were Irish. It may be that Lupus' memory muddled the names, but there is no evidence and no reason to suppose that he did. Pict, Irish and Saxon were old allies, and Hengest's small Saxon force was not the only one of its kind that tried its luck in western waters in these years. But whoever the enemies were, there was a real danger that the triple alliance of the past might be renewed, this time in support of a Pictish attempt to conquer all Britain. Vortigern forestalled the alliance, detaching the Saxons by purchase, the Irish by a blend of diplomacy and force.

Germanus' campaign was fought when Vortigern's strategy was beginning to take shape. It formed part of that strategy; for so important a decision, the despatch of an eminent continental bishop to bless a British expeditionary force and advise its commanders cannot have been taken without the goodwill of the British government. The political consequence of the victory is related in another life of Germanus, transcribed among Nennius' documents after it had been lavishly embroidered by the story-tellers. In this account, Germanus, on his first visit to Britain, destroyed the stronghold of a wicked king named Benli, and replaced him with one of his subjects, Catel, 'from whose seed the whole country of Powys is still ruled to-day'. Vortigern is not named in the text, but an inscription set up by the king of Powys about the year 800, termed the 'Pillar of Eliseg', claims Vortigern as the political authority who established the kingdom. The origin of the dynasty was traced to Brittu, who is made a 'son' of Vortigern, 'whom Germanus blessed'; and Vortigern's own legitimate authority is asserted by making him son-in-law to the emperor Maximus, who 'killed the king of the Romans'.

Native tradition placed Germanus' military activity in a countryside that fits the eye-witness description of mountain and river that Constantius learnt from Lupus; though tradition did not know that account. The names of places and persons add detail. The term 'Powys' is a Welsh spelling of the Latin *pagenses*, the 'people of the rural districts'; it implies a separation of the upland rural territory of the Cornovii from the city of Wroxeter, set in the flat lands of the Severn valley. It also implies that the separation took place when Roman administrative terminology was still in use. The names of the first rulers, Catellius and Bruttius, are ordinary Roman family names, appropriate to the landed families of the *civitates*. By contrast, the dynasty of the Cornovii themselves favoured somewhat different names, above all the two personal names Constantine and Gerontius, used by many men for many centuries. These two names may have owed their popularity to the emperor Constantine III and his general Gerontius;

they are recorded among the Cornovii alone, until later accident made Constantine popular among the northern British and the Scots. One medieval Welsh poem appears to echo a tradition that a commander who fought with Germanus was named Gerontius.

The personal and district names associate Germanus with the notables of the Cornovii in a campaign, fought in 429, that recovered their hill territory from the rule of aliens, presumably Irish; and thereafter made it a separate political state, under the rule of men with Roman names. The native tradition concentrates upon the reduction of the principal enemy stronghold. Constantius describes a battle, evidently fought before the siege of the stronghold, against a mobile force of Picts and Saxons; since they also fought the Romans and British, they were necessarily *de facto* allies of the entrenched foreigners, the Irish, very possibly their formal allies.

Local place names add topographical detail. The hill fort of Moel Fenli in Ruthin in northern Powys preserves the name of Benli, or else inspired it. An exceptionally large late Roman coin hoard there buried argues that it was in the fourth or fifth century the residence of a powerful ruler. Twenty miles to the south, on Deeside by Llangollen, Moel-y-Geraint bears the name of Gerontius. Places and churches named after Germanus abound in Powys, but are rare elsewhere in Wales, though they occur in three or four scattered groups in England.

All this diverse evidence hangs together. Each of the several items, considered on its own out of context, bristles with obscurities and tempts the unwary modern critic to speculate without evidence that its statements are 'untrue', or to replace them with others that occur in no source at all. But in context they tell a plain tale. Hostile Irish had settled in numbers in northern Wales; when a force of Picts and Saxons appeared in the area, they threatened to renew the alliance of the barbarians and to establish a firm operational base for continuing attacks upon lowland Britain. A British force was sent to prevent the establishment of that base, to deal with the Picts and Saxons before they reinforced the Irish. Germanus' neat stratagem brought them victory, and Vortigern's political solution prevented a repetition of the threat. The enemy kingdom of the upper Dee was overthrown. A Roman British authority was established in the hilly rural districts of the Cornovian state; though its first commanders doubtless held the rank of Roman military officers, protectors and rulers of the *pagenses*, their command endured, and became the kingdom of Powys.

The establishment of the new kingdom was the first step towards the reduction of the Irish settlements of western Britain. Success required the neutrality of the mainland Irish. In 431, two years after Germanus' visit, the pope sent a Roman priest, Palladius, to fortify the orthodox of Britain and to convert the Irish. He was ill-received in Ireland, and returned after a few months, to die in Britain; in the following year he was replaced by Patrick, a British monk trained in Germanus' cathedral monastery. The young High King Loegaire received him without enthusiasm, but gave him licence to preach. The next event recorded in the Irish Annals, in the same year or the year after, is 'the first Saxon raid on Ireland'. It does not say whence the Saxons came. But the Irish coast is far from the Elbe, and British harbours are nearer. Vortigern may well have let his allies loose against the Irish, to warn Loegaire that it was henceforth dangerous to aid Pictish adventures or to succour colonists in Britain. Vortigern profited, whether or not he was responsible for the attack. No Irish aid to Picts or to colonists is recorded, in British or Irish texts; as far as the evidence goes, the Irish stood idly by while the British mopped up their kinsmen. Two generations later, at the end of the century, Irish attacks were resumed for a few years, and failed. No more are mentioned, and the ancient threat from Ireland ended as abruptly as the Pictish danger.

The sudden end to hostilities is said to have been accompanied by the marriage of Vortigern's daughter to the son of the Irish king, and by the conversion of a number of Irish notables and plebeians to the religion of Britain and Rome, preached by Patrick. The lasting peace, the dynastic marriage, and the admission of the Roman religion of Britain suggest the conclusion of a formal treaty. Such agreement could not have been reached unless a significant body of Irish opinion was ready for it. Recent experience had prepared them. Many of the Irish had seen something of the Roman world and of the Christian religion; some had served with the previous king, who was killed 'in the Alps' in 428, presumably in Roman employ, and a few individual Irishmen had already adopted Christianity. But agreement was reached only by the active diplomacy of lay and clerical leaders. Patrick's biographers assert that his mission was undertaken with the approval of the Gallic bishops and of the Pope; and Patrick himself recalls the prior approval of the British bishops. Such approval was necessary; Patrick would not have been heeded as a private visitor, without the backing of the British church and of the Head of Christendom. But the mission could not have been undertaken without the consent of the Irish government; and the political agreement required the interested participation of the British government, for its secular consequences were plainly considerable. The despatch of Germanus' pupil to Ireland, three years after Germanus had intervened among the Irish settlers in western Britain, indicates some negotiation, discussion and agreement between the governments of Britain and Ireland and the churchmen of Britain, Gaul and Italy.

The basis of agreement lay in identity of interest. The Gallic bishops' main purpose was to confound heretics. They made little headway among the churchmen, and needed what help the government could give them. Vortigern had cause to avoid dispute with the orthodox catholics of Gaul, for he had enemies at home who might seek their aid. Native British tradition is quite clear that relations were friendly during Germanus' first visit, when the bishop blessed the king, and were hostile only during the second visit; the contemporary record agrees, for the army could not have taken the bishop's advice unless secular authority approved. Their interests also coincided in the Irish problem; Patrick is said to have been Germanus' pupil, whom he proposed to send even before the Pope sent Palladius; and the British government required catholic approval for a mission to win the Irish to the religion of Britain. The timely understanding with the Irish was hardly reached without the exercise of considerable diplomatic skill; and the advice of the shrewd experienced bishop is likely to have guided the diplomacy. Constantius credits the bishops with a bloodless victory in Wales; it may also be due to them, at least in part, that Ireland was pacified without bloodshed.

Cunedda

Once the neutrality of mainland Ireland was assured, Vortigern was free to subjugate the Irish colonists of western Britain. They were reduced, not by the conventional Roman method of sending campaigning armies who returned to base after victory, but by the drafting of settlers from other parts of Britain, who made their permanent homes in the territory they regained. A document in Nennius' collection specifically describes the reconquest of Wales

> Cunedag, ancestor of Mailcunus, came with his eight sons from the north, from the district called Manau Guotodin, CXLVI years before Mailcunus reigned, and expelled the Irish ... with enormous slaughter, so that they never came back to live there again.

The genealogies have much to say of Cunedda. He was the great-grandfather of Mailcunus, or Maelgwn, and his alleged descendants ruled north Wales for eight centuries. The later kings of Cardigan and Merioneth also claim descent from him, and he is said to have recovered Cetgueli, Kidwelly, the eastern Carmarthenshire coastal region. The figure of 146 years is given in Roman figures, that are easily corrupted in copying. It conflicts with the evidence of the genealogies that place Cunedda in the 430s. Since the figure occurs once in a single text, whereas the genealogies are repeated by many writers, and in this instance date both the descendants and the ancestors of Cunedda, their evidence is stronger. It is probable that the figure was miscopied, and that Cunedda was a contemporary of Vortigern.

Cunedda was a portent. Posterity has popularised his name, nowadays spelt Kenneth. His origin, his career, and his name link the Roman past with the medieval future. He was a grandson of the Paternus who had been appointed, probably by Valentinian, to rule the Votadini of the north-east coast, between Tyne and Forth. Like Vortigern's sons, he is one of the first persons in authority in Britain who were known only by a native personal name. His father, grandfather, and great-grandfather had all borne normal Roman names, and are given an origin among the cultured Romans of the south. His own 'sons' and 'grandsons' divide equally between those with Roman names and those with native British or Welsh names; but their later descendants almost all used Welsh names. The memory of Rome was fading.

Cunedda's northern territory had been incorporated within the empire for a short while, centuries before his time; and had thereafter remained a border state dependent on Rome. The lands of the Votadini are naturally divided by the Tweed, and each portion contains a large prehistoric hill fort, evidently the centre of government until the English conquest. Traprain Law in the north, in the Lothians, has been excavated; it contained quantities of Roman coins and other objects, and a remarkable early fifth-century treasure, of silver vessels smashed ready for smelting, looted by someone from Gaul, and presumably received as a gift by the Votadini. Traprain Law was plainly the residence of rulers long in contact with Rome, and northern tradition makes it the residence of a sixth-century Lothian king. The southern fort, Yeavering Bell, by Wooler, in north Northumberland, has not been excavated. But when the English subdued the region, they established a royal centre at its foot, on a hideously uncomfortable windy site that was abandoned a few decades later; their choice of so unsuitable a site cannot easily be explained, unless it was a dynastic centre similar to Traprain Law before they arrived. Cunedda's movement, and later northern tradition, suggest that he ruled at least over the southern Votadini. He may have ruled the north as well, for the Nennius text gives his home as the Manau of the Gododdin, or Votadini, the northernmost of their territories, about Stirling. If the text is literally accurate, he ruled there, but since the Manau was the last portion of Votadinian territory to remain in British hands after the English conquest, an eighth-century writer may well have used it as synonymous with the whole Votadinian country.

Only a portion of the Votadini are said to have accompanied Cunedda; his eldest son is reported to have remained behind, but his heirs followed in the next generation. One group of inscriptions seems to concern a Votadinian family who moved to north Wales; and implies that the immigrants also brought settlers from the Clyde, as well as from more southerly territories in Liddelwater. The inscriptions also show something of the nature of the reconquest of Wales, for some were found in and near Roman forts. Reconquest was evidently the work of several decades, not of a short campaign; Cardigan takes its name from Cunedda's sons, Merioneth from his grandson; Irishmen remained in the north to renew the war at the end of the century, and Cunedda contained Demetia in the south-west, but did not subdue its Irish dynasty. The inscriptions show that some Roman forts were occupied in the fifth century, during or just after the reconquest, though excavation cannot yet recognise their occupants. Other forts were doubtless held, whose defenders have left no inscriptions, and Caer Rhun on the Conway bears the name of one of Cunedda's descendants. Cunedda's strategy and his military organisation were necessarily geared upon the Roman roads and forts; and it is hard to suppose that any such war, fought to regain control of north Wales, can have had any other main base than Chester.

Cunedda's arrival changed the history of Wales. His departure brought consequences scarcely less important to the north. At home, he may well have been as much an enemy as a friend. His ancestors had been installed to protect the Roman army against the Picts, replacing the unreliable *Areani*. The single written reference to Cunedda in the north suggests that the new guardians may have become as unreliable as their predecessors. A late poem incorporates and adapts verses whose meaning was forgotten, and uses the place names current in its own day. They tell of Cunedda's wars in the north, singing

> Splendid he was in battle, with his nine hundred horse, Cunedda
> ... the Lion ..., the son of Aeternus,

and two obscure corrupt lines appear to say that he fought against the inhabitants of the north east, the future Bernicia, and that 'the forts will tremble', thanks to him, 'in Durham and Carlisle'. Whatever lies behind these lines, they imply that Cunedda attacked the lands south of Hadrian's Wall. He can only have done so before he moved to Wales. The story is not improbable. Gildas' report of enemy settlement between the walls early in the century convicts the Votadini either of collusion or of inability to resist. The Traprain treasure has similar implications. Either the Votadini accepted gifts from the enemy; or they required expensive presents from the British to ensure their loyalty and alliance. Cunedda's removal may well have relieved the north as much as it benefited Wales.

Cunedda's migration implies an authority accepted by the whole of the Roman diocese. The movement cannot have been accomplished without agreement between Vortigern and the army command of York. It left a gap in the defence of the north that required filling; and separate accounts indicate the measures taken both by Vortigern and by the northern army to fill it. Vortigern sent Octha north with English federates; they left traces in and about Dumfries, slight enough to suggest a short-lived settlement, but established permanent homes on the north Northumbrian coast, in the southern Votadinian lands south of the Tweed. The genealogies place at about the same date an offshoot of the dynasty of York, that appears to be located in or about the Lothians, headed by Germanianus, 'son' of Coel. There is nothing to show whether both movements were simultaneous, or were separated by an interval of years; nor whether they were agreed between Vortigern and the northern army, or were separate settlements undertaken in rivalry. But they are linked by geography; Octha and Germanianus both moved into lands that the Votadini left.

The Cornovii

Cunedda's migration was matched by another, equally vaguely dated to about the time of Vortigern. The territory of Roman Dumnonia had also been settled by Irish colonists. It comprised the modern counties of Devon and Cornwall, with much of Somerset. It retained its name, but accepted rulers called Cornovii, whose homeland lay on the upper Severn, with their capital at Wroxeter, near Shrewsbury; and centuries later, when the English conquered its eastern portion, the ancient name of Dumnonia, pronounced Dyfneint in Welsh, and Devon in English, was restricted to English territory, while the still unconquered west became known by the dynastic name of Cornovia, Cornwall, the land of the Cornovian Welsh.

The date of the Cornovian migration is given in no text. But Docco, said to have died in old age about 473, and Gerontius, killed about 480 in youth, are both represented as sons of Dumnonian Cornovii. The date should therefore lie in the first half of the fifth century, not far removed in time from Cunedda's migration. The two movements were similar in aim and nature. The purpose of both was to expel or subdue Irish settlers. Both involved military peoples who bordered on the highlands.

The Cornovii were the only *civitas* of Roman Britain with a military commitment. The *Notitia Dignitatum* lists a unit called the *cohors I Cornoviorum* at Newcastle-upon-Tyne. It was not there in the early empire; it is the only unit in the Roman army that took its name from a British *civitas*; and it is the only British unit known to have served in Britain at any time. The origin of the unit is readily explained. The territory of the Cornovii included a number of forts in Wales, whose likely Roman garrison was not regular units, but the *iuventus* of the Cornovii, their men of military age. It was probably some of them who were raised to the status of a cohort and posted to Newcastle, in the late third century or the fourth. It is likely that the Newcastle cohort continued to recruit among its own people, and that with their *iuventus* and their cohort, the Cornovii had a long military tradition not shared by other *civitates*.

Though the date of the move to Dumnonia is uncertain, this military tradition suggests its context. The changes on the northern frontier are likely to have ended the connection of the Cornovii with the cohort at Newcastle, if it had not earlier ceased; and the establishment of the new state of the *Pagenses*, Powys, ended whatever military responsibilities the Cornovii may have retained in their own territory. The creation of the new state is likely to have meant that some Cornovian notables lost lands and lordships, that some troops experienced in fighting Irishmen in hill and moorland lacked employment. The opportunity to seize and settle lands occupied by enemy aliens in the south-west compensated their loss, and profited the government.

The Dumnonian end of the migration suggests the same context as the movement of the Votadini, for it also presupposes a strong central government. Though it was legal to billet native armies upon the same terms as foreign federates, the existing civil authorities of Dumnonia could hardly be expected to undertake the permanent maintenance of such a force, unless constrained thereto by a superior government able to enforce its will. No evidence suggests that either the predecessors or the immediate successors of Vortigern enjoyed such authority, and it was therefore probably he who organised the migration of the Cornovii, as of the Votadini.

Vortigern's Success

The precise date and sequence of these important events cannot be determined, but the crowded energy of Vortigern's first ten years fills the sources. Later ages vituperate him as the unhappy author of the English occupation of Britain, but in the early 430s disaster had not yet come. Judged by his early achievement, Vortigern assumes the stature of a major statesman, whose enterprise came near to salvaging a powerful and enduring state from the wreckage of the western Roman empire. The British frontiers were intact, more securely held than at any time in the previous two hundred years, and past losses were in process of recovery. The problems that had outwitted the generals of the empire were permanently solved. Mediterranean opinion might wonder that

> the British had freed their states from the barbarian threat . . . and set up a native constitution on their own,

for no other region of the west could claim as much. The orderly household of bishop Fastidius' widowed correspondent, the quiet estate of Patrick's father, betokened a security then rare in Europe, so that the last years of the Roman British seemed to their nostalgic grandchildren a legendary time,

> affluent . . . with abundance beyond the memory of any earlier age.

CHAPTER FIVE

THE OVERTHROW OF BRITAIN

Civil War

It was civil war, not foreign invasion, that destroyed Vortigern and opened Britain to the English. A Nennius text pinpoints the three main dangers that he faced on his accession. He was threatened by

> the Picts and the Irish, by a Roman invasion, and, not least, by fear of Ambrosius.

The Picts and the Irish were successfully contained. The other two dangers were linked. Ambrosius, who was Vortigern's enemy in the 430s, was too old to be identical with Ambrosius Aurelianus, the resistance leader of the 460s; but the elder Ambrosius may well have been father of the younger, and the father of Ambrosius Aurelianus ruled for a while as emperor, either in Vortigern's time, as his rival, or before him. Nennius' Chronographer reports that the elder Ambrosius made war on Vortigern in or about 437, and one late tradition exiles him to Gaul and brings him back with an army from Europe. Whether or not he managed to persuade the Roman government to invade Britain, Vortigern had good grounds to fear that he might. Any dispossessed British emperor must necessarily look for aid to Roman Europe, though his chances of arousing sufficient interest in a distracted Gaul were doubtless slim. There, army commanders had their hands full at home; barbarians and peasant rebels made more urgent demands than the domestic affairs of the British. But the church had a greater interest, for un-orthodox opinion might cross the Channel. If the government of Britain were shown to be heretical, its enemies might count upon the support of the bishops.

From the standpoint of Europe, the church of Britain was no longer orthodox. After 410, the trenchant theology of Augustine prevailed in the western empire, but it had not penetrated Britain, where the milder philosophy defended by Pelagius escaped challenge. The imperial government had proscribed the Pelagians in 418, but its writ no longer ran in Britain; there, laws enacted in Italy had no validity, unless the British government chose to enforce them. It is unlikely that it did, for there is no sign that the controversy bit deep in Britain. Fastidius was shocked and amazed to discover that there were churchmen abroad who discounted the efficacy of good works; but he treated them as eccentric rather than as dangerous, and for the next several centuries there is almost nothing to show that Christians in the British Isles were aware of Augustine. Augustine's triumph was decisive for the Christianity of Europe, but in Britain it made no change.

The indifference of the British was matched in parts of northern Gaul. There, the Chronicler who wrote in 452 casually observed that 418 was the year in which

> Augustine is said to have invented the heresy of Predestination.

He chronicled a remote event that for him had little immediate local consequence. But the vigorous churchmen of southern and central Gaul could not so easily dismiss the new philosophy of the mediterranean; whatever their personal estimate of Augustine, their concern was to preserve the unity of the church against schism. They could ignore Britain so long as the British church left Gaul alone. But latent conflict became acute soon after Vortigern's accession. According to Prosper, the reason why Germanus came to Britain in 429 was that the British bishop Agricola had 'revived' Pelagianism. Prosper was a staunch Augustinian, in close touch with senior ecclesiastical opinion. The bishops of Gaul could not ignore Agricola; he had evidently restated the views of Pelagius, forcefully enough to bring aid and comfort to the critics of Augustine in Europe.

The dispute gave the British government an embarrassing choice. If Vortigern championed the Pelagians, he offended catholic Europe, and heightened the risk that his enemies might find foreign support; but if he opposed the Pelagians, he offended an influential section of his own people. What is reported of the sequel indicates a judicious compromise. Germanus came, and failed to win the churchmen. Vortigern welcomed him and gave him licence, but used no coercive secular authority to aid him against the heretics; instead, he diverted the bishop's energies into help and advice on secular problems.

Judicious compromise might soothe and postpone impending conflict; it could not remove its causes, and the relatively mild antagonisms of religion were soon overshadowed by the political and financial consequences of the government's defence policy. While the foreign danger remained acute, men acquiesced in the mounting cost of federates, and in the drastic demands of the central government upon each individual state. But, so soon as the crisis was past, the states protested. The Kentish Chronicle tells the story plainly.

> The king undertook to supply the Saxons with food and clothing without fail; and they agreed to fight bravely against his enemies. But the barbarians multiplied their numbers, and the British could not feed them. When they demanded the promised food and clothing, the British said, 'We cannot feed and clothe you, for your numbers are grown. Go away, for we do not need help.'

The Chronicler accurately distinguishes between the 'king', and the 'British'. An assembly of the states of Britain had endorsed the original invitation to

Hengest's three keels; whether it had been consulted about their heavy reinforcement is doubtful. At all events, a Council now determined to end the agreement, evidently after Vortigern had found that the taxation necessary to maintain the federates was no longer forthcoming. Compared with the real wealth of the province, the cost was probably not excessive. The barbarians cannot yet have numbered more than a few thousand, nor could their upkeep have cost much more than the annual income of the owner of the North Leigh or Woodchester villa. But to Roman noblemen costs on such a scale seemed insupportable; twenty years before, the ransom that Alaric exacted from the defenceless Roman Senate appeared enormous, yet the sum he demanded was little more than one year's income of a rich senator. But paying an adequate army would have cost even more. Rome fell because its great men would not pay for its defence. So did Britain.

Indignation at the cost of barbarians was inflamed in Gaul by resentment at their uncouth manners and simple arrogance. The same causes operated in Britain; and there, if the magnates of some regions declined to deliver the subsidies due, an added burden fell upon the areas least able to bear it. For Vortigern's authority rested upon the willingness of individual states to obey his government. In the east, where the federates lived, their presence gave him the physical power to enforce payment, but it was less easy to coerce the states of the south and west, the Belgae, the Durotriges and the Dobunni, if their magnates induced their state councils to discontinue supplies, or if numerous wealthy individuals decided to withhold or diminish their contributions. These states comprised the richest areas of Britain, and if they defaulted, the full cost fell upon their poorer eastern neighbours, who could not so easily avoid payment.

The Council's decision to dismiss the Saxons was understandable; but it presented an insoluble problem. The barbarians were the main military force in the areas where they lived. If their promised supplies failed, they at once became a danger; the only alternatives were to feed them, to pay them to go away, or to expel them by force. The only force strong enough to oust them was the northern army; but even if its commander was able or willing to lead his men to the Thames, it is unlikely that he was asked, for his victory might depose both Vortigern and the Council in favour of a military monarchy. Yet some such military intervention must have seemed for the moment possible, for the cautious Hengest, though he 'took counsel with his elders to break the peace', held his hand for several years more.

The open breach between Vortigern and the Council gave Ambrosius an opportunity. Nennius' Chronographer baldly reports the event.

> From the beginning of Vortigern's reign to the quarrel between Vitalinus and Ambrosius are twelve years; which is Guoloppum, that is the battle of Guoloph.

His date is 437. The place is perhaps Wallop, in Hampshire. The genealogists knew Vitalinus as ruler of Gloucester, closely connected with Vortigern; he was perhaps identical with him. The struggle was between the adherents of Vortigern and those of Ambrosius; Vortigern's opponents now included a majority of the magnates who composed the council and had voted to expel the barbarians; many of them doubtless rallied to Ambrosius.

We do not know who won the battle, but the ultimate victor was the Saxon. Vortigern, rejected by a powerful section of his subjects, had no choice but to lean upon his federates. The Saxons were not a well-knit people, but they had a leader.

> Hengest was a man experienced, shrewd and skilful. Sizing up the king's weakness, and the military inexperience of his people . . . he said to the British king, 'We are few; if you wish, we can send home for more men, to raise a larger number to fight for you and your people.' Envoys were sent across the sea, and returned with nineteen keels full of picked men.

This was a force to be numbered in thousands rather than in hundreds. The first modest contingent had been enlisted to repel foreign invaders; civil war compelled Vortigern to bring over larger reinforcements to fight his British enemies. He was now irrevocably committed to his federates, a tyrant holding down his own people with their aid. He had to pay dearly for their support.

> In one of the keels was Hengest's daughter, a very beautiful girl. . . . Hengest arranged a banquet for Vortigern, his soldiers and his interpreter, named Ceretic. . . . They got very drunk . . . and the devil entered into Vortigern's heart, making him fall in love with the girl. Through his interpreter, he asked her father for her hand, saying, 'Ask of me what you will, even to the half of my kingdom'.

The romantic morality is sensational journalism · marriage alliances between emperors and barbarian generals had august recent precedents; the emperor Arcadius' cousin married the Vandal Stilicho; and on the strength of another sister's romantic promise, Attila the Hun demanded half the empire. The husbands may or may not have loved their brides, but the motive of their marriages was political.

Marriage demanded a gift to the bride's father.

> Hengest took counsel with the elders who came from the island of Angel; they agreed . . . to ask for the district that their language calls Canturguoralen, ours Kent. Vortigern granted it, though the then ruler of Kent, Gwyrangon, was unaware that his kingdom was being made over to the heathen, and he himself abandoned to their control. So the girl was married to Vortigern and he slept with her and loved her deeply. . . . So Hengest gradually brought over more and more keels, till the islands whence they came were left uninhabited, and his people grew in strength and numbers, established in Canterbury.

Canterbury is the only city in Britain that the Saxons are said to have acquired by treaty, rather than by conquest; it is also the only city where Saxon pottery of the earliest period has yet been excavated from dwellings, set side by side with the homes of the latest Romans. Its new inhabitants were presumably billeted as federates in the normal manner, but in numbers sufficient to make them masters of east Kent, in control of its native ruler.

It is at this point that the Kentish Chronicler inserts the expedition of Octha and Ebissa to the lands about the Wall. His date may be right. If so, their settlement may have had an additional purpose. Placed on the flank of the northern armies, it may have helped to deter any possibility of their intervention in the affairs of the south on behalf of Vortigern's enemies; other local leaders might fear to be overridden as rudely as Gwyrangon of Kent, and might be dismayed at the extent of Vortigern's dependence on his federates.

The First Saxon Revolt

Tension increased. Hengest, confident in his swollen numbers, now openly threatened both parties. The federates

> complained that their monthly deliveries were inadequately paid; deliberately exaggerating individual incidents, they threatened to break the treaty and waste the whole island, unless ampler payments were heaped upon them.

The formal complaint was doubtless accurate, for it is doubtful if Vortigern commanded sufficient revenue to pay the growing number of immigrants. Hengest must have valued him less as a paymaster than as a legal cover for the increase of his own following; but as his numbers grew the legal sanction of a weakening government mattered less. In or about 442, Hengest was ready to strike; Britain 'passed into the control of the Saxons'.

The disaster was final and all-consuming; a century later Gildas still shuddered at the horror.

> The barbarians . . . were not slow to put their threats into action. The fire of righteous vengeance, kindled by the sins of the past, blazed from sea to sea, its fuel prepared by the arms of the impious in the east. Once lit, it did not die down. When it had wasted town and country in that area, it burnt up almost the whole surface of the island, until its red and savage tongue licked the western ocean. . . .
>
> All the greater towns fell to the enemy's battering rams; all their inhabitants, bishops, priests and people, were mown down together, while swords flashed and flames crackled. Horrible it was to see the foundation stones of towers and high walls thrown down bottom upward in the squares, mixing with holy altars and fragments of human bodies, as though they were covered with a purple crust of clotted blood, as in some fantastic wine-press. There was no burial

save in the ruins of the houses, or in the bellies of the beasts and birds.

The rhetoric leaves little to the imagination. The drama is heightened. Some excavated towns ended in scenes of horror; thirty-six bodies lay unburied in one burnt building at Caistor-by-Norwich, but other houses were undamaged; several bodies were buried beneath the charred remains of a gate at Colchester, but the interior of the town seems to have escaped destruction. Lincoln itself was little damaged, but the east gate was forced by an enemy, who burnt down the wooden gate and the timbers in the stone guard chamber.

Excavation can uncover the traces of such disasters, but it cannot date them. The revolt of the 440s is the probable occasion of the final destruction of Caistor, in the centre of the strongest English kingdom, where nothing suggests that the British ever regained control; but Colchester recovered, for the same gate was stormed on two widely separate occasions, and was therefore rebuilt after the first disaster. But not all towns suffered. There is nothing to suggest that Wroxeter, far from the English districts, was then attacked, and the city is said to have remained in British hands for two hundred years thereafter. Lincoln might have fallen in the revolt; but the occasion might as easily have been the campaigns of Arthur in Lindsey; or the English conquest at the end of the sixth century, or even the later wars between Northumbria and Mercia. Yet it is likely that in some places civilised Roman life ended abruptly and permanently in the 440s, for where 'there is no burial save in the ruins, or in the bellies of beast and bird' men have ceased to dwell; if life had been resumed before grass concealed the ruins, the bodies would have been swept away. But the sensational discoveries of lurid archaeology are rare. More characteristic are some hundreds of hoards of the latest Roman coins, buried by men who never came back to reclaim them. They are the memorials of those who fled before the sudden onslaught, taking their valuables or hiding them, leaving empty undefended homes that were not worth the burning. In town and country, the majority of excavated buildings were destroyed by time and weather, not by human violence; most were abandoned in their prime, their painted plaster walls not disfigured, their floors intact, occasionally scorched by ashes from an overturned brazier. No evidence dates the desertion of these houses. Common sense suggests that many among them were left empty when the Saxons rebelled in the 440s.

Men fled because raiders came; they failed to return because the raiders destroyed the economy upon which town and villa rested. The surest index to that economy is its ceramic industry, for fragments of broken pottery are virtually indestructible, and are numerous enough to warrant well-based conclusions. For more than three hundred years, the homes of Roman Britain had relied upon the marketed manufactures of professional potters. Their output was suddenly cut off; save in a few areas, there is no sign of a slow decline, of clumsier workmanship, of any growing mixture of home-made substitutes found side by side with commercial products; a prosperous and sophisticated industry was pulled up short in full production. With their customers gone, the shops closed, the roads unsafe for pedlars, the kilns ceased to work. The extinction of the potteries is a symptom of the whole economy, for the same causes cost the villas their market and their income, deprived the towns of food, and ended the manifold trades their craftsmen served. In much of the lowlands, the ferocity and the long duration of the revolt snapped the customary compulsions which held society together; for no peasant freely offered rent, or grew a surplus for the townsman, unless constrained; and those who survived the catastrophe had enough to do to feed themselves and their families.

Gildas' horror and the sharp epitome of the Gallic Chronicler at first sight suggest that the fury of destruction burnt itself out in a matter of months or days; but the wording of Gildas, the narrative of the Kentish Chronicler, and a quantity of other evidence describe a long uneven struggle that followed the uprising. The first blow was enough to shatter the economy and the political cohesion of Britain, but it did not give Hengest a kingdom like that of the Goths in Gaul, or of the Germans of the next generation in Italy. Hengest already held Canterbury and East Kent. The destruction at Colchester and at Caistor-by-Norwich, probably during the revolt, suggests that in East Anglia the federate rebellion was successful. In Yorkshire, an English tradition held that in the mid fifth century Soemil 'separated Deur from Bernicia'. 'Deur', Deira, is the East Riding, Bernicia the rest of the north-east. The tradition implies a revolt whose context and meaning the genealogist did not comprehend; all that Deira could be 'separated' from at that date was the authority of the British of York.

It does not follow that the rising was successful everywhere. The archaeology of Saxon cemeteries is the principal guide. In Yorkshire, the early English settlement about Sancton and Goodmanham, by Market Weighton, continued unbroken; but there was very little expansion until the end of the sixth century, and at York itself there were two extensive cemeteries; only a few grave goods are preserved, but they are all early, with virtually nothing of the sixth century, and little that need be late in the fifth. At Elmswell, by Driffield, and perhaps elsewhere, British and English seem to have lived peacefully together. It looks as though the rising was soon suppressed; the federate settlement was permitted to continue in the Market Weighton and Driffield areas, but not at York itself. In Lincolnshire, open country sites are more numerous, and most continue; but at Lincoln itself, very few burials are known, and these few may be as early as at York. There may be undiscovered cemeteries whose grave goods would tell a different tale; but the present evidence does not suggest that Lincoln or York became English in the mid fifth century, like Caistor and Canterbury. Elsewhere, however, the great majority of the earliest cemeteries remained in use, and it is likely that the English at once mastered many of the districts where they lived.

The immediate reaction of the British is known. They sought help from Gaul, in or soon after 446, pleading with Aëtius that,

> the barbarians push us to the sea, the sea pushes us to the bar-
> barians; between the two kinds of death, we are either slain or
> drowned.

There is ample evidence for a drastic change in the sea level of Europe and the mediterranean towards the end of the Roman empire; its severity affected the coast and rivers of southern and eastern Britain. It has not yet been comprehensively studied; its date is uncertain, and it is not yet known how much of it was sudden, how much gradual. The letter to Aëtius means that in parts of Britain the flooding was extensive, sudden, and recent in the 440s. But, since the British put the danger from floods and the danger from the barbarians on the same level, the letter also implies that, after the initial rising, the extent of the enemy menace was not disproportionately greater than the threat from flooding. The rebels of the mid fifth century destroyed the economy of Roman Britain; they controlled the districts where they themselves lived, and made the open country unsafe for many miles around. But they were too few to exploit their success, for the

> fire of their vengeance licked the western ocean . . . but . . . after
> some time the savage plunderers went home again.

The rebels raided the west, but did not conquer it; and they raided westward only after they had 'wasted town and country' in the 'east of the island'. The magnates were not all consumed at once in a single dramatic holocaust; they perished more slowly, as the economy that had made them rich withered away. It was mortally wounded in the 440s, when it lost the communications that had sustained its elaborate distributive trade. But it died piecemeal; in much of the west, fragments of the disintegrating Roman society lasted for generations, but in much of the east, decline was plainly sharper and sooner.

The experience of Severinus in Noricum, Austria, in the same years, shows something of how Roman towns, as well as the Roman army, ceased to be. There, the barbarians controlled the open country, but Roman urban life long struggled on, and ultimately ended on a definite occasion; but only because Italy was near enough for the whole remaining population to walk there, with an armed escort provided by the government of Italy. Previously, several towns had been abandoned, one by one, on separate occasions, their shrunken population often doubling up with the inhabitants of another town. When each town was evacuated, opinions often divided; some left home, and some decided to remain; sometimes those who stayed were too few to man their walls, and soon succumbed to barbarian attack. Once, an unexpected raid carried off 'the men and the cattle who were outside the walls at the time', and one lively tale focuses the chances that threatened dying towns.

> The citizens and refugees from the upriver towns sent scouts
> to explore the places that looked suspicious, to guard themselves

against the enemy as far as human precautions could. The Servant of God . . . arranged . . . for them to bring inside the walls their poor property . . . that the enemy might be starved. . . . Towards evening he said . . . 'Post proper sentries on the walls tonight, but keep a sharper watch, and be on the look-out for a sudden . . . enemy attack.' They replied that the scouts had seen no sign at all of the enemy. . . . 'If I prove a liar, stone me,' he replied; so they were constrained to post sentries.

They went on guard. But a nearby haystack was accidentally set on fire by a torch, and lit the city up, though it did not burn it down. Everyone began shouting and screaming. The enemy, who were lurking in the woods, thought that the sudden light and shouting meant that they had been observed, and so stayed quiet. In the morning, the enemy surrounded the town, and ran around everywhere; they failed to find food, except that they seized a herd of cattle whose owner had obstinately despised the saint's prophetic warning to make his property safe.

The enemy withdrew . . . and the citizens went outside. They found ladders near the walls, which the barbarians had prepared for their attack on the city, but had abandoned when they were disturbed by the shouting during the night.

These are the realities of a Roman population, sheltered by town walls against barbarians who mastered the open country but were not yet strong enough to break inside. The citizens lived within the walls, cultivating as best they could the lands immediately nearby, bringing the cattle and agricultural gear within the town when they had reason to suppose that raiders were near; though it is evident that such raids were relatively infrequent, since the citizens clung to a false security. Occasionally excavation suggests similar conditions in parts of Britain. At some time in the fifth century, a large corn-drying oven was constructed in the centre of Verulamium. Such ovens are a normal feature of open country farms, though they are rarely so large, but they are not elsewhere reported inside towns. It is evident that corn was grown outside the walls, conceivably also on deserted sites within the town, and processed within the walls as soon as it was harvested. The reason was presumably fear that the countryside was no longer safe after 441; the presence of considerable numbers of English near Dunstable, thirteen miles away, is sufficient explanation of the fear. But Verulamium survived, and undertook further skilled Roman building work, long after the oven had gone out of use. It is clear that the conditions of each town varied, that the history of the Roman British fragmented into a number of separate local histories. Just as Severinus negotiated with the barbarian king, so the inhabitants of Verulamium might reach an understanding with the English of Dunstable; guaranteed immunity from raids might be bought for a price. Such risks, however, varied greatly. Verulamium, very close to English villages, was exposed to frequent attack. Cirencester or Bath, farther from the fifth-century English, had less to fear, but doubtless risked occasional danger from larger and bolder expeditions that roamed further.

The British asked help of Aëtius in Gaul. He could not help, for he was heavily committed to the defence of Gaul against the Huns. But Germanus paid a second visit, a few years after the outbreak of the revolt. Germanus was on this occasion more successful against the heretics. Accompanied by the Bishop of Trier, he was received by 'Elafius, the chief man of the district', and

> the whole province followed Elafius. . . . The bishops sought out the authors of heresy, found and condemned them. . . . They were expelled from the island, handed over to the bishops . . . who returned home.

As before, there is no sign that any churchmen or any synod rejected Pelagianism; but on his second visit Germanus found a secular government, willing and able to arrest and deport heretics, in some part of Britain. The locality can only be guessed. Common sense suggests the south coast, Selsey or Southampton the probable landing area, since Kent was in enemy hands. Elafius may have been the chief citizen of the Belgae of Winchester. He may or may not have still acknowledged the authority of Vortigern; in the British tradition reported by Nennius, Germanus on his second visit attacked and condemned Vortigern, 'with all the clergy of Britain'. After the catastrophe, it is likely that many of the British states ceased to obey Vortigern; but there is no tradition of an alternative government, or of any other force yet able to focus resistance against the enemy. Elafius may have been among the British who asked help of Aëtius. He gave Germanus greater aid than Vortigern had done in 429, and doubtless urged the bishop to use his influence to gain help. Perhaps he did so. But if so, it was unavailing. Germanus shortly after went to Italy, and there died. He is said to have urged the imperial government to pardon the defeated Armorican rebels, but is not said to have carried or furthered any plea from the British.

Counter-attack

After the immediate shock of the revolt, Vortigern and the British fought back. The chronicles of the British and the English independently record a protracted campaign. At first, the British were successful; Hengest tried and failed to capture London, and was expelled from Kent; but he returned. The Kentish Chronicler sets down two parallel versions, the first a general summary of the fifth century, the second a fuller account of part of the earlier fighting.

> Vortigern's son Vortimer fought vigorously against Hengest and Hors and their people, and expelled them as far as the island called Thanet, and there three times shut them up and besieged them, attacking, threatening and terrifying them, and drove them out for five years. But they sent envoys overseas, to summon keels full of

vast numbers of warriors; and later they fought against the kings of our people, sometimes victoriously advancing their frontiers, sometimes being defeated and expelled.

This first account distinguishes two stages, a war in the east, in the course of which Vortimer drove Hengest back to Thanet, and a later campaign when the heavily reinforced enemy fought, not the single Vortimer, but the 'kings of our people' over a wide area with shifting frontiers, evidently against Ambrosius Aurelianus and his captains. The second account gives details of the first stage, of Vortimer's wars. He fought on the river Darenth; also at the ford called *Rithergabail*, 'Horseford' in British, or 'Episford' in English, where Hengest's brother, Hors or Horsa, and Vortimer's brother Categirn both fell; and won a third battle at the 'Inscribed Stone by the Gallic Sea'. The place was evidently Richborough, whose most prominent monument was a massive arch of marble, fragments of whose dedicatory inscription still survive. Then

> the barbarians were beaten and put to flight, drowned as they clambered aboard their keels like women.

The Saxon Chronicle also lists three battles, with the same results, in the same areas, but gives them different names, and reverses the order of the first two. In the English story, Horsa was killed at Aylesford. Neither version claims a victory; the two fords might not be identical, but the word limits the choice to places where a road crossed a river, as at Aylesford, and is likely to mean a major road and a major river. It was then that 'Hengest took the kingdom'. At Crayford the English claim a victory, when the 'British forsook Kent and fled to London'; the place is two miles from the junction of the Cray with the Darenth, where the British name a battle but claim no victory. The third battle was at 'Wippedsfleot', the estuary of 'Wipped', where the English record the death of twelve British leaders and of the 'thane' Wipped, but claim no victory. The third battle was a decisive British victory that expelled the English from Kent. The estuary or inlet of 'Wipped' must lie in east Kent, and is likely to be the Wansum channel at Richborough, between Thanet and the mainland.

The two versions correspond too closely for coincidence. Each names its own dead, reports its own victories, uses the place names of its own language. Neither is likely to have borrowed from the other, and their common origin is plainly events differently remembered, rather than invention by either side. The Kentish Chronicle gives no dates. The Saxon Chronicle spreads the events over ten years. Its dates are late additions, but its wording shows the time that its compiler intended. The first battle is placed in the year in which Hengest 'took the kingdom'; the words regularly mark the beginning of an independent reign, and are also used of the foundation of later kingdoms after the second revolt in the late 6th century. Here, the first assertion of independence indicates the outbreak of the first revolt, in or about 442. The intervening ten years date the British victory at Richborough to about 452.

The strategy of the campaign is implicit in the places. Hengest's base was in east Kent, beyond the Medway. His first two battles were fought outside his territory, between the Medway and London. He needed London, for he was not only the leader of the Jutes of Kent. He was the captain and the main architect of the migration of all the English. Outside Kent, the strongest of the early settlers were the East Angles, between Yarmouth and Cambridge. Their location compelled Hengest to reach for London, and compelled the East Angles to push southward to join him there. But though the British fell back on London after their defeat by Crayford and Dartford, English tradition does not claim that Hengest was able to pursue them and take the city. His effort failed.

No account survives of the fighting north of the Thames; nor does any report of what Vortigern was doing himself while his son was fighting in Kent. His principal concern was necessarily to hold London, and to prevent the junction of the main enemy forces. It is probable that the East Angles tried and failed to reach London; and that Vortigern fought them off.

In the south-east, the British held their own. To the north, in Lincolnshire and Yorkshire, tenuous evidence suggests that the revolt was locally contained. The few small inland pockets of English, about Dunstable and about Abingdon, maintained their existence, but did not expand; both were too small to send useful forces to other areas without leaving their own wives and children unprotected.

In ten years' fighting Vortigern and his son had defeated the federate rebellion. Kent was cleared, the East Angles were contained, and the rest of the English were subjugated or overawed. A strong government might have been able to restore an economy and a civilisation that was severely damaged, but not yet destroyed, if the government had been accepted and financed by the effort of the whole of Britain. But there is no sign that the wealthy west and south contributed to Vortigern's victories, or continued to admit his authority. Many of his enemies must have been tempted to see his troubles as a well-deserved retribution. Shrewd men might sanely calculate that the distant English were too few to menace the west, and might thank them for weakening the tyrant's power. They might equally fear that if Vortigern wholly subdued the English, or struck a bargain with them, he would be able to turn his arms westward or northward.

The Kentish Chronicler's closing chapters hint at the divisions that followed the defeat of the Saxons, and gave the enemy a second chance. Vortimer died soon after his victorious campaign, and told his 'warband' to bury him on the coast in the port whence the enemy had fled, prophesying that then the enemy

> will never again settle in this land, whatever other British port they may hold.

But his men ignored his request, and buried him elsewhere.

The mystique of protection by the tomb of a dead leader veils the content of his injunction, that the enemy could not everywhere be expelled, but must remain held in some areas in subjection; and that the strategy essential to continuing British supremacy turned upon the control of London and of Richborough. Kent had been recovered. This was the land that the English could not subdue, so long as the British held its key fortresses. But to be held, they must be manned. Yet the maintenance of an adequate force on the Thames estuary was a heavy charge that could not be met without the financial backing of the whole country, willingly and regularly contributing money and men to the central government, an expense that fell heaviest upon the magnates of the still undamaged west.

Vortimer's dying charge was not heeded, for Vortigern lacked the means to enforce contributions. He was obliged to make an ally of his vanquished enemy, presumably to defend himself against Ambrosius the elder, or other aristocratic dissidents. The Kentish Chronicler reports that

> the barbarians returned in force, for Vortigern was their friend, because of his wife, and none was resolute to drive them out again. Britain was occupied not because of the enemies' strength, but because it was the will of God.

Vortigern's affection for his wife is an inadequate motive; it had not availed to limit the bitter fighting of the last decade. The Kentish Chronicler explains how the Council was obliged to accept harsh realities. The barbarians

> sent envoys to ask for peace and to make a permanent treaty. Vortigern called a council of his elders to examine what they should do. Ultimately one opinion prevailed with all, that they should make peace. The envoys went back, and a conference was summoned, where the two sides, British and Saxon, should meet, unarmed, to confirm the treaty.

The advocates of partition recognised that the existing English settlements were too strong to evict, at least for the present. Their critics objected, but were ultimately persuaded to agree. The policy reflected the common attitude of Roman realists, ready to absorb barbarians they despaired of expelling. In Britain, as in Europe, it aroused opposition, but its opponents could offer no viable alternative, for they could not or would not raise and maintain an adequate native army. There therefore seemed no prospect of decisive victory for either side, for the enemy were still too weak to conquer Britain. They had failed to take London; they had been chased from Kent, and might be chased again; but the obstacle to a total British victory was the powerful force entrenched in Norfolk, behind natural and man-made defences of river, dyke and forest. Moreover, renewal of the war threatened a double danger to the British; defeat risked opening all Britain to the enemy, but the success of an army raised and officered either from the west or from the north was likely to eclipse the power of Vortigern; or if Vortigern broke with Hengest and led a united Britain to victory against the Saxons, then the west and north must permanently submit to his authority.

Massacre and Migration

A stable treaty might have given Britain a chance to recover her strength; but the 'shrewd and skilful' Hengest did not afford that chance. At the conference, he

> told his men to hide their daggers under their feet in their shoes, adding, 'When I call out, "Saxons, draw your knives", take your daggers from your shoes and fall on them. . . . But do not kill the king; keep him alive, for the sake of my daughter, . . . and because it is better for us that he be ransomed.' The conference met, and the Saxons, friendly in their words, but wolfish in heart and deed, sat down to celebrate, each man next his British neighbour. Hengest cried out as he had said, and all Vortigern's three hundred elders were killed; the king alone was taken alive and held prisoner. To save his life, he ceded several districts, namely, Essex and Sussex.

The catastrophe was final; the three hundred 'elders', deputed by the Council of the Diocese to sign and celebrate a momentous treaty, must have comprised most of the great men of the island, the natural political leaders of both parties, many of them born in the distant age of the great Theodosius, school-fellows of Fastidius and of Faustus of Riez. Their death, at the moment when their fellows anticipated a permanent peace at the close of a long war, left the battered states of Britain leaderless and unready, open to Saxon assault. The old king survived, a disgraced and impotent wreck; hated by all men of his own nation,

> mighty or humble, slave or free, monk or layman, wandering from place to place, till his heart broke and he died without honour.

Vortigern's tragedy was not the failure of one man, but the tragedy of Britain, and of the empire which had schooled her people and shaped her institutions. His early mastery of the 'old enemies' from Ireland and the north, and the early checking of the Saxon revolt, owed nothing to good fortune; these successes were the achievement of a more than ordinary ability and courage, then rare in Europe. Lasting victory was twice snatched from him at the moment of triumph, because he was left dangerously dependent upon an enemy as able as himself. He was exposed to the barbarians by the same feckless infirmity that had opened Italy and Gaul to the Goths of Alaric forty years before, and 'none was resolute to drive them out again'; a leaderless nobility too proud to condone a government that hired Germans, but too tight-fisted to free it from the need, too divided and inept to construct an alternative, drifted to disaster, and stood amazed when catastrophe destroyed them, blaming their own futility upon the will of God.

The Great Raid

Retribution came swiftly to the British; 'the fire of righteous vengeance . . .

burnt up almost the whole surface of the island'. When Hengest was hard pressed in Thanet he had sent urgent appeals to Germany for more keels; they did not arrive in sufficient numbers to give him victory over Vortimer, when his prospects offered a greater chance of heroic death than of British plunder. But, 'later', when the island lay open at his feet, 'huge number of warriors' crossed the sea to 'fight against the kings of our people'. It was this second stage of the war that left the midland, the south and the west defenceless against raiders who inspired panic flight from town and villa, and destroyed the economy that nourished them. Gildas recalled how

> some of the wretched survivors were caught in the hills and slaught-
> ered in heaps; others surrendered themselves to perpetual slavery
> in enemy hands . . . ; others emigrated overseas, loudly wailing and
> singing beneath their swelling sails no shanty but the Psalm (*44, 11*):
> 'Thou hast given us like sheep appointed for the eating.
> And among the Gentiles hast thou scattered us.'
> Others entrusted their lives . . . to the rugged hills, the thick forests
> and the cliffs of the sea, staying in their homeland afraid, until,
> after some time, the savage plunderers went home again.

This is a familiar account of raiders who came to plunder and destroy, but not to settle. Excavation confirms Gildas' accuracy, for except in ceded Sussex, there is little sign of settlement in new areas in the middle of the century, though graves and cemeteries in the older areas are more numerous. Hengest's return re-established the kingdom of Kent, but the strongest concentration of the English was in Norfolk and in the Cambridge-Newmarket region, a secure base conveniently sited at the head of the Icknield Way, the highroad to the west. Yet the English did not take London. Modern building operations have repeatedly uncovered extensive Roman cemeteries outside the walls, but have found no pagan English burial ground, though much less intensive disturbance of the soil has revealed such cemeteries in large numbers in the districts that the English held.

The two main groups of English settlers, in Kent and in East Anglia, were still separated by the inhospitable clay lands of the Thames basin. They were no longer rootless federates, whose only security lay in the political success of their captain; many of their villages had been established for twenty years and more, and many of their men had been born in Britain, and now fought to defend and enrich their native land. The Jutes of Kent had been expelled and recently restored, but in his old age Hengest no longer retained the supremacy that had been his in his prime. Though he is said to have survived another fifteen years, his descendants credited no more victories to him and his men. Primacy among the English had passed to the better established East Angles, whose early traditions are not preserved; while the British were left without a rallying point.

These calamities are quite closely dated by the memory of the English, and the firm witness of contemporary Gaul dates the emigration of the British in the late 450s. Some five or eight years after Wippedsfleot, therefore in the late 450s, the Saxon Chronicle noted Hengest's part in the great raid, when he

> fought against the Welsh and captured countless plunder, and the Welsh fled before the English as from fire.

This is the last Kentish annal for a century, apart from the record of Hengest's death. It is immediately followed by the first Sussex annal, setting down the consequences of its cession, the arrival of its first Saxon inhabitants, seven leap years, over a quarter of a century, after the coming of Hengest to Thanet; a date also about the late 450s. These dates are fallible, rough approximations when they were first written down by English Christians many generations later, probably in the margins of an Easter Table; and they were easily liable to corruption by later copyists. But they coincide with the Gallic record of the migration. The massacre of the elders of Britain is dated not long after 455; the chaos and the fearsome raid that followed are sufficient motive for the mass migration.

The common ruin of Vortigern and his British opponents ended the half century of independent Britain, still Roman in its civilisation but governing itself. Its early success contrasted with the lethargy of the European provinces that remained nominally subject to the Emperor Valentinian III, but its fearful overthrow seemed to commend the cautious common sense of European magnates; for timely surrender had preserved the bulk of their property and many of their institutions. Yet it was this independent resistance to the barbarians that for the first time distinguished Britain from Europe, whose civilisation had hitherto dominated her history and her economy. Even its failure snapped the old compulsions that had constrained the British to imitate and adapt the changing fashions of the mainland; and set her people free to begin to evolve their own society.

CHAPTER SIX

THE WAR

The years of Arthur's lifetime are the worst recorded in the history of Britain. Some two generations, a little over half a century, separate the age of Vortigern from the Britain that Gildas described. Gildas' world and Vortigern's differed greatly, and there is just enough evidence to distinguish their chief differences; Vortigern ruled in the last age of Roman Britain, but when Gildas preached the future nations of the British Isles were beginning to learn their identity. Yet almost all that happened in between is misty, its detail forgotten. When Gildas was young, most elderly men had been born and schooled in a world still Roman, and had witnessed its destruction. Their names are not remembered, and their successors preserved only hazy notions of what they did and how they did it. Later centuries knew only one outstanding name, Arthur, the last emperor of Britain. They portrayed him as an all-conquering military commander, a paladin who ranked with Caesar and Alexander; and as a mighty ruler, a just and admirable protector of humble men. The portrait is stylised; in each version, its features are those of the age in which it was painted. The authentic features have all but vanished, because later men had no use for them. The power of Arthur crumbled soon, and when it was gone, men dwelt upon the single fact that that benevolent power had once ruled all Britain. How it had been achieved and what it meant in its own day mattered little. The future needed a legend, not a history. Men yearn for the gleam of a golden age, not for an analysis of its metal.

To modern men, the gap in the evidence is tantalising and frustrating. The change that turned Roman Britain into England and Wales is the sharpest snap in British history, and the enquirer is irritated that so little can be known of its crucial central years. Yet the seeming blank is natural to the historical record of quick and drastic change in distant times. The history of the Roman empire itself suffers from a similar baffling vacuum of knowledge in its crucial transformation in the third century; for the story of the early empire, when Rome was unchallenged mistress of the known world, was eagerly remembered; the church remembered Christian Rome, but the age of change between is reported only in stark and jarring outline, so that the middle decades of the third century constitute the dark age of Roman history. Sixth-century Britons, like fourth-century

Romans, preferred to remember that their world had once been stable, and to forget the mournful story of its disintegration.

The sources that describe the overthrow of Roman Britain have little to say of the immediate sequel. The Kentish Chronicle ends with the death of Vortigern, and Gildas gives no more than a couple of sentences to the next several decades. Their silence cannot be mended by guesses. The evidence is not there, save for a few scattered random details. But what can be known is the circumstances in which these details are set, the limits which men's ideas and their physical resources set upon their possible action. We cannot grasp the personality of Arthur. We can only understand the man and his achievement by inference from what is known of the age in which he lived, the circumstances that explain the few incidents that later writers report. These inferences and incidents become intelligible only when they are seen in the context of the Europe of their own day.

Britain and Europe in the 460s

The ruin of Britain was sudden. Her Roman noblemen perished or fled abroad at almost the same time as the death of the last legitimate emperor of the west. Valentinian III was murdered in 455, and thereafter 'the western empire fell, and had no strength to rise again'. His short-lived successors commanded little respect in Italy, and what was left of the provinces slipped from Italian control. Valentinian's widow rashly invoked the aid of the Vandal king of Africa; Rome fell for a second time, and Gaul proclaimed its army commander, an elderly nobleman named Avitus, as emperor. He appointed Aegidius, a fellow-nobleman, to take over the armies of Gaul, and himself hastened to Italy, where he was acknowledged by the senate; but he was soon deposed by Ricimer, captain of the German federates. Ricimer thereby attained in Italy the factual sovereignty that had eluded Hengest in Britain. But his authority was confined to Italy; the general Marcellinus in Dalmatia and Aegidius in northern Gaul withheld obedience to the nominal emperors he enthroned.

Aegidius was a provincial noble, who owed his military command to a transient

---

Map 4

B   Places named *Bretteville*

+   Dedications and place names of British Saints

    Inset
//   Area of sites shown on main map

MAP 4 THE BRITISH IN GAUL

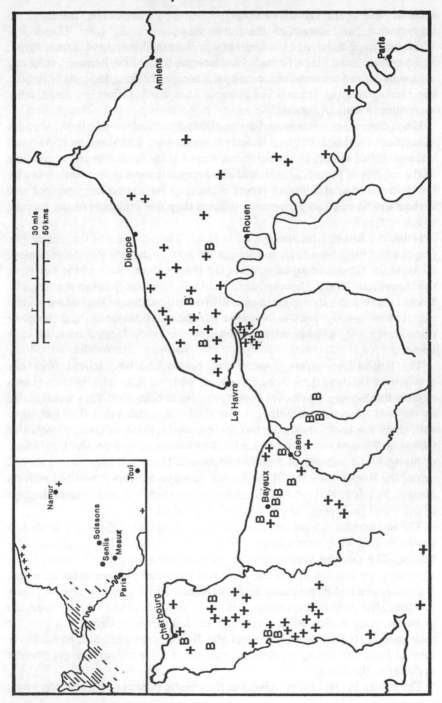

emperor. He could not impress upon Goth and Burgundian the inherited majesty that had surrounded the feeble grandson of the great Theodosius. Western Europe dissolved into a series of separate kingdoms, equal in sovereignty, and Aegidius found himself transformed into the 'king of the Romans', ruler of a state with defined frontiers, bordered by the comparable kingdoms of the Franks, the Goths, and the Burgundians, whose own further frontiers faced other sovereigns in Italy, Africa and Spain.

When German rulers mastered the mediterranean and the Rhine, the Romans of northern Gaul and of Britain looked to one another. The kingdom of Aegidius was established too late to aid Vortigern, almost at the same time as the massacre of the nobility of Roman Britain; and its own stability was gravely threatened by the destruction of the Roman power in Britain, for the Saxons acquired safe harbours in Sussex and Hampshire, whence they freely plundered the Atlantic coasts of Gaul.

It was the British who brought aid to Gaul. The survivors of the catastrophe despaired of their homeland, and sought security in the still Roman dominions of Aegidius. He welcomed them, and gave them estates 'north of the Loire', in the 'Armorican Tract', that the *Notitia* extends from the Seine to the Atlantic. It was probably already sprinkled with British settlers, descendants of army units placed there seventy years earlier, after the defeat of Maximus; and the place name Bretteville, widespread in Normandy, probably locates some of their homes.

The British immigrants were Roman provincials, who moved from one province to another, from Britain to Gaul, with no more of a wrench than a modern Englishman who moves from Yorkshire to Somerset. They were headed by the well-educated and well-born, for Gildas complains that they had taken with them the books that were no longer available; and in Gaul, Sidonius of Clermont-Ferrand wrote to their leader, Riothamus, to seek redress for a friend of his against a substantial British landowner. These were the men who had owned the Roman mansions of the British countryside, whose rents and markets Hengest had destroyed; and all the adults among them had been born in the days of peace and prosperity, before the English rebelled.

The immigrants did not come empty-handed, receiving their new lands as a charitable gift. They were a fighting force of 12,000 men, whom Aegidius badly needed. The German armies upon his borders were not the only threat to his authority; much of the Armorican Tract had long been exposed to the insurgent *Bacaudae*, who had dispossessed landowners, and had repeatedly resumed their rebellion after punitive expeditions had come and gone, most recently some ten or twelve years earlier, when Germanus carried to the government a plea for their pardon. It may be that some of the British were settled upon lands recovered from the rebels, where their resident military strength might prevent uprisings in the future.

The British in Gaul are prominent in the chaotic politics of the next ten years;

and so are the Saxons, hitherto rarely named in the history of Gaul. In or about 468, the Gothic king, 'observing the frequent changes of Roman emperors, decided to master Gaul in his own right'. Anthemius, a nobleman of Constantinople temporarily enthroned as emperor in Italy, enlisted the British, who sailed up the Loire to Bourges; they were beaten before the Romans could arrive, and driven into Burgundian territory, but the Goths failed to master Gaul. Yet the struggle was not a clear-cut division between Goth and Roman; each leader played his own hand, and the last Roman Prefect of the Gauls, nominally the viceroy of Anthemius, urged the Gothic king

> not to make peace with the Greek emperor, but to attack the British beyond the Loire instead, asserting that the Law of Nations partitioned Gaul between Visigoths and Burgundians.

The last imperial act of the Roman senate, obedient to Anthemius, was to impeach the Prefect for the treasonable incitement of Goths against the loyal British; but the charge was framed in terms that had lost their meaning, for many Romans of Gaul already preferred the firm rule of a resident Goth to the intrigues of a remote Greek manipulated by a German in Italy.

A fragment of a local history of the lower Loire, preserved by chance, gives a jumbled list of events in these years, whose complexity must have dazed contemporaries almost as much as the modern reader. The Franks had for a while chosen Aegidius as their king, when their own young king Childeric had suffered exile to Thuringia for his too great freedom with his subjects' wives. But Childeric's friends secured his recall, and after his return he fought at

> Orleans, while Odovacer and the Saxons came to Angers. There was a great plague, and Aegidius died, leaving a son, Syagrius. Then Odovacer took hostages from Angers and other towns. The Goths drove the British from Bourges, killing many of them at the village of Dol.
>
> The Romans and Franks under Count Paul attacked the Goths and took booty, but when Odovacer reached Angers, king Childeric arrived the next day, killed Count Paul, and took the city, burning its church in a great fire.
>
> The Saxons and Romans then fought each other. The Saxons turned tail; many of them fell to the Roman pursuit, and the Franks seized and overthrew their islands, killing many of their people. There was an earthquake in the September of that year. Odovacer and Childeric made a treaty, and conquered the Alamanni, who had overrun part of Italy.

Most of the dates and places and people are known. Aegidius died in 464; the Goths took Bourges about 468, and Dol is perhaps Déols, its border village, thirty or forty miles south-west of the city. Paul is otherwise unknown, but was apparently Syagrius' general. The events are confusing, because four or five different armies changed alliances rapidly; and the account is unclear, because it is no more than a local report of what the armies did in one district, and does not say why or whence they came to Angers. But the context makes its meaning plainer. Syagrius or his father had evidently stationed the British on the frontier where the main Gothic attack was expected, well south of the Loire. The survivors of the British army evidently withdrew towards their homes north of the Loire, and were thenceforth numbered among 'the Romans'. The Romans enlisted other allies. The Franks had been subjects of Aegidius until Childeric's return; and, whether Childeric had fought against Goths or against Romans at Orleans, he fought with Romans against Goths after the British defeat. On the Roman western borders, the Saxons had sailed up the Loire, either as enemies or as invited allies; they were evidently enlisted by Aegidius against the Goths, and were stationed on islands to hold the river against the Goths from Angers downstream. But both allies rebelled. First, the Franks killed the Roman general; but when the Saxons also rebelled, the Franks helped the Romans against them. In the end, Syagrius held the Loire; the Gothic bid to master Gaul was checked; and the Saxons and Franks went off together to Italy.

This isolated flash of detail warns of the intricacies that lie behind the summaries of the history of fifth-century Gaul and Britain given by short chronicles. It is true that in the end Gaul passed from the control of Rome into the control of Goths and Franks, but the detail is not simple; in Britain, as in Gaul, engagements when all the Romans fought on one side, and all the barbarians on the other, are likely to have been the exception rather than the rule; and both countries felt the impact of far-off decisions taken in Italy or Constantinople.

Though the narrative concerns only incidents in the local history of a small district, the campaign it reports was decisive. The Goths were held, so that Gaul did not become Gothia, and was able to become Francia, or France, in the next generation. The campaign also involved both British and Saxons in the wars of Europe. Continental British tradition preserved its own memories of the campaign. It knew the Saxons of the Loire, and recalled the

> devastation of the Frisians, and of their leader Corsoldus

which took place just before south-western Brittany was permanently mastered by the British, whose commander 'John Reith', also called 'Regula' and 'Riatham', is evidently identical with Riothamus. A later poet celebrated Gradlon, the local British leader who controlled Quimper in the mid fifth century, who,

> when the enemy race was laid low after the barbarian wars, defeated the 'keels' of five chiefs, and cut off their heads ... Let my witness be the river Loire, by whose fair banks so many battles were then so keenly fought.

Bitter memories of the massacre and of the great raid at home gave the British immigrants a keener hatred of the barbarians than continentals could experience or understand; and preserved their pride in permanently denying the Loire to Saxon keels. But they had not saved the coasts of Britain itself, and Saxon ships were for a period free to distress the people of the Atlantic coasts. The Irish Annals place the 'second Saxon raid on Ireland' in 471, and in 478 Sidonius, poet, senator and bishop of the Auvergne, called them 'masters of the sea', whose raids on the Biscay coast were deterred by a Gothic admiral's

> half-naval, half-military duty of coasting the western shores, on the look out for the curved ships of the Saxons.

The notices of these far-ranging raids are limited to the twenty years or so after the fall of Vortigern, while the unconquered Saxons of Britain controlled the south-coast harbours, their seamanship not yet obliterated by the habits of settled farming. These were dangerous years, for while they kept their sea power, the Saxons might still carve themselves a kingdom in Europe. If the settlers on the Loire had managed to retain their foothold, they might have done so, for in Odovacer they had a commander as capable and as ambitious as Hengest had been. In the end, he won himself a kingdom, but he led no nation and he left no heir. He was the son of a general of Attila the Hun, and was probably Saxon by birth. When he was defeated on the Loire, he led the surviving Saxons to Italy to fight the Alamanni, in alliance with the Franks; and he may also have enlisted some of his British enemies, for the later British entertained the otherwise surprising belief that in the late fifth century a son of one of their emigrant leaders became king of the Alamanni. What happened to the allies when they reached Italy is not reported; the alliance may well have broken and reformed as rapidly as it had in the campaign of the Loire. The one known result is that Odovacer did not immediately prosper; he is next reported on the Danube a few years later, a leader without a following. He soon found one, and led a mixed German force to conquer Italy, where he ended the appointment of puppet western emperors, acknowledged the nominal suzerainty of the emperor in Constantinople, and ruled as the first German king in Italy.

Britain in the 460s

In such an age, the simpler ties of nation, tongue and kinship melted into a world of warlords, whose miscellaneous following obeyed whichever paymaster offered a more promising reward. National cohesion was somewhat more easily preserved in Britain, for geography shielded the British lands from most of the rival armies whose wanderings disturbed the loyalties of Europe; moreover recent memories united the British in fear and hatred of the Saxons, and obliged the Saxons to stand together against the superior numbers of a nation whose government and state they had destroyed, but whose will to resist was not yet crushed.

Organised resistance did not everywhere collapse as absolutely as Gildas' dramatic picture would suggest. In the occupation of Sussex the Saxon Chronicle reports that

> Aelle and his three sons, Cymen, Wlencing and Cissa, came to Britain in three keels, at the place called *Cymenes Ora*, and there slew many Welsh, driving some of them in flight to the wood called Andredsleag.

The landing place was near Selsey Bill, close to Chichester. The Kentish Chronicler understood that Vortigern had formally ceded Sussex to the English; and Aelle may have hoped that Chichester would respect the remnant of his authority, and submit. Instead, he was opposed. His force is said to have been small, and he did not take the city. Part, but not all of the British army withdrew to the Weald, behind Anderida, Pevensey. Aelle followed, but his men were confined to the coast of east Sussex. There, pagan burial grounds are numerous, with plenty of fifth century grave goods, but none that proclaim a date in the first half of the century. But in west Sussex, the first English graves are more than a hundred years later. Chichester is not called Elchester from Aelle, but bears the later name of Cissa, one of his three 'sons'; the earliest English object in the area is a brooch found in the Roman cemetery of St. Pancras, that dates to the time of Aelle's grandchildren. Its isolation suggests a Saxon woman who lived and died in a British community rather than a Saxon settlement. The absence of pagan burial grounds in west Sussex argues that the English did not reach Chichester until more than a hundred years after Aelle's time; Cissa was more probably his remote heir than his son.

Aelle was hard put to maintain his tiny kingdom. Eight years after his arrival, he had to fight the Welsh at 'Mearc Redes Burna', the agreed frontier river, and he did not take Pevensey till six years later. British and English tradition, and the excavated evidence, agree upon the date and nature of the origin of Sussex. The Kentish Chronicle puts Vortigern's cession of the territory immediately after the massacre of the Council, at about the same time as the migration to Gaul, at the end of the 450s; the Saxon Chronicle enters Aelle's landing nearly thirty years after Hengest's, also in the late 450s. The name of the river where Aelle fought argues that within a few years he made a formal treaty with the British of Chichester, defining a frontier; the pagan English sites reach near to the Arun, but no further west, and suggest that the Arun was the frontier. Their northern limit is the crest of the Downs to Beachy Head; and even after the fall of Pevensey, early in the 470s, Aelle's men ventured no further eastward. But they had won good harbours, and might raid by sea more safely than by land.

In ceded Sussex, settlement was limited and opposed. Vortigern is also said to have surrendered Essex, but there further evidence is wanting. No written tradition has survived, and the pots and brooches from the few known sites seem earlier, nearer to Hengest's first years. In Middlesex and Hertfordshire sites are even rarer, and none are known to the south or west of London, save in districts where the first federates had settled. The London clays are unfriendly soils for primitive farmers, and the city has prospered only when safe communications have made it the centre of trade and government. But it remained a strategic stronghold, keeping the main English regions apart; if the men of Kent or the East Angles tried to reduce it, they did not succeed. A few seals, stamped with the name of Syagrius, who reigned at Soissons from 464 to 468, show that some merchantmen might still trade between Gaul and the port of London, in spite of Franks and Saxons.

Ambrosius

London and Chichester were held; Verulamium and some other cities still did not admit English settlement near their walls. Though evidence survives only from Sussex, it is likely that the men of other cities had to fight as stoutly as those of Chichester. But the enemy could not be contained by local defence alone. A well-organised offensive was needed. In the panic of the great raid, 12,000 men who might have undertaken it had gone to Gaul. Those who stayed at home took time to recover from the shock. When the enemy returned to their homes after the great raid,

> God strengthened the survivors, and our unhappy countrymen gathered round them from all parts, as eagerly as bees rush to the hive when a storm threatens . . . 'burdening the air with prayers unnumbered' (Vergil, *Aeneid*, 9, 24). . . . To avoid total destruction, they challenged their conquerers to battle, under the leadership of Ambrosius Aurelianus, perhaps the last of the Romans to survive, whose parents had worn the purple before they were killed in the fury of the storm; though his present-day descendants have greatly degenerated from their ancestor's excellence. . . .

> To them the Lord granted victory; for, from then on, sometimes our countrymen won victories, sometimes the enemy, that the Lord in his accustomed manner might test in this people a modern Israel, to see whether they loved him or no. This continued until the year of the siege of Badon Hill, almost the last defeat of the bandits.

The alternating struggle corresponds to the later stage of the war, summarised in a Nennius text, when 'vast numbers' of fresh arrivals from Germany fought against the 'kings of our country', 'sometimes victoriously advancing their frontiers, sometimes being defeated and expelled'.

The resistance evidently began at some time in the 460s. It lasted some 30 or 35 years. It was conducted by the 'kings' of the country, leaders military and civil thrown up in the several states of Britain. 'To avoid total destruction', they took the offensive, leading their forces out of their own territory, and accepting the overall command of Ambrosius. Ambrosius headed the early years of the resistance, but by the time of the final victory Arthur was the 'commander of the kings of the British in the war'. Whether Ambrosius was killed, died, or was superseded by a younger general we do not know. His successor was a man of similar background. Artorius is a Roman family name, like Catellius of Powys, or Calpurnius the father of Patrick; in the fifth century it places his birth and origin among the owners of villas, from whose ranks came the leaders of the separate states, the members of the council, the 'elders of Britain'.

The nature of the war compelled an unusual strategy. The early poetry of the Welsh consistently sings of mounted warriors wearing scarlet plumes and using swords, riding well-fed horses, who fought an infantry enemy equipped with spears. Their picture of the English is accurate; Germans nearer to the mediterranean used cavalry, but further north among the Franks, the kings and their bodyguards alone had horses, while the English had none, and were said not even to know what a horse looked like. Horse gear does not begin to appear among their grave goods until the late 6th century, and then only in the occasional possession of a leader who rode to battle while his men marched.

The evidence for the fifth-century British is slighter. Most early Welsh poems concern the sixth century. Then, though men fought on foot in mountainous Wales, the heroes of the Pennine kingdoms and of the west midlands were almost all mounted men; and cavalry was the outstanding arm of the Armorican British. Only one surviving poem sings of a battle of Arthur's. It describes a defeat of his horsemen by English infantry. Otherwise, there is no direct evidence that Arthur's men fought like their children and grandchildren; but no evidence at all suggests that they fought differently, for there is no contemporary account of how the Romans struck back at the barbarians in Britain. But in Gaul, there is first-hand evidence. There, fifth-century success was entirely due to the use of cavalry alone against an infantry enemy. About 471, Ecdicius routed thousands of Goths at Clermont-Ferrand with only 18 mounted men, for the Goths, like most German forces, were poorly armed. Sidonius describes the consequence.

> You were welcomed with an ovation. The courtyards ... were crowded with people, some kissing the dust of battle from your person, other unharnessing bridles slimy with blood and foam ... and sweat-soaked saddles. ... The crowds danced for joy. ... You had to put up with the most fatuous congratulations.

Thereafter Ecdicius, from his private resources,

> raised what was in practice a public force ... that curbed ... the audacity of the barbarian raiders. ... Surprise attacks wiped out entire regiments. ... To the enemy these unforeseen onslaughts proved disastrous.

Ecdicius' horse 'never lost a moment in following up the rout' so that the enemy had no time for the proper burial of their dead; sometimes 'bodies piled on dripping carts' had to be hastily shovelled into cottages that were then fired over the corpses 'till the debris of blazing roofs formed their funeral pyre'.

Ecdicius in Gaul was a lone hero, whose single campaign had no sequel. He received 'small help from the magnates'. They lived in a relatively stable Gaul, side by side with barbarians whom they did not fear. Their homes and estates were normally secure; and would become the first casualties in any attempt to extend the adventure of Ecdicius into a national effort. In Gaul, such resistance was unthinkable. The Goths were too firmly rooted, and the Gauls had too long acquiesced in their rule. Ecdicius' campaign was soon over, and three years later, when Sidonius wrote, he had abandoned the struggle.

Ambrosius' resistance had begun in Britain some ten years before Ecdicius attacked; and it is not improbable that Ecdicius had himself been fired by stories of Ambrosius. His strategy was the only effective way in which Romans could fight back with hope of success, and was as valid for lowland Britain as for Gaul. Sixth-century British and late fifth-century Gauls relied on cavalry alone, unencumbered by slow-moving infantry; tradition held that the late fifth-century British fought in the same manner, and is plainly right.

The most brilliant strategy fails unless it has the supplies it needs. Ecdicius was a magnate who raised a force from his own resources. Those resources were lands where horses might be bred and pastured, and corn grown for their fodder, peopled by dependants able and willing to tend the horses and to ride them. Any well-stocked estate might send a few bold raiders on a single expedition, but a war that lasted for a generation required ample lands secure from enemy counter-attack. In Britain such resources were to hand in the Cotswold country from Dorset to Gloucester, in Salisbury Plain and in Hampshire. There, if the remaining magnates and their dependants had the will, cavalry forces could be raised and trained, sheltered between campaigns, their losses replaced. No central government could any longer extract the taxes to maintain a professional army or pay mercenaries; but landlords could still raise forces among their tenants.

The Cymry

Gildas says that during the great raid those who did not emigrate fled to the rough country, some of them to hill forts. When the raid was over, 'a remnant' took up arms, and were thereafter joined by great numbers of their fellow countrymen, *cives*. In distinguishing a 'remnant' from the mass of the population, and in describing their leader as the 'last of the Romans', he means that the initiative was taken by what was left of the political and military leadership of Roman Britain. The first authors of the resistance were men of standing, Roman landowners who, like Ecdicius in Gaul, could raise forces from their own estates. Some still remained; and in the west country, though raiders had come and gone, the enemy were not near, and the old social relationships were not yet wholly overthrown.

But resistance was not long confined to those who began it. In Gaul, the first successes of small mounted units had inspired wild enthusiasm among humbler citizens, who 'danced for joy'. In Gaul, bold young men infected with that enthusiasm had no opportunity to join and spread the movement, for one campaign opened and closed the resistance. But in Britain, opportunity increased for more than thirty years. The counter-offensive was begun by the remnant of the Roman nobility of Britain, raising forces to defend their own lands against raiders and robbers; it became a national war of liberation, and its successes created a nation with a new identity.

As that identity was born, the forces of Ambrosius and Arthur adopted an enduring name, that distinguished them not only from the English, but also from Romans abroad. For Gildas' *cives* is the Latin equivalent of the British word *Combrogi*, fellow-countrymen, whose modern form is *Cymry* or *Cumbri*, still the national name of the Welsh and of the north-western British. The name is shared between them, and therefore originated before they were separated by English conquest. It existed in or before the sixth century, and was adopted throughout the former Roman territories of Britain; for when the English gave names to villages whose population was still Welsh, they called a number of them Comberton, Cumberlow, or the like, in the London region and the south-east, as well as in the west and north. They did so because their inhabitants called themselves *Cumbri* at the time of the English conquest.

The new name was born when Roman Britain died. The armies of Ambrosius recruited men who had lost respect for the fallen majesty of Rome; and it registered a change in the outlook and structure of their society. The values of Roman civilisation were enshrined in Latin literature; and, though most men in all classes knew something of both languages, Latin alone was written. Roman values died sooner among men who could not read, or read but rarely; and when the material civilisation of Rome was gone, the need to know Latin disappeared among laymen. The word Britain meant the whole island. *Cymry* was the name adopted by the native population in the former Roman diocese, after Britain ceased to be Roman. Their descendants were called Welshmen by the English.

The armies of the *Combrogi* were mainly cavalry, acting alone; those of the English were infantry alone, without any mounted men. Such warfare imposed strict and unusual demands upon both sides. The tactical success of the British depended upon surprise, that put the enemy to flight and killed him as he ran. But since the stirrup was not yet known, the horsemen could not strike hard; to attack spearmen who held their ground invited the loss of horses that could not be replaced without return to base, and left unseated riders unprotected. Even if the enemy were overridden, the winning of a battle might lose a campaign if losses were too heavy. But disciplined cavalry wisely led had little need to engage an enemy who did not flee. Their tactical success required them to concentrate stronger numbers against weaker enemy forces; free of footmen, able to move four or five times as fast as the English, their scouts were in a position to locate the enemy quickly, and to make such concentrations possible.

The existence of such mounted units was clearly able to deter the English from raiding in small parties and to hinder the assembly of larger armies; for men drawn together in numbers from scattered small villages left their homes weakly defended, and the British cavalry was free to ignore the ordered army and attack its villages. Immediately, such warfare enabled relatively small numbers of British to curtail the English raids; but cavalry was less well equipped to conquer, destroy or expel its enemies. To overrun even a small stockaded village, held by the men whose wives and children it sheltered, required more than a single charge. Though the smaller English settlements about Dunstable and Abingdon might be exposed to unexpected assaults, whence the British might speedily withdraw into friendly territory, no such cavalry army could hope to reduce the denser populations of Kent or East Anglia. The nature of the fighting invited a stalemate, with little hope of decisive victory by either side.

Cavalry skilfully led might easily escape attack in the open; but they were weak and defenceless when dismounted, and men must sleep at night. An infantry army may carry spades and palisade posts like the Roman legion, to throw up speedy defences when it bivouacs, but cavalry so encumbered loses speed. If infantrymen are attacked without warning, they have only to jump and seize their weapons; dismounted cavalry taken by surprise may find their horses hamstrung or dispersed before they can mount. Tactical needs therefore required the British to seek out enclosures with defined ready-made defences. There they risked only siege by a force much larger than their own, surrounding them tightly enough on all sides to prevent them breaking through in a concentrated charge. In much of the lowlands, small walled Roman towns, eight to twelve miles apart along the main roads, offered such protection; elsewhere, ancient Iron Age forts, often on sharp-sided hills, provided comparable security; excavation has shown that many western forts were refurbished in the Arthurian centuries, particularly where Roman roads are farther from each other, and towns correspondingly fewer. The excavation of these forts suggests that some, like South Cadbury Castle, became permanent strongholds, especially in districts far removed from English settlement, while others may have protected forces that stayed for a few days or a few weeks in the course of a campaign.

Inferences from the circumstances of the war show only the problems that the fighting thrust upon a prudent commander. They do not show whether commanders were prudent, nor how much or how soon they learnt from experience. But oral and written tradition has preserved something of Ambrosius. His name passed into Welsh legend as Emrys, and spread thence into modern usage. One or two sites in Wales, and perhaps in Cornwall, bear his name. Features of the landscape named after heroes, like Dinas Emrys or 'Arthur's seat', are never by themselves evidence that the hero had anything to do with the place. What they show is that when they were so named the local population knew and loved stories told about those heroes, and liked to imagine that their exploits were performed in their own familiar countryside. The urge to localise a national hero is strong in every generation, in the twentieth century as in the middle ages; antiquarian fancy buries Boudicca and king Arthur in half a dozen different parts of the country, and it does the same for Oliver Cromwell.

Places named after stories of Ambrosius are fewer than those inspired by the

Arthur legend, and are evidence of when and where the stories were told. The Arthur names derive almost entirely from the Norman romances of the 12th and later centuries; but they are fewer in Wales than in England, and in Wales the legend of Ambrosius was well established by the eighth century, though it was not long-lived. It may be that during the sixth and seventh centuries the name of Ambrosius was as well loved as that of Arthur.

It is also possible that Ambrosius' name survives in England for reasons that owe nothing to legend. 'Ambros' or 'Ambres' is considerably commoner in English place names than is Emrys in Welsh. Strenuous efforts to find an English origin for these names have failed; since they are not English, they are names that were used before the English came. The syllables have no meaning in any relevant language; the early spellings suggest that they usually represent the name of a person, and probably always do so.

In late Roman usage, cities often bore the names of emperors, but lesser places were rarely so distinguished, save in one particular context. Army units often named the places that they garrisoned, and in the late empire army units commonly bore the names of the emperors who raised them; the 'Theodosiani' and the 'Honoriaci' were regiments raised by the emperors Theodosius and Honorius. It is likely that any units raised by Ambrosius were known as 'Ambrosiaci', and possible that they named the places where they were garrisoned, in lands they had recovered and pacified. The English towns and villages called Ambrosden, Amberley, Amesbury and the like are found only in one part of the country, in the south and south midlands, between the Severn and East Anglia, on the edges of the war zone between the Cotswold heartlands of the *Combrogi* and the powerful English kingdoms of the east. Half of these places are suitably sited to defend Colchester and London against Kent and the East Angles, and three more border on South Saxon territory. Several of them are the names of earthworks. If garrisons were there stationed, they were established when the Thames basin was securely held, and they stayed long enough to leave their names behind, into and beyond the time of Arthur.

The conclusion is no more than an inference from a puzzling group of place-names. The solution to such puzzles must be sought by strict logical deduction from what is known of the late Roman Empire and early English Britain. These problems may not be evaded by the feeble and self-evident assertion that we do not know the answer, or that the conclusion might be different if we had more evidence. In this instance, the conclusion is the most probable inference from the available evidence. It may be overset by other evidence or by sharper logic; until it is, it suggests that Ambrosius raised numerous units during the war, and that when the British regained secure control of the Thames basin Arthur stationed them in permanent garrison upon its borders.

The War Zone

The archaeology of the war is as inferential as its place names. Excavation has

MAP 5 THE WAR ZONE

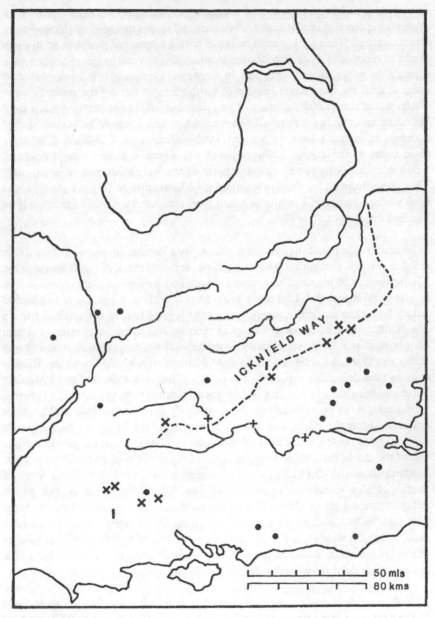

ICKNIELD WAY

50 mls
80 kms

X 'Massacres'
+ Concentrations of weapons
   in the Thames

| Burials with fatal bone wounds
• Ambros- Place Names

uncovered a number of groups of executed prisoners, of warriors buried with broken weapons and fatal wounds, of swords and spears dredged in quantity from river crossings. None of them can be dated within a hundred years; most of them might be relics of raids earlier than Ambrosius, or of the campaigns of the late sixth century, or of incidental struggles in between. Common sense suggests that some at least are the material traces of battles fought during the main British–Saxon war of the late fifth century. Their distribution is precise; they reach from Wiltshire and the borders of Gloucestershire to the Cambridge region. Large numbers of weapons have been found in the Thames by Wallingford, where a main route of the Icknield Way crossed the Thames, others near Cookham, below Marlow, perhaps the crossing point of the Verulamium–Silchester road. They were dropped by Saxons who had no opportunity to retrieve them, for at both places a competent swimmer could have recovered a valuable weapon if he had had time.

Sometimes the detail suggests an incident. On a Roman farmstead at Dunstable a Saxon warrior was buried beside the upper summer track of the Icknield Way. The underside of his skull was stove in, smashed by a blunt instrument before he was buried; and with him was a broken spear without a point. He was buried hardly later than the fifth century, for by the second half of the sixth century a Saxon village and its cemetery occupied the site, and these later burials cut into his grave; it was therefore already forgotten and unrecognisable. A mile away across the Watling Street a spur of the Chilterns rises sharp above the Roman town to a flat defensible top. Half-way down the hillside, a ditch of unknown date is cut into the chalk. It was dug in an unusual place, unlike the ditches of normal earthworks, at the point where the slope suddenly ceases to be sharp and becomes gradual. Above the ditch, the descent is too sharp for horses to be ridden on slippery grass; at the ditch men might mount to charge down the gentle incline. Below the ditch, men on foot might run uphill; above it they could only walk. Nothing dates the ditch; but the site suggests the possibility that a force of British cavalry encamped upon the hill-top, intending to attack the Saxon villages grouped about Dunstable, and took precautions against counter-attack. The injuries to the dead man's skull are those that a horse's hoof could have caused. But if it were so, the result was not a decisive British victory. The villages of the Dunstable Saxons continued uninterrupted, and the survivors were able to carry their dead from the battlefield for decent burial.

Such dramatic reconstructions can never be more than possible interpretations of the evidence; and interpretation is possible only on the rare occasions where precise detail has been carefully recorded, at the time of excavation. Most accounts are looser and vaguer reports, of skeletons with their hands behind their backs as though tied, or with their heads cut off, published without detailed study of the bones or examination of the surrounding countryside, usually with even weaker evidence of date. Guesses about the possible occasion of each tragedy remain guesses. But the geographical limits of the area where such discoveries have been noted are more important than speculation about individual sites; and, as with most distributions, the blanks upon the map are as informative as the symbols. Map 5 shows the sites that might concern the wars; where none are shown, there is not even suggestive evidence. These sites do not intrude into English Norfolk or Kent, and penetrate only the borders of the British west. Neither side could overwhelm the other. The hesitant witness of the archaeology and the place names concurs with the generalities of the British writers, that the war was a long struggle of alternating victory and defeat.

Arthur

The battles and campaigns of Ambrosius are unremembered; it may be that he was still in command about 470, when Pevensey fell to the enemy; and it may be that he used the fort as the base for an unsuccessful attempt to recover the Sussex harbours at the mouths of the Cuckmere and the Ouse; for if he could deprive the Saxon ships of their mastery of the Channel, there was some chance that some of the British of Normandy might be induced to sail home to reinforce their countrymen. The strategic importance of the place is obvious; but the only evidence is a brief English report, that for reasons unstated Aelle besieged the formidable walls of a fortress beyond his borders. But whatever the occasion, the Sussex campaign is the only incident that any source reports from the earlier years of the resistance war that Ambrosius began.

There is no indication of when Ambrosius died or retired. Since he earned a place in legend, he is likely to have lived for several years after the beginning of the resistance, in the early 460s; and since his successor was probably in command by about 480, a date in the 470s is probable. Ambrosius was replaced by Arthur as the supreme commander of the British. The change roughly coincides with a change in the character of the war. When the resistance began, it was a simple patriotic struggle between all the British on one side, and all the English on the other. But the notices that concern Arthur and the second stage of the fighting point to a more complex situation. The early West Saxon entries in the Saxon Chronicle are exceptionally confused, duplicated under different dates and, at first sight, contradictory. The confusion has a special cause. The easier ambiguities of the Kent and Sussex annals are the consequences of fading memory and of tradition ill-understood; but the Wessex entries are the deliberate contrivance of ninth-century scholars, devised to serve the political needs of their own day. Their story is that the kingdom of Wessex owed its origin to Cerdic, who was in command of a number of separate Saxon forces under named leaders, at a date that was originally set at about 480. Cerdic is the only founder of an English kingdom who has an unequivocably British name. His pedigrees alone are patent inventions, for his 'ancestors' are lifted from the straightforward traditions of other English dynasties, and later Wessex kings are represented as his descendants by improbable and contradictory links, that credit some of them with two or three different fathers. A ruler with a British name, with no ancient tradition of English forebears or English descendants, is plainly British. Though he was the earliest ruler of the future Wessex whom the later English knew, the claim of ninth-century Wessex kings to suzerainty over all the English could not be built upon the authority of a British king. He had to be treated as an Englishman. The relationships are invented; but the substance of the tradition that had to be disguised is itself ancient.

Cerdic was regarded as the ruler of the Winchester–Southampton area in the late fifth century; as the commander of the Saxons who landed in that area; and as a king who consistently fought with the English against the British armies. This is a tradition of a British ruler of the *civitas* of the Belgae who rebelled against the authority of Ambrosius and of Arthur, and hired English federates to hold his territory against them. Excavation locates and dates the homes of his federates, and suggests where he raised them. The earliest English of Hampshire were stationed at and near Portchester, perhaps by Vortigern. But towards the end of the fifth century they were reinforced by people who used grave goods akin to those of Kent and Sussex; and Bede includes them, with the men of Kent, among the Jutes. At the same time, the newcomers began to bury their dead outside the city of Winchester. It is also the time at which Cerdic is said to have ruled in the same territory.

Two accounts explain how the English came. The entries of the Saxon Chronicle land one force in Southampton Water and another on the Isle of Wight. A third contingent came to Portsmouth harbour.

> Port and his two sons, Bieda and Maegla, came to Britain at the place called Portsmouth, and slew a young Welshman, a very noble man.

The name of Port is plainly invented to explain the name of Portsmouth. Of his two 'sons', Maegla is the British Maglos, Bieda straightforward English. The local British and the English were allies. They beat off the attack of a British army, which had evidently been sent to suppress Cerdic's rebellion.

The battle of Portsmouth harbour inspired the only detailed tradition of the war that the British remembered. One Welsh poem, the 'Elegy for Geraint', describes a battle of Arthur's.

> Before Geraint, the enemy's scourge,
> I saw white horses, tensed, red.
> After the war cry, bitter the grave. . . .
>
> In Llongborth, I saw the clash of swords,
> Men in terror, bloody heads,
> Before Geraint the Great, his father's son.

In Llongborth I saw spurs
And men who did not flinch from spears,
Who drank their wine from glass that glinted. . . .

In Llongborth I saw Arthur's
Heroes who cut with steel.
The Emperor, ruler of our labour.

In Llongborth Geraint was slain.
Heroes of the land of Dyfneint,
Before they were slain, they slew.

Under the thigh of Geraint swift chargers,
Long their legs, wheat their fodder,
Red, swooping like milk-white eagles. . . .

When Geraint was born, Heaven's gate stood open;
Christ granted all our prayer;
Lovely to behold, the glory of Britain.

The poem is not early; its language is not that of the earliest Welsh poems, and
no Welsh poem could be anywhere near as old as Arthur's time, for the profound
changes that turned the British language into Welsh did not take full effect until
about a century after the death of Geraint. Any elegy composed in or near the
time of Arthur would have been in British, not Welsh. But the poem has nothing
in common with the twisted concepts of Arthur current in the eighth and ninth
centuries. It is fresh and vigorous, shot through with a sense of personal loss, as
close to its hero as are the laments for the late sixth-century heroes of Gododdin
and of Reged. It vividly describes a battle, fought as battles were fought in the
fifth and sixth centuries, before the final English conquest, not in the manner of
Welsh battles thereafter. The genealogies record its hero Geraint, prince of
Dumnonia, now called Dyfneint in Welsh, Devon in English. The poem reads
like a late written version of an older Dumnonian poem, originally composed
while the memory of its hero was still green, its language modernised and
translated from British into Welsh as the original wording became difficult and
archaic.

The English tradition dates the battle to about 480. The Welsh poem puts it
in the later stages of the war, after Arthur had replaced Ambrosius, but before
the war ended at Badon, somewhere between the 470s and the 490s. Llongborth
is the 'ship port'. 'Llong' in Welsh carries the general meaning of ships of all
sorts; but when the word was first taken into British from Latin it had the more
precise meaning of warship, *longa navis*. A port of warships, a naval base where a
prince from Devon fought and died in the fifth century, can hardly be other than
Portchester, the westernmost of the Saxon Shore forts listed in the *Notitia*, at

the head of Portsmouth harbour. The poet describes the same event as the prosaic entry in the chronicle. It would be absurd to suppose that the native poet learnt English, read, interpreted and elaborated the pedestrian language of the chronicler; or that the chronicler learnt Welsh and condensed a poem. The common source of the two accounts is an event, differently remembered.

Neither poet nor chronicler says who won the battle. The Dumnonian leader was killed, and the Saxons retained Portchester fort; at best the battle was a strategic defeat for the British. Wessex tradition names two other battles in southern Hampshire, and the Saxons were also settled at Winchester. But they did not reach the Salisbury area until the second Saxon revolt seventy years later. Cerdic lived to fight again; his rebellion was contained, and his authority was perhaps limited to the Winchester–Southampton area, but it was not crushed. The south coast was not recovered, and the independent Saxons held Portsmouth and Southampton Water as well as their Sussex harbours.

The English as well as the British found new leaders in the later stages of the war. Hengest's death is put in the 460s, not long after Ambrosius began the resistance. Later kings of Kent claim descent from the Bernicians of the far north, whose leader Oesc returned to rule Kent, either immediately after Hengest's death or some time later. Reinforcements arrived from Germany.

> The Saxons increased their number and grew in Britain. . . . But when they were defeated in all their campaigns, they sought help from Germany, and continually and considerably increased, and they brought over the kings from Germany to rule over them in Britain.

All evidence agrees that the flow of immigrants in the later fifth century much increased. Bede and Nennius' text both say that the homeland of Angel by Schleswig was left empty, and the archaeological evidence on both sides of the North Sea assents. In Britain recognisable burials of the later fifth century much outnumber those of the earlier fifth century, while in Germany burials virtually cease before the end of the century. As with other migrations, the movement of the dynasty was decisive; kings tend to move when the bulk of their subjects have gone before; the remnant left leaderless and undefended at home is likely to succumb. In Britain, older settlement areas on the east coast acquired a denser population, and the dynasty from Germany appears to have established itself at first among the East Angles; but few new regions were settled. In the north Midlands, about Leicestershire and Northamptonshire, there was some extension of territory as far as the evidence goes, though it is possible that further study may show that the earlier fifth century settlement was more extensive than the record at present reveals. In the south-east the evidence is somewhat clearer; a small group of newcomers with a strong Scandinavian background

MAP 6 PAGAN ENGLISH SETTLEMENT 2
THE LATER FIFTH CENTURY

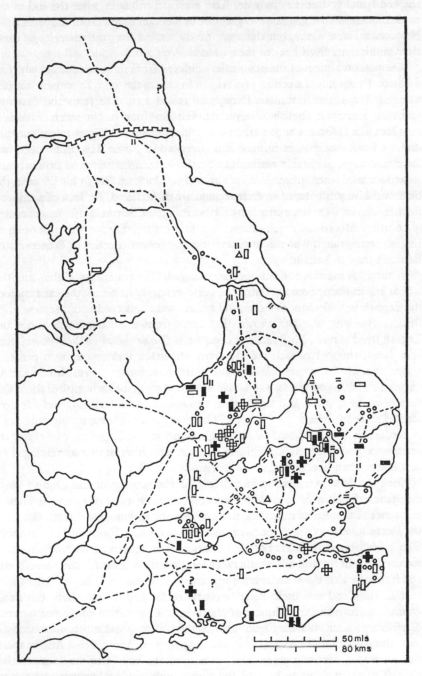

o Sites shown on Map 3, p. 59. Other symbols as for Map 3.

reached Ipswich, but they may not have arrived until later, after the end of the wars. Danish influence is also recognisable in Kent, at much about the same time. Newcomers were many, but the areas newly settled few; the majority of these later immigrants lived near to their predecessors.

The aims and hopes of the new settlers differed from those of the men who had followed Hengest half a century before. In his time, the western empire was still in being. He was an ambitious Dane, who raised a band of Jutes and Frisians, and then recruited English adventurers. His ambition might reach towards a kingdom like Odovacer's, or to the power that a *magister militum* might exercise under a weak emperor, as Stilicho had governed in Rome. His prime need was for armed men, preferably maintained by the Roman taxpayers in Britain; they looked for land when other means of support was lacking. But in his lifetime, the bulk of the English stayed in Europe; and when he failed, for lack of numbers, further recruits were not extensively forthcoming, for he could offer no guarantee of security. Moreover, much of northern and central Europe was still open to English immigrants, who might expect less dangerous enemies in Pomerania or Bohemia than in Britain.

By the 480s the shape of Europe had changed. The empire had fallen, and the barbarians in Europe moved faster and grew stronger. At home, the expansion of the English was blocked, and their old homes were squeezed and threatened. In Britain, the long war had shown that away from the main battle-zones the English lived secure. They had not conquered the British, but their young men had shown themselves well able to ward off attack and to ensure a peaceful agricultural life for women, children and older men. Emigration to Britain was no longer an exciting appeal to warriors in search of glory and adventure; there was land to be had, easier and richer than the soil of the homeland, and life now seemed safer in Britain than Europe. The main wave of new immigrants came as settlers rather than soldiers. Though there was still plenty of fighting to occupy the younger men, their elders had a greater interest in maintaining their new homes than in conquering the British.

None the less, extensive immigration and the coming of the English kings threatened the British. It made the prospect of reconquest of the main English territories almost impossible. Nor perhaps was it the only new threat. The Irish wars were for a brief space renewed, in north and south Wales and in Cornwall. The Irish were contained; but they cannot have been held without diverting men and resources that would otherwise have been available for the Saxon wars; and it may be that the Irish invaded in concert with the English.

Both sides had lost their earlier incentives, for neither now had reasonable grounds to foresee the conquest of the other. The British could not overrun Norfolk and Kent, but they held most of the country, and most of its strategic strongholds, above all London. London, holding Kent and the East Angles apart, was an essential strong-point at any stage of the war. Ordinary unmounted citizens might man its walls, and the walls might shelter horsemen who were able to enforce the submission of the nearby countryside. It was not only a fortress that could stand a siege; it was able to secure a wide surrounding territory. There is some evidence of the nature of that control. Eight miles south of London lies the small cluster of fifth-century English villages about Mitcham and Croydon. They are too few to have constituted a threat to the city; their grave goods are not found in or around the walls, and when they did expand, they spread southward on to the arable downs, not northward towards the river. But the city threatened them. Their agriculture was quite impossible if it was exposed to raids from nearby enemy horse. The villages continued, and can only have done so by the consent and agreement of London. The nature of their grave goods emphasises their dependence. In Surrey, and in the West Kent sites in the Darenth valley, their ornament is wholly different from that of Kent, beyond the Medway, closer to that of the middle Thames Saxons. The differing ornament means that they had little or no contact with the kingdom of Kent across the Medway, but had contact with Saxons on the other side of London. It had been the long experience of Roman governments that barbarian settlers in Roman territory, if securely controlled, might both cultivate the soil for the benefit of Roman townsmen and landlords, and at the same time defend the lands Rome gave them against other barbarians. That was the function of the *Laeti* of Gaul; it was the necessary function of Saxon villages that remained in contact with the lands across the Thames beyond London, but were denied intercourse with Kent.

Between London and the Medway there are no such dramatic signs of war as in the south midlands, and though there was doubtless some unrecorded fighting, there is no evidence that the men of Kent made serious attempts to break out of their Medway frontiers towards London before 568; and then it was Saxons who opposed them and defeated them. In the fifth century, the successors of Hengest are not known to have revived his earlier wars against the British of London. Their frontiers were secure, their lands were fertile, military ambition was dangerous and unprofitable. The trade of London implies that at least for some periods the English agreed to live in peace with their British neighbours; for vessels could not have risked the long voyage round the Kentish coast if Kent had been at war, its longships intent to seize merchantmen that used the port of London.

Similar considerations indicate the defence of London north of the Thames. The nearest formidable enemy were East Angles many miles away. It is not likely that they were held without heavy fighting, and perhaps one or other of the Cambridge dykes constructed in the years after the Romans may constitute a frontier, erected in defence, accepted by agreement. But, as in Surrey, the differences of ornament among the English command attention and require explanation. The fifth-century ornament of the East Angles is abundant in and around the town of Cambridge. But nearby were a different people. Five miles south-west of Cambridge, the Roman road from Wimpole and Sandy climbs a slow but sharp ridge just after the village of Orwell. Behind that ridge, stretching southward to the Royston–London road, is a small group of large cemeteries, one of which, Haslingfield, 'the open land of the Eslingas', records the name of the people who used them. There, the 5th-century ornament is matched on the middle Thames; only in the 6th century did these people acquire Anglian jewellery from Cambridge as well. They were at first as sundered from Cambridge as were the men of Surrey from Kent. But they were nearer the town, in sight from the top of the ridge, and their difference argues a firm unfriendly frontier that admitted no intermarriage and no exchange.

Such frontiers seem puzzling only if it is assumed that all the British fought all the time on the same side, all the English on the other. It had always been a main principle of Roman diplomacy to subsidise nearer groups of barbarians against the potential attacks of their farther neighbours, and to guarantee them protection when necessary and possible. The Eslinga Saxons lived on the edge of the large Anglian complex, but no sizeable English settlement lay between them and London. If they were enemies of the British, there was nothing to prevent British horsemen raiding and burning their homes, and riding off towards Essex or London long before help could come from nearby Cambridge. It may be that some such raid had taught them that alliance with the British was safer. But there is a more probable explanation. Present evidence suggests that the cemeteries differ in kind from those of Cambridge, and also began somewhat later, after rather than before the middle of the century. If it be so, the people may well have been placed there by the British. Throughout the history of the empire, terms dictated to conquered barbarians frequently exacted the surrender of fighting men or family groups, to be settled where the Romans needed them. Such had been the origin of the Sarmatian units in the army of second-century Britain, and of the family groups of the *Laeti* in third-century Gaul. The fifth-century British had ample precedents to follow if they subdued the Saxons about Oxford and obliged them to send a part of their population to curb the aggression of the Angles of Cambridge.

All such inferences derive from what is now understood of the grave goods. New discovery may suggest different conclusions. But until it does, the implications of the evidence now to hand is that the war began with an alliance between the English and Vortigern's party among the British against another British faction; that for a short period in Hengest's later years, his success turned it into a clear conflict between the English and the British; but that it ended with a more complicated pattern of local variation. The little evidence that shows Saxon sundered from Saxon, British at odds with British, warns that such divisions are likely to have been more numerous than we know.

The English held
The scattered evidence suggests that the British cavalry units gradually ended the threat from raiders, and confined the English behind recognised frontiers. The East Angles, the men of Kent and the men of Sussex were each checked, perhaps

before the dynasty of the English moved to Britain. Outposts drawn from the peoples who accepted the name of Saxons were placed upon the borders of the Angles and the Jutes, and behind them the places that bear the name of Ambrosius may locate some of the permanent garrisons established to consolidate territory regained and secured by the British in the middle years of the war.

The whole of the known operations of the British–Saxon war are located in the south and the south midlands. Nothing suggests that the northern armies and the Pennine kingdoms intervened; and some considerations hint that they did not. Within their territory, English settlement remained extremely small, and did not extend beyond small regions of the East Riding and the poor sparse settlements in the 'region about the Wall'. There are a few English burials outside the walls of some of the Pennine Roman forts; but they are too few to be the cemeteries of communities, as in the East Riding. They show the presence of some English men and women among the defenders of the forts, rather than the advance of enemies. The Saxon rebellion was contained in the north; some English settle-ments were suffered to continue, and the fort burials imply that some of their young men were enlisted in fort garrisons, perhaps that some of their women married British husbands.

The southern border of the Pennine kingdoms was the river Trent. English settlements stretched along its right bank in considerable quantity, in Lincolnshire and Nottinghamshire. But no cemetery of the 5th or 6th century has yet been reported from the opposite bank. The Trent became a clear-cut frontier between the British and the English. There may have been unrecorded fighting, but whether there was or no, the lasting frontier demonstrates that agreement was reached, either in formal compact or informally in practice. The northern British forebore to attack the English, but forbade them to cross the river, so that the English were enabled to live safely by the river bank, not confined to lands more safely withdrawn.

The principal casualty was the *civitas* of the Coritani, centred upon Lincoln and Leicester. Its countryside was settled by the English in numbers large enough to argue that they were in political control, or at least were strong enough to coerce whatever British government remained. But English expansion halted on the west at the Watling Street, and did not penetrate westward into the territory of the Cornovii. The Cornovii had a military tradition that gave them easier possibilities of raising their own defences than the Coritani.

Apart from the struggle at Portsmouth, the only direct statement about the wars of Arthur is a document in Nennius that lists twelve of his battles, evidently victories, the last of them at Badon. The list looks like a prose summary in Latin of a lost Welsh poem. Most of the sites named cannot be located with any confidence; but a few can. Celidon Wood is located in the north, and one or two other sites may also be northern. The City of the Legion is either Chester or Caerleon. It is unlikely that such battles had anything to do with wars against the English. If the text accurately reports the poem, and if the poem was close to reality, these were campaigns fought in later years by Arthur to subdue the highlands after he had beaten the English and recovered the lowlands.

But one identifiable site is the river Dubglas in the district of Linnuis, made the scene of four battles. Linnuis translates *Lindenses*, the men of Lindsey about Lincoln; the only significant river of Lindsey is the Witham, whose ancient name is not known, but might have been Douglas. A campaign may have entailed four nearby battles, but the more likely explanation is that this battle received four stanzas in the poem, the others one each. On any interpretation, it was evidently regarded as the most important of the battles, apart from Badon. It is the only other identifiable site where the enemy is likely to have been English, and its special importance may be that it was a major campaign against the national enemy. The effort was needed. The British had contained the older settlements, but in the later 5th century almost all the remaining Angles crossed to Britain with their king. If he would unite the East and Middle Angles with the men of the East Riding, he must hold Lincoln.

The text implies a British victory and an English failure; and the consequence of victory was more than local. The rescue or recovery of Lincoln meant that the British army must first march through and reduce the numerous settlements of the Middle Angles in Coritanian territory in the north-east midlands. Victory in Lindsey made the British masters of the island; London and Lincoln held the main enemy concentrations apart, and the inland groups about Dunstable and Oxford lay isolated, deep in British territory, too small to be more than a local menace. It is more likely than otherwise that the Lindsey campaign, remembered only in a paraphrase of a forgotten poem, is a real event, and belongs to the later years of the war, giving the decisive check to English expansion. But whatever the details, English expansion was halted.

Both sides had fought themselves to a standstill. Hitherto the English had been able to summon new reserves from Germany. Now there were no more left to come. The reinforced English were far too strong, far too long established for the British to expel them. But their interests and character changed. They were no longer raiders, and there was no longer a wealthy lowland economy to raid. They were settled farmers and there is no reason to suppose that they were yet gravely short of land, or under any compelling need to attempt a conquest that experience had shown to be difficult, dangerous and unprofitable. Though some might urge a desperate renewal of the struggle, prudence constrained the kings of the Angles to heed the sentiments of all their subjects, and to discourage rash enthusiasm. Both sides were ready for agreement and peace.

Badon

The southern English made a last effort at total victory. Badon was in the west country; one direct statement, and several early English spellings, identify Bath with Badon. An English army that could penetrate so far to the west must have been exceptionally large, the joint force of a number of kingdoms. Only one

English king is directly stated to have fought at Badon, Oesc of Kent. Little is known of the man, save the name he chose for his son, Eormenric, who was apparently born and named at about the time of the battle. The great Eormenric, dead more than a hundred years before, had been the mightiest of the kings of the Ostrogoths, conquering a vast empire in eastern Europe from the Baltic to the Black Sea. The king who revived his name and gave it to his heir at the end of a long war was a man who dreamt of empire.

A few texts indirectly suggest Oesc's probable allies. Wessex tradition places the death of Cerdic at the same time as the death of Oesc and the battle of Badon; and Aelle, of the small obscure kingdom of Sussex, is the first of those whom Bede believed to have exercised superior authority over other English kings. There is no possibility that the south Saxons fought or conquered the West Saxons, the men of Kent or any other English kingdom; Aelle's authority can only have been voluntarily bestowed. At the end of the fifth century, Sussex was the smallest of the southern English kingdoms, but Aelle was the eldest of their kings. These notices suggest that the English force comprised the armies of Kent, and of the south and west Saxons, under the overall command of Aelle. There is no hint that the Angles took part. Had they done so, it is unlikely that the high claims of their kings could have admitted the supremacy of Aelle, however senior his age. Moreover, if East Anglian expansion had been checked by Arthur's victory in Lincolnshire, recent defeat is likely to have deterred them from further adventure.

The aim of a large infantry army advancing deep into British territory must have been to overwhelm the main force of the British cavalry by weight of numbers, and to destroy the bases whence it drew remounts and fodder. Gildas calls Badon a siege. Though he does not say who besieged whom, it is probable that the infantry besieged the cavalry. He describes the site as *Mons Badonicus*, a distinct and separate hill at or near Badon. Hard-pressed cavalry required the shelter of a steep sided hill not too large for their dismounted men to hold against superior odds. There are many hills and hill forts in the neighbourhood of Bath. Most are defended spurs, easily attacked from the rear, or forts placed on the flat tops of large hills. One hill only is a separate *Mons*, sharply escarped on all sides, small enough to be defended with ease by a body of dismounted cavalry, Solsbury Hill by Batheaston. Though there are endless possibilities, this site best fits both Gildas' choice of words and the nature of the campaign.

Whatever the precise site, the circumstances are the same. The size of the forces engaged cannot be known, but there is no reason to suppose that the British cavalry numbered above a thousand men, if so many. To entertain hope of success the English required an army several times as large as the British. A siege of cavalry on a steep hill demanded more of logistics and supplies than of tactics; if the siege had been in English territory, only time was needed before starvation forced the besieged to try to break out whatever the odds. But in British territory, time favoured the defenders. An exceptionally large infantry army must needs live on the country; and any supplies available in the immediate neighbourhood of the siege must quickly have been consumed. In British territory, small foraging parties of the English risked encountering larger forces of armed men on foot, for men without horses might fight in their homelands near the shelter of their walls. The despatch of larger parties in search of food also risked weakening the encirclement. Nennius' poem allots the siege three days. The figure might be chosen to suit the metre, but it is not unreasonable. Competently organised cavalry with well-stocked saddle-bags might last three days with greater ease than a larger infantry force hungry in an alien land. At the end of the three days, the poem makes Arthur charge, slaughtering 960 of the enemy. Few of the English can have had hope of escape. Unless the survivors were very numerous, able to withdraw in good order, those who escaped the first charge were at the mercy of the pursuit, in enemy country where none would give them shelter.

Badon was the 'final victory of the fatherland'. It ended a war whose issue had already been decided. The British had beaten back the barbarians. They stood alone in Europe, the only remaining corner of the western Roman world where a native power withstood the all-conquering Germans. Yet the price of victory was the loss of almost everything the victors had taken arms to defend. Ambrosius and Arthur had fought to restore the Roman civilisation into which they had been born. But in most of Britain, the society of their fathers was ruined beyond repair. What emerged was a new world, startling not only because it differed from the past, but because it differed from the rest of Europe.

The war had begun when the emperor Valentinian was newly dead, while his successors still claimed an authority over Gaul, that men did not yet know was soon to die. Throughout the greater part of the war, the territory of Aegidius and Syagrius was still Roman, and the British might hope for aid from Gaul if they could regain control of the sea coast. But permanent change came to Gaul as well as to Britain. In 486 Clovis, the new king of the Franks, killed Syagrius and took his kingdom. Ten years later he overran the Alamanni of south-west Germany, and the Franks occupied Bohemia; he accepted catholic baptism, and in 507 he acquired the kingdom of the Visigoths in Aquitaine, chasing their survivors over the Pyrenees into Spain. The Burgundian kingdom acknowledged his authority, and was annexed by his sons. Gaul had become France, the land of the Franks; and the Franks dominated central Europe. Italy changed no less. Odovacer had discontinued the appointment of western emperors. He was a military captain grown great, but in 489 the Ostrogoths destroyed him and set Theodoric the Great upon the throne of Italy, the heir of an ancient national dynasty. What had been the western Roman empire in the childhood of the victors of Badon was now wholly comprised within the powerful Germanic kingdom of Gaul, Italy and Vandal Africa, with the smaller states of Spain. In Europe, German notables merged with the Roman nobility, and, in the words of a shrewd observer

the poor Roman copies the Goth, but the rich Goth copies the Roman.

In Britain alone no such fusion was possible. The English were left to build their society in their own territories, almost wholly free of direct Roman influence. The British were faced with the challenge of rebuilding a successor state in half an island, all that remained of western Rome.

CHAPTER SEVEN

THE PEACE OF ARTHUR

The Reign of Arthur

Arthur is celebrated as the supreme commander who defeated the English; and as a just and powerful ruler who long maintained in years of peace the empire of Britain, that his arms had recovered and restored. Arthur the ruler is as elusive as Arthur the conqueror. Contemporary and later writers honour and respect the government he headed. A few notices describe events and incidents that happened while he ruled. None describe the man himself, his character or his policy, his aims or his personal achievement. He remains a mighty shadow, a figure looming large behind every record of his time, yet never clearly seen.

Arthur's name and fame were honoured by men who lived soon after, and had known his contemporaries, before legend had had time to obscure reality. The oldest mention of his name is in a tribute to a warrior who died about 80 years after his time; the poet praises the warrior's prowess but adds 'still, he was no Arthur'. A little later, the last lowland British armies, destroyed in the middle of the 7th century, were remembered as 'the heirs of great Arthur'. The name of Arthur meant a famous commander of the past, greater than any in the poet's time. The name itself says something of his origin, and of his reputation, for Artorius is a normal Roman name. It is not previously reported in Britain, but in the half century after his death, half a dozen rulers gave their children the name of Arthur. Thereafter, the name altogether dropped from use, and is not known to have been used by anyone anywhere for some six hundred years, until the Norman romances gave it lasting popularity. But in the sixth century Arthur was a great name, held much in honour.

The sixth century is silent. No text at all that could have named Arthur survives, except Gildas; for the memory of later ages dwelt upon the monks who lived after Arthur, and the kings who helped or hindered them. Gildas praises Arthur's government, but does not name him, for he names no one at all in the 80 years before his own day, save only Ambrosius; and his name is invoked in order to reproach his degenerate living descendants. No other 6th-century texts survive before the old Welsh poems; but traces of lost texts are many. Nennius in the 8th century epitomised a poem that was already old; the Llongborth poem probably translates a lost original. Later Welsh verse is rich in allusions to lost poems about Arthur. Catalogues of old tales, and chance incidents, assert that during the 8th and 9th centuries tales of Arthur were commonly told in Britain, in Brittany and in Ireland. Arthur's exploits did not go unrecorded; but the record perished early, because from the 9th century onwards it ceased to interest the British and the Irish, who remembered only his name. Yet though the older stories are not now preserved, they lingered long enough, at least in oral tradition, for the Norman poets to found upon them their romances. Why the Normans chose Arthur as their central hero is a problem that concerns the history of France and England in the 12th and later centuries; it does not concern the history of 6th-century Britain, or of Arthur himself. That history must derive from the notices that concern Arthur's lifetime.

The Cambrian Annals place twenty-one years between Badon and the death of Arthur. These were the years in which Gildas grew to manhood. He looked back upon them with nostalgia as years of good stable government, when

> rulers, public persons and private, bishops and clergy, each kept
> their proper station;

when the 'restraints of truth and justice' were still observed, not yet 'shattered and overthrown'. Gildas was a contemporary, a subject of the state Arthur ruled, and his statement of what his readers well knew is the starting-point of any attempt to understand and interpret the reign of Arthur. Gildas' outlook was conservative, and other men of his day, with less respect for the institutions of the past, may have disliked the government that he admired. His value judgement is personal. But his statement is not to be disputed, that a stable government persisted for a generation, so long as the men who had known Badon and the wars still lived. He distinguishes political rulers from public servants and private persons, and these laymen from an established episcopalian church. These institutions existed. They are not the institutions of a society that had entirely disintegrated, but of a society whose rulers were at least trying to rebuild the administrative order of the past. Arthur's government had only one possible and practicable aim, to restore and revive the Roman Empire in Britain.

The Legend of Arthur

Gildas' historical Arthur headed a strong orderly government that upheld the 'restraints of truth and justice'. It did not endure. But in its failure it won everlasting fame, so that millions of unlettered men who have never heard the names of Roman emperors and medieval kings know at least the name of Arthur. The stories of Arthur's knights have retained their popularity for so many ages that anything that may ever be learnt of the historical Arthur must always be overshadowed by the power of the legend. From all the past heroes that it might have chosen, western Europe selected the short reign of Arthur as the pattern of a golden age of good government.

The legend developed late, several hundred years after the event; but it is one of the great tales of Europe, told again and again in all lands that speak a Latin or Germanic language, still loved today. In the twelfth century, the spoof history of Geoffrey of Monmouth made Arthur a conqueror who subdued not only the Saxons, but most of Europe as well; Geoffrey's Arthur served the ambition of Plantagenet kings, but their subjects welcomed and perpetuated a different Arthur, the hero of the Norman poets, gentle, wise and courteous, whose chivalrous knights, just champions of the afflicted, were all that medieval lords should be, but were not. Their legend first appeared in the twelfth century, its source vaguely described as *Matière de Bretagne*, or *Leis des Bretons*, a story taken from the British of Normandy, or from Brittany. Soon, king Arthur's court became a central tale that drew to itself stories of other heroes, whose tragic loves and brave quests made them worthy knights of the Table Round. Some of them had origins in other lands, and some brought with them stories from the repertoire of international folk-tales. But many were British. Peredur of York, killed in 580, grew into Sir Perceval. Chance has preserved the prosaic historical basis of one among them, Tristan, in legend nephew to king Mark of Cornwall and lover of Iseult, who lived in Castle Dore, by Fowey in Cornwall. The real Tristan was an ordinary mid sixth-century British kinglet. He lived at Castle Dore, but he was son, not nephew, of king Mark, and lived three generations after Arthur. Many of the other legendary heroes are likely to have a similar origin that chance has not preserved. They were real people. They had little to do with Arthur; but the story-tellers depicted them as his companions, because his was the best loved name of all.

Tales of king Arthur existed in Wales as well as in Brittany well before the Norman romances seized upon them; but it is from the Norman stories that the legend grew, retold in succeeding ages in words and sentiment adapted to changing taste. The classic English version is Malory's, written in the later fifteenth century; the taste of his day, as of Shakespeare's, required that the heroes of romance and drama should wear modern dress, so Malory's knights wear fifteenth-century armour, as fitly as Hamlet the Dane wears an Elizabethan doublet. In English literature, the story was for a while obscured by Tennyson's misty Pre-Raphaelite version, with its banal explicit comparison of Arthur with the Prince Consort, 'Albert the Good'; and such vulgarity invited mockery, in the American cinema, or in English musical comedy. But the straightforward retelling of the tale in this century has rescued its essentials from their temporary degradation, and proved by commercial success that the legend has not yet lost its popularity. Its appeal remains extraordinarily potent. Even today it is possible to raise large sums of money for the excavation of archaeological sites that later tradition associates with Arthur, though no such sums are offered by the public for the exploration of sites connected with Julius Caesar or Claudius, Edward I or Henry VIII. The response is not simply due to the mystery that surrounds Arthur; Vortigern and Old King Cole are as mysterious, but their names do not inspire the public to finance the solution of the mystery. Arthur remains popular because of the content of his story, even when it is only dimly remembered by adults who read the tales in childhood.

The core of the story has always been melancholy regret for a strong and just ruler who protected his people against barbarism without and oppression within, but was in the end defeated by treachery and disunity. The moral varies in each age. Malory wrote towards the end of the Wars of the Roses. He made his king Arthur rescue Britain for a short space from 'great jeopardy', at a time when 'every lord that was mighty of men made him strong, and many weened to be king', so that at the final catastrophe his knights exclaim

> in this realm will now be no quiet, but ever strife and debate. . . .
> For by the noble fellowship of the Round Table was king Arthur upborne, and by their noblesse the king and all his realm was in quiet and rest.

Tennyson's Sir Bors was

> a square-set man and honest; and his eyes,
> An outdoor sign of all the warmth within,
> Smiled with his lips . . . a smile beneath a cloud.

He is the pattern of a Victorian hero, just, benevolent, protective to his inferiors of any class or colour, so long as they keep their station; and the twentieth-century version sees in Arthur's kingdom

> the model of chivalry and right, striving against the barbarism and
> evil which surrounded and at length engulfed it.

Each retelling of the tale clothed Arthur in the ideas of its own day. Malory wrote for readers weighed down by the licence of the barons. Tennyson's readers had been taught to admire benevolent and chivalrous empire-builders. In the 1950s, men believed in the defence of western civilisation against evil eastern barbarism.

It is this timeless universality which gave the legend its power over men's minds; it spread wherever Norman poets sang or were imitated, and even the sad destruction of the golden age gave men hope for its future restoration. Many peoples in many lands dreamt of a distant hero who is not dead but asleep, who will one day awaken to rescue his people from conquest and oppression; and in Europe king Arthur sleeps beneath Mount Etna in the legend of Sicily, as well as in Scottish rocks or English hill-forts, his second coming a commonplace of country fancy.

This central feature of the legend, the portrait of the strong just ruler whose good government was overthrown by the jealous ambition of lesser lords, is fully historical. It is the contemporary picture painted by Gildas, who was probably over twenty years old when Arthur fell. But all the rest is the painted fancy of later centuries; some of the legendary companions of the Round Table may have lived at other times and places, and the origin of many is unexplained. The idealised picture of the courtly king attended by heroes delighted the poets of early medieval Wales and their princely patrons, and is told most fully in the story *Culhwch and Olwen*, which is older than the Norman tales, and independent of them.

Ecclesiastical tradition preserves a more rugged attitude to Arthur, plebeian and nationalist, portraying a foreign lowland enemy, cruel, lascivious, and fearful, and is found in all three highland zones. In central Wales, at Llanbadarn Fawr, near Aberystwyth,

> a certain tyrant came from foreign parts. . . . He cast eyes on bishop Paternus' tunic and greedily demanded it. Paternus answered: 'This tunic is not for wicked men to wear, but for priests.' Arthur left the monastery, raving furiously, and came back in a rage, trying to take the tunic by force . . . cursing and swearing and stamping the ground. Paternus said: 'Let the earth swallow him up.' The earth straightaway opened and swallowed Arthur up to the chin. . . . He begged forgiveness; the earth spewed him up . . . the saint forgave him.

In south Wales, St Cadoc's father Gwynlliw abducted the king of Brecon's daughter, escaping across the frontier with the girl on the back of his horse, closely pursued by the angry father.

> But lo, three noble heroes, Arthur and his two knights, Cai and Bedwyr, were sitting on top of a hill, playing dice. When they saw the king and the girl, Arthur's heart was fired with lust. . . . Full of evil thoughts, he said to his knights: 'I am on fire with desire for the girl that that warrior is carrying on his horse.' But they replied: 'You must not do anything so criminal; we are supposed to help the needy and distressed. Let us go and help these people who are hard pressed.' Arthur answered: 'All right; if you would rather help him than grab the girl for me, go and ask whose land they are fighting on.'

Since the land was Gwynlliw's Arthur helped him, and he 'came to his palace under Arthur's protection'. The old tale was too strong for the author who copied it; his readers knew the character that Arthur ought to assume, and so he awkwardly made Cai and Bedwyr remind him of the role in which he was cast. The story is told in the Prologue to a Life written about 1100, preserved in a manuscript of about 1200; the author's emendation is one of the earliest traces of the chivalrous Arthur, and if the prologue is of the same date as the Life, it is earlier than the time of Geoffrey or of the Norman poets.

Another tale from the same Life, certainly written down in about 1100 from an earlier original, shows no such compunction.

> A great general of the British, Ligessauc Longhand son of Eliman, killed three knights of Arthur, the illustrious king of Britain.

> Arthur pursued him everywhere, and no man dared shelter him,
> for fear of the king, until . . . he found sanctuary with Saint Cadoc
> . . . who feared Arthur not at all. . . . He stayed seven years. . . .
> Then he was betrayed to the king, and Arthur came with a great
> army to the river Usk.

Arthur demanded compensation, and arbitrators awarded him a 'fine of 100 cows', since 'from ancient times among the British this kind of judgement and price had been laid down by the lawmen of kings and chiefs'. Arthur 'arrogantly rejected cows of one colour, but after much wrangling accepted cows coloured red before and white behind'. The saint's magic however tricked him by turning the cows into bundles of ferns, and restoring the animals to their owners' stalls.

The tradition of Wales is matched in Dumnonia and in Scotland; in northwestern Somerset, in Dumnonia,

> Cato and Arthur ruled, living in Din Draithov. . . . Arthur tried to
> use the altar as a table,

but was constrained to repent and to grant estates to the church of Carantoc. In the far north, Arthur encountered the 'sons of Caw', who ruled 'beyond Bannauc', north of the Clyde, probably by the upper Forth. The eldest, Cuill (Hueil), represented as blood brother of Gildas,

> was a vigorous warrior and famous soldier, who submitted to no
> king, not even Arthur. He would often come down from Scotland,
> burning and raiding with victory and honour. The king of all
> Britain, hearing what the high-minded youth was doing, persecuted
> the victorious and admirable young man although the people used
> to hope and avow that one day he would become king. He killed the
> young robber . . . and after the murder, Arthur went home, very
> pleased to have killed his strongest enemy.

When he is not hated and feared, Arthur is still a remote suzerain, commanding a power and prestige far beyond the local prince's. The young Illtud, allegedly an Armorican,

> hearing of the magnificence of . . . king Arthur, longed to visit the
> court of so great a conqueror. . . . When he arrived, he saw an
> abundance of soldiers . . . and received an appointment suitable to
> his military ambition. When he had earned the honours he wanted,
> he withdrew from the court in high favour . . . and came to
> Poulentus, king of Glamorgan, who retained him because he was a
> royal soldier . . . preferring him to all his own military companions
> . . . and appointed him as his *magister militum* (commander-in-
> chief).

These stories are not historical; Arthur was dead before most of these saints preached. But they record an attitude that was certainly taken by some people.

They describe a ruler of the lowlands who succeeded in imposing his authority on all Britain, on Wales, the south-west and the north, and even beyond the borders of Britain, north of the Clyde and Forth. The tyrant came from 'foreign parts', from 'beyond the Usk', but he is not resisted by the kings within Britain; rather, he is the patron of Gwynlliw, the respected overlord of Poulentus, sovereign of king Cato's Dumnonia. He ruled over them, but not among them. The centre of his power lay east of Wales, in the lowlands that are now England.

His army was much larger than the regional warbands; it attracted the ambitious, even from overseas, rewarding their loyalty with a standing that of itself earned honour in the separate states, mastering rebels so effectively that 'none dared shelter' them. The Arthur thus portrayed is the same great sovereign whom the literature of the kings held in honour; but he is seen from a different angle, through the eyes of humbler men, whose children and grandchildren revered the saints and first composed their praises. They suffered and resented the depredations of the subordinate kings, and fastened their greatest resentment upon the person of their author, patron and supreme head of all predatory warbands, the alien emperor in the lowlands.

The stories are the fancies of a later age. But their viewpoint is not. Some of the places named are mentioned because they serve a medieval interest, but other places, and the regions defined, derive from earlier traditions. When the medieval author brought Arthur to the monasteries of Paternus and Carantoc, he did so for the benefit of their medieval inmates. But the monk who wrote a life of Gildas in southern Brittany had no such interest in reporting Arthur's campaigns beyond the Clyde; and he wrote out his northern proper names in the spelling of the 6th century, revealing that he copied from an early original. Cadoc's biographer had no interest in locating Arthur's captains and armies upon a barren mountain moor, or at a particular crossing of the Usk. His interest and invention was to link his patron Cadoc with stories set in a generation earlier than Cadoc's.

These places belong to an older tradition, secular and local. That tradition preserves the highland view of Arthur, a tyrant who came to conquer, and came from foreign parts, east of the Usk, outside Wales and the west. The tradition of an alien Arthur, an enemy who ruled the lands that became England, is not a medieval invention. It conflicts with the legend of the hero Arthur, but it is not the product of a different age; it stems from a different social class. The concept of the warrior Arthur was popular with princes. It was already old in the 8th century or earlier, repeated in the translation of a Dumnonian poem and in the verses epitomised by Nennius; it was an established legend by the time of Aneirin's *Gododdin*, early in the 7th century, and was widely accepted in the middle of the 6th century, a generation after Arthur's death, when kings named their sons after him. It was already yielding to the notion of the gentle and courteous Arthur when the author of the Cadoc prologue doctored his rough original to fit it.

The stories of the detestable Arthur, the national enemy, reflect the outlook of humbler folk, who had no love for kings and lords, warriors and rulers. They are preserved only in the Saints' Lives, for the early monastic leaders also quarrelled with kings, and many of the monks themselves came from humble homes, in later centuries as in the 6th century. Their stories preserved the outlook of the subject in the kingdoms of the Welsh. They are not part of monastic experience, for Arthur died before the monastic movement developed. The monastic tradition picked up and perpetuated a viewpoint that it found in the world around it, a plebeian tradition of deep-rooted local resentment against the suzerainty that Arthur powerfully and successfully asserted over the peoples of the highlands of Britain.

Arthur's Frontier Wars

Arthur's authority, and the campaigns that enforced it, were the inescapable consequence of the victory of Badon. The war had been won principally by the effort of the lowlands. Once it had been won, the necessary business of a government that sought to restore the past was to recover and reunite the whole of the former diocese of Roman Britain, and to restore its ancient frontiers. A number of separate stories, one of them preserved in considerable detail, describe campaigns fought to re-establish the Roman frontiers, near to the year 500. A few of them name Arthur as the victorious commander, but all of them fall within the early years of Arthur's empire, soon after Badon, and all the British commanders named lived within or on the borders of Roman Britain, and therefore owed allegiance and obedience to a restored Roman government. Some are said to have been chastised as rebels; those who did not rebel prudently accepted the new government, and fought their wars as Arthur's generals, the military *duces* of the revived empire.

In the south-west, the Dumnonian poem accepts Arthur as emperor and superior ruler over its own hero Gerontius during the wars; after the war the Life of Carantoc accepts Arthur as well as the local king, Gerontius' son Cato, as rulers over Dumnonia. The tradition of the Cornovian forces in Dumnonia makes them steadfast allies and main supporters of Arthur's rule; and their loyalty appears to have been rewarded by a large eastward expansion of their dominion, into Hampshire, that was to make them for the next several centuries the rulers of the most considerable British state; their preponderance is obscured because few of their records have been preserved.

In the north, the Nennius poem gives Arthur several battles in the Cheviot region north of Hadrian's Wall. There his enemies were certainly not the English, and the date is therefore probably after Badon. The story of Cuil carries his northern campaign farther, to the line of the Antonine Wall, between Edinburgh and Glasgow. The campaign reasserted imperial authority on the furthest borders that Rome had reached, and effectively reunited the Clyde kingdom with the rest of Britain. The genealogies name its king, at about 500, as Dyfnwal, whom they honour more prominently than any of his northern contemporaries. The extent of his power is not reported, but the independent traditions of the Lothians also acknowledge a king Dyfnwal at the same time; he was a mighty ruler, whom early medieval Wales regarded as the legendary lawgiver of the nation, who took a census of his dominions to establish the financial and taxation system of the future. That system was in practice heavily indebted to the conventions of Roman administration, and it may well be that Dyfnwal of the Clyde was Arthur's ally, rewarded with a larger territory as a trustworthy guardian of the northern frontier, who there undertook a census that Arthur enforced throughout Britain.

The faint memories of Dyfnwal are one part of a major reorganisation of the northern frontier, attributed in several stories to these years. When Britain had last obeyed a single government, seventy years before, Vortigern had solved the frontier problems by a double-sided movement of military forces. The troublesome Cunedda of the Votadini was moved away from the north to be employed against the Irish in north Wales. The government of Arthur exploited the connection between north Wales and the north-east, and repeated Vortigern's policy. The Votadini of the north-east received Dyfnwal; and Marianus, grandson of Cunedda, head of that branch of the dynasty which had stayed in Votadinian lands in Vortigern's time, was now moved south to Wales, to name the territory still called Merioneth. He did not move alone. A few inscriptions of southern Scotland name others who migrated at about the same time; and Cauuus, or Caw, the father of Gildas, was also transported to Powys, in his son's early childhood, about 500.

The settlement of the north removed commanders of doubtful loyalty and imposed trusted local rulers. It also involved the enlistment of Irish allies. Fergus of Dal Riada ruled a tiny north-eastern people whose home was squeezed by powerful neighbours, and was immediately threatened by Mac Erca's alliance with the Ulaid. He moved the seat of his dynasty to safety overseas. The date given by the Irish Annals is 503. Fergus settled in Kintyre, the long peninsula that commands the estuary of the Clyde, and stretches southward to within a dozen miles of the coast of Dal Riada in Ireland. It is probable that he settled among colonists who had long preceded him, perhaps by several centuries, but the movement of the dynasty entailed a considerable increase of Irish strength on the Clyde. For many years there is no record of conflict between Dal Riada and the Clyde, but ample record of wars between Dal Riada and the Picts. The Clyde kings could not have tolerated the establishment of a hostile dynasty in command of their seaways; and were powerful enough to reduce enemy invaders. Fergus' peaceful migration is likely to have been undertaken with the goodwill of the Clyde kings, who had cause to welcome allies against the Picts; and in the context of Arthur's northern campaign it required the approval of Arthur, and was perhaps due to the initiative of the central government of Britain.

The Irish were a problem, for in Britain they were ready to fight on either side.

Arthur's British had enlisted Irish allies before, during the war; two surviving inscriptions name Irishmen, Cunorix at Wroxeter and Ebicatos at Silchester, who probably commanded hired Irish troops; and a generation after Arthur's death Cynric of Winchester bore the same name as Cunorix of Wroxeter, and perhaps was also Irish. But considerable numbers of Irish colonists remained unsubdued in western Wales and in Dumnonia, after the first force of the fifth-century campaigns of Cunedda and of the Cornovii was spent. Several British stories report successful campaigns by British generals in Arthur's time to reduce the pockets of independent Irish in Britain, and a number of Irish traditions report the support that the Irish in Britain were able to secure from Ireland.

In north Wales Cunedda's grandson Catwallaun Longhand is said to have expelled the Irish from Anglesey about 500, at the close of a long campaign; their commander is given a Leinster name, and the Caernarvonshire peninsula of Lleyn bears the name of the men of Leinster, evidently because they had there settled in considerable numbers. Early Leinster tradition independently remembers that king Illan, who reigned from 495 to 512, fought eight or nine campaigns in Britain; but it knows nothing of any other wars by Leinster kings in Britain at any other time. Catwallaun's victory was final. Thereafter, Irish place names remain, and there are a few traces of Irish monks, but there is no further record of independent Irishmen in arms in north Wales. Nennius' poem records a battle of Arthur at Urbs Legionis, either Chester or Caerleon. If it were Chester, either Illan's armies struck deep, or else Arthur had to fight to impose his authority upon Catwallaun.

But the strongest Irish colony in Britain was in south-west Wales. In the earlier fifth century, Cunedda's forces had recovered Kidwelly, eastern Carmarthenshire, but not Demetia, Pembrokeshire and western Carmarthenshire. There, a branch of the Ui Liathain of Munster had ruled an Irish kingdom for a century or more. Both the Irish and British have preserved quite independently the list of the succession of Demetian kings; in both versions the kings have Irish names until about 500, when suddenly they are replaced by kings with British names. The names of the first new rulers are not merely British. They are Roman; and in contemporary record as well as in later genealogies, they use the titles of senior officers of the imperial army of the late empire. They begin with Agricola, son of Tribunus. It may be that the genealogist has turned two names of one person into two persons, and that in his original he found Agricola the Tribune; but it is also possible that Agricola was the son of an officer whose personal name has been forgotten, and who is remembered only by his title 'the Tribune', just as Vortigern before him is remembered by a title rather than a name. Agricola is well dated to about 500, for he was father of Vortipor, who was old and grey when Gildas wrote about 540. Vortipor bore a British personal name, but his tombstone survives, and on it he is styled, not king, but Protector. The term is a Roman military rank, and meant in origin an officer who protected the emperor, much as in later armies a guards officer guards a king; and the genealogists use the same term, for the rulers of Demetia and of Demetia alone, though their uncomprehending transcripts turn the title into the personal name of an ancestor of the dynasty.

Chance has recorded a large number of fragments of the story of Arthur's recovery of south Wales, and of the generals to whom the armies were entrusted. Many of them are embedded in nonsense even wilder than is usual in medieval story, but the separate items are independently preserved in the accounts of Wales, Cornwall, Brittany and Ireland; and when they have been extracted from the fantasies of their context, they combine to tell an intelligible tale. Their story begins with an Irish invasion of Wales towards the end of the fifth century. The crazily perverted documents of Brecon derive the name of the town and region from Brychan, the son of an Irish chief, who is also dated to the beginning of the sixth century. The traditions of south Cardigan make Brychan's father land on their coasts, accompanied by the Irish king of Demetia and by captains with Munster names, at a date that seems to mean the 490s. An isolated line of Irish place names leads inland from their alleged landing-place to the Roman fort at Llandovery, whose site commands the approaches to Demetia from the west.

These movements make strategic sense, if the Demetian Irish took the offensive, renewing the alliances of the past and intending to help the last effort of the English at Badon; or if they stood on the defensive after Badon, anticipating attack from beyond the Severn. Other stories report such attacks. One of the Glamorgan tales brings Arthur to the Usk, and if his battle at Urbs Legionis were not at Chester, then it was also on the Usk, at Caerleon. Another Glamorgan tale takes him farther, and makes him fight against Brychan, and check his advance, at a strategic point on the Roman road from Cardiff to Brecon, half-way between the forts of Gelligaer and Merthyr Tydfil; it puts him in alliance with the local forces of the Cardiff region. The tales are in themselves jejune miracles; their purpose is to claim the authority of Arthur for privileges granted to monasteries that did not exist until after his death. The connection between the saint and Arthur is invented; but the localities are not. The monks of Llancarfan served their interest and honoured their founder by associating him with Arthur; but no such interest was served by placing one incident upon the Usk, and another upon a remote and windy hilltop above Merthyr Tydfil. In detailing one particular spot upon a Roman road in deserted country, the monastic writer transcribed a statement that he found in a tale told before he wrote; which he annexed to his patron and turned to his own purpose.

Theodoric

The Brecon narrative extends the geography of the fighting, with new names. A general named Theodoric advanced down the Roman road that runs from Gloucester to Brecon through Hay, and reached Brecon. He then despatched a force under Marcellus, which drove on down the Roman road through Llandovery and Carmarthen to Porth Mawr, Whitesands Bay by St. David's, and lost a hundred men at each of two named places on the way, staged 25 to 30 miles apart. The visible ruins of Porth Mawr stand above a little estuary harbour, that the recession of the sea has now dried up; but in other texts it is named as a principal port for voyages to and from Ireland, whence Patrick was held to have sailed. Four miles inland, directly on the line that links Porth Mawr with the nearest known stretch of Roman road, lies Caer Farchell, the 'fortress of Marcellus'; and Llan Marchell lies 5 miles west of Hay.

The Brecon texts make strange fancies of their story, reading Marcellus as Marcella, and turning 'Marchel' into a woman, whom they represent as the daughter of Theodoric and the mother of Brychan. But what they describe is a military expedition, for armies are commanded by men, and when they lose men by the hundred, the cause is battle with an enemy. The texts name six places in all. They are not medieval inventions, for after the starting-point, they serve no recognisable Brecon interest. They relate to a military campaign, for they are all sited on or close to the Roman road, at staged intervals and strategic points, though the texts do not remark the fact. The names and tales of the people are also not the creation of fancy, nor are they invented for the benefit of later ages. Agricola and Marcellus, *Tribune* and *Protector*, reek of the Roman past that Arthur tried to revive, and have some contemporary confirmation; Vortipor's stone gives his rank, and his father is the only sixth-century king whom Gildas praised. The places and the people belong to the time in which the tale is set, and owe nothing to the world of the medieval author who preserved its fragments.

The name of Theodoric, son of Theudebald, also belongs to the 5th century rather than the 12th. It is remarkable because it is German, neither British nor Roman; and not only German, but, at this date, specifically Gothic, not yet adopted by Frankish kings. The employment of a Goth in Britain fits the date and context, for Arthur, like other late Roman rulers, had elsewhere engaged foreign captains. The appearance of a Goth in Britain suggests a date and context, for such commanders are commonly enlisted with their men, not empty-handed. Theodoric's later career implies that he had ships at his disposal, and argues that a Gothic admiral who lacked employment was available to aid the British. The troubles of Gaul suggest that such an officer was driven out in the middle years of Arthur's reign, and at no other time. The kingdom of the Visigoths had maintained a Biscay fleet in the later fifth century, but in 507 the kingdom was destroyed by Clovis the Frank, and the Goths were expelled over the Pyrenees into mediterranean Spain. Their fleet lost its Atlantic harbours. No writer reports what happened to the ships and crews; but it is evident that a commander who had lost his homeland and his base might find it prudent to transfer all or part of his fleet to the service of the British; and Arthur's campaigns had a use for a naval force.

Theodoric was a Goth by name. That he brought the Gothic navy to Britain is no more than a possibility; but it is a natural and normal possibility, not an improbable oddity. Nor was he the only German to find employment in Demetia.

MAP 7 THE DEMETIAN CAMPAIGN

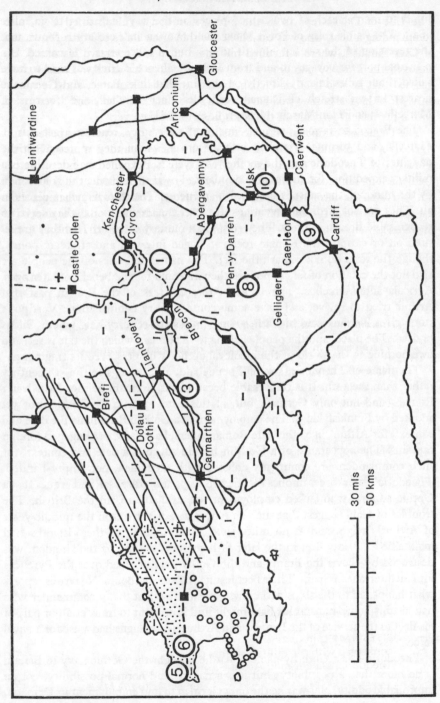

The Life of David reports in the next generation a ruler named Boia, also commanding a fleet, who was established within a few miles of Porth Mawr and of Caer Farchell, where a fortified hill and a cove still conserve his name. He annoyed the saint by parading naked women before his monks. Later writers guessed that he was Irish or Pictish, but his name is Germanic, and Germanic only. He or his father may well have been a subordinate of Theodoric's, rewarded with a permanent lordship in the lands he helped to recover.

The Demetian campaign was successful. The Irish dynasty was expelled, and Agricola was installed as the new ruler; his heirs founded a new, British, dynasty. Irish rule was ended, but the Irish were not expelled or exterminated. Demetia long remained a bilingual state. There, and there alone, the Irish word 'rath' became the normal description of small defended earthworks, whatever their date; and the use of the Irish language was officially admitted, on the memorial of the king, as well as on many private monuments, inscribed in both Irish and Latin.

Map 7

IRISH

| Inscriptions with Irish Ogam characters or Irish personal names

⫽ Place names in *-cnwc* and variants, densely concentrated

Names in *Moydir* and variants
- single sites
⁖ concentrations

— Names in *Cil-*

\ Names of Irish saints (excluding Patrick and Brigit)

+ Names incorporating *Gwyddel.*

O Earthworks termed *raths*

ROMAN

—— Roads

--- Roads, course uncertain

■ Forts and roadside towns

O SITES NAMED in texts connected with the military forces of Theodoric, Marchel and Arthur.

see Notes to the Maps

Brecon also remained in the possession of the heirs of Brychan. Language as well as geography henceforth made Demetia a principal bridge between Britain and Ireland, a region where in the next generation the experience of civilised Roman and of barbarian Ireland was fruitfully mixed. David, the most forceful of the British monastic reformers, placed his chief monastery close to Porth Mawr; the bishop who baptised him, and his outstanding pupil and successor, were both Irishmen, and his stern but popular plebeian rule was most eagerly welcomed in and about Demetia and Brecon, where Irish settlers were most numerous.

Memories of Theodoric's wars against the Irish extend to Cornwall and Brittany. Tradition names the Cornish parishes of Trigg, north of the Padstow estuary, after the 'daughters' of Brychan; and is confirmed by an inscription dated to the decades on either side of 500, that commemorates Brocagnus son of Nadottus. The name is identical with Brychan, but it is common all over Ireland, and the Cornish Brychan, with a different father from his Welsh namesake, is probably a different person. But he was one part of the same substantial Irish migration, noted in many sources at the turn of the century, in Arthur's time. Theodoric is reported to have contained another invasion further south. After an unsuccessful attempt to land in Brittany, an Irishman named Fingar disembarked an army of 770 men, with an Irish king, at Hayle Bay, near St. Ives, where he fought in alliance with a second army, commanded by Guiner, whose name is British. They were met by Theodoric, who anticipated their attack, patrolled his coasts, and caught them as they landed, defeating both armies separately. In Cornish tradition, the survivors were absorbed into the native population. They included Findbar of Fowey, Breaca, and other followers of the early monks of the Shannon, Ciaran of Saigir and Senan of Inis Cathy; between them they name many south Cornish parishes. Irish tradition preserves independent echoes of the migration; it knew nothing of the battle, but, though it rarely remembers Irishmen abroad, it stresses the activity of the Shannon saints in Cornwall.

Cornish tradition thereafter gives Theodoric a permanent lordship south of the Padstow estuary, where he was remembered as the subordinate associate of the Dumnonian king. His principal residences are located near St. Ives and near Falmouth; the ruins of both are visible, but neither has yet been excavated. He is also reported to have sailed across the Channel to fight in Brittany; for Guiner, the ally of Fingar, whom he killed at Hayle Bay, is said to have been on his way to help his 'uncle Maxentius', whom Theodoric had previously 'deprived of part of his territory'. The name of Maxentius is as startling and as unusual as Theodoric's. Even in Gaul it is rare, reported only once in these centuries among laymen; that report is placed at the same date and in the same region, and is also linked with Theodoric. The brothers Budic and Maxentius, heirs to the British kingdom of Quimper in south-western Brittany, are said in Breton tradition to have returned from abroad at the beginning of the sixth century, and to have recovered their patrimony from a ruler named Marcellus. The name Marcellus, though common enough in earlier Roman centuries, is also very rare in Gaul, unique among the British. These relationships concur, for the Marcellus of Demetia and of Brittany were both allies of Theodoric, and may well have been the same person.

The quite independent traditions of south-east Wales connect the dynasty of Brittany with Theodoric's Demetian allies. Maxentius' brother Budic was subsequently expelled, and found refuge in Demetia; the story does not name his enemy, but, in Brittany, as in Wales, a common cause of a king's expulsion was the superior strength of a brother or near relative. Budic was restored to his territory with the help of a powerful fleet provided by Agricola of Demetia. The probable sequence of the events told in separate stories is that after killing Marcellus, the brothers divided the kingdom of Quimper; that Maxentius expelled Budic and seized his portion of the kingdom; and that thereafter Theodoric, commanding Agricola's Demetian fleet, restored Budic, thereby 'depriving' Maxentius of 'part of his kingdom'.

The substance of the story is preserved only in disjointed morsels of medieval tradition. But Budic, and his connection with Theodoric, were known to the contemporary historian Gregory of Tours, who wrote at the end of the 6th century. He reports that Budic died about 557, and gave the name of Theodoric to his own son, who was born about the year 510 to 530. At that date, it was a quite exceptional choice for a British father; among the thousands of British persons known, no other is reported to have given a Gothic, or any German name to his child. The exceptional choice implies that the father was beholden to a friend who bore that name and earned his gratitude. Theodoric had fought to enthrone Agricola. He sailed the seas, and perhaps commanded the fleet that Agricola sent to restore Budic to his inheritance.

In yet another local Cornish tradition, Theodoric is said to have lived long as the local lord in the Falmouth region, and to have died in a hunting accident between 530 and 550. His career is not in itself exceptional; it is less remarkable than the history of Odovacer, or of many another bold adventurer dispossessed by a quick change of fortune, and lifted up again. It is unusual only because chance has preserved so much vivid detail, in so many different records. Portions of his story are remembered in medieval texts that are wholly independent of each other, in Ireland, in south-west Wales, in two distinct traditions of south-east Wales, in three separate regions of Cornwall, in Brittany and in Ireland; in two contemporary inscriptions, and in the contemporary witness of Gregory in Gaul. The diversity of these notices, and the chance that three among the people involved in the tale bore exceptional names, while two more used Roman titles, rule out the possibility that the story derives from a late legend. Most of the detail is presented in a grotesque context concerning a particular saint in one locality. These accounts have no common written origin; each ultimately derives from an original that was first set down when the memory of Theodoric was green in the district that each story concerns, and reported only local events, knowing nothing of the wider story.

Theodoric came to Britain in the maturity of Arthur's empire, and outlived him, to die about the time that Gildas wrote. He was a wartime captain who became the peacetime ruler of a small territory, far from the land of his birth. He was a relatively unimportant officer of Arthur's armies, and became a subordinate local lord. His story matters because chance reports more of him than of other men. It outlines the unromantic portrait of one of Arthur's lesser 'knights'; and explains the origin of one among the 'generals' and 'tyrants' of whose upstart independence Gildas complains. His career typifies the experience of hundreds of his contemporaries, who are nameless, or known by name alone, who lived like him with their retainers in small defended halls, local replicas of the greater commanders, whose heirs Gildas was to denounce as 'ill-starred generals', the curse of Britain when Arthur was dead.

Arthur's Civil Government

These several stories of Arthur's frontier wars describe the restoration of the territorial integrity of Roman Britain. The Irish were finally subdued or expelled wherever they had survived, in the south-west, in south Wales and in north Wales. The northern frontier was recovered to its farthest limits. Some stories of the frontier wars survive because it was in these western and northern regions that the language of the British remained in use long enough for medieval writers to salvage a few scraps of their history. In the lowlands, the language died out much sooner, and no such incidents were remembered even in twisted forms; for in the lowlands no one transcribed the lives of British ecclesiastics or copied out the genealogies of lay rulers. But the traditions of the highlands are emphatic, and are agreed upon one chief essential of Arthur's rule. He was the emperor, the all-powerful ruler of the whole of Britain, and the seat of his power was in the lowlands; in the western and northern highlands he was a foreigner whose authority was accepted resentfully, and asserted by superior force.

The government of a lowland emperor is an earlier and more credible tradition than medieval folk-tales told of a western king in Wales and Cornwall. The men who followed Ambrosius and Arthur had fought to preserve and restore the Roman civilisation of their fathers; when they won the war, they could not do any other than try to restore its political institutions, and 'emperor' is the natural title for the head of those institutions. Gildas' description of Britain a generation after the fall of Arthur frequently mentions institutional titles, and Gildas is a writer who consistently and carefully uses technical terms precisely and accurately; *foederati, annona, hospites, praepositi, consilium,* and *consiliarii* are late-Roman terms correctly used, as is *cuneus* for a military formation; *cyulae* and *curucae* are exact terms for the ships of the Saxons and of the Picts and Irish, *naves* for Roman ships; and each term is used rightly for the people concerned. In his preface, Gildas mentions the titles of his own day. He apologises for speaking out; others should be more competent than he to redress the evil, for

Britain has *rectores*, she has *speculatores*.

These also are technical terms. *Rector* means a provincial governor. Gildas else-where uses the word several times for governor, once for the Deity; he never applies it to any of the rulers whom he calls *reges, tyranni, duces,* for these words also have a defined meaning and describe other offices. *Speculator* also has an exact meaning; it is the normal term for the executive officers who served the *rectores,* their watchmen or police.

Gildas means what he says. Though sixth-century provincial governors in Britain seem startling to modern notions, there was less cause for surprise at the time of Badon. Their revival was a necessary part of restoring the administration that a Roman emperor must re-establish. Imperial government also required the appointment of a praetorian prefect, and of a *magister militum,* with *duces* and *comites* to command the armies. Gildas makes no mention of prefect or *magister,* for these were the officers of the central government, and could not have survived its collapse, on Arthur's death, years before Gildas wrote. But he has much to say of the *duces,* the regional and local army commanders. On the rare occasions when he names them without reproach, he accords them their formal title, *duces patriae,* 'the generals of our country'. But when he abuses them, he attacks their factual authority, and denounces them as *reges* and *tyranni,* 'kings' and 'tyrants'. He follows the usage of Europe in his own day. In Europe, the Roman generals Aegidius and Marcellinus had become kings in Gaul and Dalmatia; in Africa, a Moroccan inscription of the year 508 honours

Masuna, king of the Moorish peoples and of the Romans

and records the official Roman titles of his subordinates, 'prefect' and 'procura-tor'. Among the British of Armorica, Gildas' younger contemporary Gregory of Tours remarks that their rulers had in the 5th century called themselves kings, but that when they admitted the nominal suzerainty of the Frankish kings, after 511, they consented to adopt the more modest title of *comites*; and the Lives of the Armorican saints accurately observe the change of usage that Gregory reports, naming 5th-century kings and 6th-century *comites.*

In Britain, as elsewhere, men used the appropriate term in its right context. Later Welsh usage in Britain called Arthur *ameraudur,* emperor. Gildas includes Vortipor of Demetia among the *reges* he abuses, and calls him *tyrannus.* But on his official public monument, Vortipor is described by his official title of *Protector,* and is not called *rex.* Vortipor and his father had owed their title to Roman imperial authority. When Vortipor died and Gildas wrote, that authority had ceased to be. The military rulers were still officially *duces,* generals, but they had in practice become *reges,* kings.

For civilian officials Gildas uses the generic term *publici*; those who administer the law he terms *iudices,* judges, and one of them is named on his tombstone in north Wales, not far from 500, with the formal title of *magistratus.* The numerous technical terms of late Roman administration, correctly used, are the debris of an apparatus of government restored or revived by the victors of Badon, though it did not long survive them. It was the government of a Roman emperor, equipped with a hierarchy of civil and military officers, on the model of that which had existed in the earlier fifth century in the western provinces, and in Britain in the childhood of the men who were old when the war was won.

These institutions endured for at least thirty years after Badon. Gildas had noted the growth of the 'crimes' he denounced over 'many years', but the total subversion of the old standards of good government was comparatively recent, for it was only over a period of 'ten years or more' that he had been moved to action, previously hesitating to speak out. The heart of his complaint is one familiar enough to late Roman experience; the excessive power of the military, overawing the civil administrators. Of his *rectores* and *speculatores* Gildas says that

> they certainly exist, and they are not short of the proper number, even if they do not exceed it. But they are under such immense pressure that they have no room to breathe.

Throughout his invective, Gildas consistently distinguishes between the *tyrannus* and the *iudex*; the *tyrannus* usurps the functions of the *iudex*, overshadows him and makes him his creature; both show a brutal disregard of established law. Gildas' *regula recti iudicii*, the rule of correct judgement, can only mean the written law of Roman Britain.

Gildas' complaint is that the *publici* of his day were corrupt, whereas those of Arthur's time were not. These 'judges' and 'magistrates' are the proper terms for the civil heads of the separate *civitates*. When Gildas wrote, they were overborne by the tyrants, generals who had become kings, but submitted to no sovereign who could compel their obedience or control their licence. His praise of the good old days, in the lifetime of Arthur, when military commanders, like civil officials and private persons, each kept to their proper station, is praise of the government established and headed by Arthur after the war. Gildas names no names, but he confidently asserts the stability of Arthur's government in the face of readers who had been his subjects and had known how he ruled.

Partition

The greater part of Roman Britain had been recovered, but a number of eastern areas remained in enemy hands. It is probable that their independent existence

---

Map 8

IIII English Areas. I I I Areas probably English. Areas with 5th-century and later 6th-century burials, without clear evidence of earlier 6th-century burials, stippled.

MAP 8 PARTITION

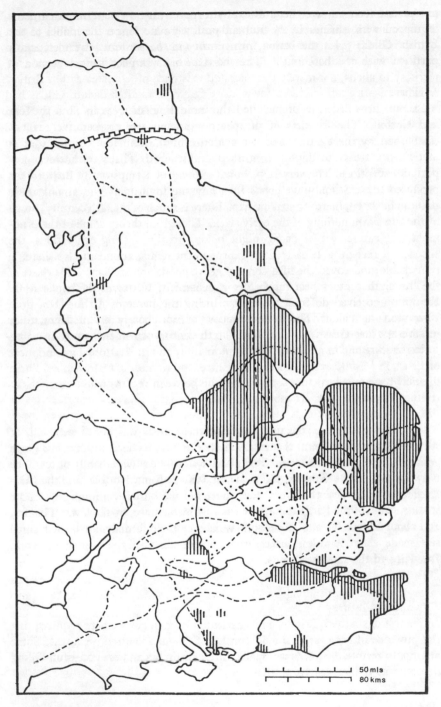

50 mls
80 kms

and precise frontiers were determined by formal treaty. In regretting that many of the martyrs' shrines of the Roman past were no longer accessible to the British, Gildas gives the reason, *lugubri divortio barbarorum*, the 'melancholy partition with the barbarians'. The word *divortio* implies formal cession of territory to aliens, not merely the tolerated existence of federates within British territory.

Plainly these ceded lands included the main English areas in Sussex, Kent and Norfolk. The frontiers of the peace must have recognised the realities established by the fighting, and the evidence of the cemeteries shows that in many other areas the English continued undisturbed. There are however important exceptions. The very large burial-ground of Kempston by Bedford has produced more Saxon grave goods than any site in Britain; but, among those that can be dated, there is a striking gap. There is much of the fifth century, much of the late sixth, nothing of the early sixth. Though in theory some of the ornament that cannot yet be dated might belong to the missing generations, the absence of recognisable early sixth-century ornaments, abundant elsewhere, is remarkable; moreover, the fifth-century grave goods are Anglian, while those of the late sixth century bear much Saxon ornament. Whatever the explanation, Kempston received different treatment during the peace of Arthur. Nor does Kempston stand alone. The scattered record of more poorly reported cemeteries in several other areas is similar. Early sixth-century ornament is rare in south Leicestershire and in most of Northamptonshire; and in Hertfordshire and most of Essex, in Middlesex and Buckinghamshire, and in most of Oxfordshire. These districts have one particular setting; they lie between regions where early sixth-century English burials are more plentiful.

On present evidence, the population of these areas was either removed, or subjected to such restraints that it was unable to bury its dead with normal grave goods or in normal cemeteries. The effect was to clear wide bands of territory between each of the main English areas, in Sussex, Kent, Norfolk, and the Mid-Anglian counties near the Trent. Elsewhere normal burials continue only in the small clusters of the East Riding, in parts of Lincolnshire, by the lower Thames, and about Dunstable and Abingdon. Whatever their formal status, their small size made them harmless, necessarily subject allies of the British of York, London and the south midlands.

Town and Country

In the rest of southern Britain, a reconstituted Roman government required that the province of each *rector* should consist of *civitates* centred on towns. Some attempt to restore the towns was made, but it was weak and unsuccessful. Gildas deplored its failure, regretting that the cities of our country are still not inhabited as they were; even to-day they are squalid deserted ruins.

St. Jerome used similar words of fourth-century Italy, meaning that cities were shrunken, decayed, dying, but not that they were grassgrown archaeological sites without human inhabitants. Gildas' complaint is that the cities were not peopled 'as they used to be'; some men lived in some cities, but they failed to make them more than 'squalid ruins'. Excavation illustrates some detail. At Wroxeter and Silchester, late fifth-century inscriptions name Irish chiefs. They were neither saints nor passing strangers, but men in authority, who left behind them followers numerous and permanent enough to erect memorials in their honour. The most probable explanation is that they had headed forces raised by the British during the wars. Later, not earlier than the sixth century, when the Silchester stone had long weathered, someone threw it down a well, together with much late Roman pottery and other rubbish. Either the well was a convenient rubbish dump, or it was a danger to the children. In either case, someone still lived at Silchester, and tidied up the debris; and in the centre of Wroxeter, men lived in solid timber houses, built over vanished Roman ruins.

Inscriptions are few. Elsewhere, evidence is less precise. Some of the excavated buildings of Verulamium lasted far into the fifth century, if not later; the latest construction on one site, a well engineered water main, is likely to have been built nearer to Arthur's time than to Vortigern's; and occasionally other evidence suggests a date as late in other towns. British cemeteries of the period are beginning to be recognised, at Verulamium and at Magiovinium near Bletchley, near Swindon, in Scotland and Somerset, and in other places. In Colchester, a substantial building was constructed over a late Roman street, but it lies beneath the medieval street; and an elegant chapel by the castle is later than the Romans, earlier than the Normans. York and London were still inhabited, but in many towns there is little direct evidence, one way or the other.

The little evidence is matched against much legend. The name of Arthur is attached to many hills, earthworks, and natural features, often named Arthur's Seat, Arthur's Leap, and the like. He sleeps till the trumpet shall arouse him to succour his people in many places, on Hadrian's Wall, in Richmond Castle and at Cadbury Castle, near Yeovil in Somerset, near Manchester, under Mount Etna, in Savoy and in Arabia, and elsewhere; but not in Wales, where tradition firmly asserts that his grave is not known. These names and local legends show where the Arthurian romances became popular in the middle ages, but they have nothing to do with early tradition. They are made-up names, invented by medieval men who read or heard the romances.

By contrast, some of the places named in the Norman romances themselves are real. They come from earlier sources; and the geographical knowledge of the Norman poets is greater than their historical understanding. King Mark's castle by Fowey is accurately named and precisely located. The misty land of Lyonesse across the sea, *pagus Leonensis* in north-western Brittany, is still called Leon. Many of the city names, London, Carlisle, Caerleon, remain in use and give no problems. The romantic Avallon is a common Roman Celtic place name; it is still the name of one small town in central France, that was known as Aballo in the Roman period. The letters 'Avallon' painted upon a dusty board on the railway station are a healthy reminder of its prosaic reality, for it means no more than 'Appleton'. A dozen modern English villages bear this ordinary name, and some of the many hundreds of small places in Roman Britain are also likely to have been called Aballo; Glastonbury may or may not have been among them.

These are places that preserve in recognisable form the names they bore in Roman times. A similar origin must be sought for Camelot, represented as among the most important of several cities where Arthur held court. Nearly all the others were large towns of Roman Britain, Chester, York, Gloucester and others, set down in their medieval spelling. Camalot, the more usual early form of the name, is therefore plainly a medieval spelling of the Latin name of a large Roman town in Britain. The only town with such a name is Camulodunum, Colchester.

Colchester had obvious advantages as a political centre in reconquered Britain. It was well sited to observe and to intimidate the two most formidable English territories, East Anglia and Kent. Easy roads linked it with the British north and west; and shipping from its harbours might reach Europe without approaching too closely the coast of English Kent. Contact with Europe mattered at the time of Badon, for then the struggle of Goth, Roman and Frank had not yet finally decided the fate of Gaul. But before the death of Arthur, the victories of Clovis the Frank had permanently turned Gaul into France. Thenceforth, there was nothing Roman left in northern Europe to comfort the British; and the collapse of a central authority in Britain ended the need for a political centre. Colchester lost its brief advantage.

Colchester was able to serve a new government for a short time because London was in decline. Throughout its history, London has prospered when commerce is busy and government secure and active. When the fifth century wars ended commerce and destroyed the government, London became a fortress, for the accidental reason that the main enemy forces were based on Kent and Norfolk. When the wars ended, London could have no health unless prosperity and strong government were successfully and permanently restored. They were not so restored.

Colchester might have been a frequent residence, but Arthur's was not a government that could rule from a single capital. It could only try to restore what had been smashed, but victory came too late for men to look back, too soon for them to start anew. The memories of the victors reached back to their own childhood, before the slaughter of the elders and the emigration of the survivors had throttled the Roman economy and the Roman institutions of Britain; and because these memories remained, men could not ignore them and devise a society that matched the actual conditions of their own day. Memory forced them to look at the past. They might recreate its outward political forms, but its economy could not be restored. Soldiers and civil servants might be placed within the walls of the decayed towns, but there is no evidence to suggest that any countryside villa was restored. Except in the west, the landlord economy was gone. So was the industry, the technology and the market economy. All that was left was subsistence agriculture, poor farmers producing food for their families, unable to procure what they could not make at home. Such an economy could not grow enough food to maintain a substantial urban population, or a numerous army and administration.

A shrunken town might feed itself from fields outside the walls, like Verulamium in wartime. But when the war was over, farmers might live more conveniently among their fields, no longer needing the shelter of walls. Government, and townsmen who did not farm, must depend upon what they could wring from small farmers; in Wales, the *duces* exacted tribute in cattle and corn, honey and beer, from reluctant peasants. In the west, tenants still paid rent. But in much of the lowlands, landlords had emigrated, joined the army, or perished and left no heirs. The old compulsions had been broken too long, and the grandson of a former landlord could not easily coerce the grandson of a former tenant into resuming a rent that had lapsed for half a century. Subsistence economy condemned each town and each warband to live on what it could get from its own area. No central government could hope to collect taxes and distribute them to its agents; its income was what it could persuade or force each local ruler to contribute. If Arthur's central army and administration were of any considerable size, no single area could afford to maintain them for long periods, save perhaps in parts of the west. East of the Cotswolds, Arthur can only have progressed from centre to centre, eating his way through his country like a medieval king. His personal prestige maintained his empire while he lived. When he fell, the empire ended. No new emperor was or could be proclaimed; actual power passed to the generals.

The Economy

The economy was not strong enough to bear a central government. Only a long period of peaceful recovery could have restored its strength, and then only if the armies were disbanded, their leadership and manpower directed to the slow reconstruction of agriculture, industry and towns. But after a generation of war the armies were made up of men who knew no trade but fighting. With no foreign enemy to fight, they fought each other. The restraints that Arthur's rule imposed checked their discords for a decade or more, but Gildas' protest that civil war was the ruin of Britain was amply justified; and it was unavoidable. Older men might dream of restoring the past, but younger men knew only the present. The realities of political power could not tolerate a strong government.

The power of Arthur's captains had rested on their ability to levy horses, men and food, much of it drawn from the peasants of the areas they protected. But aid given willingly in wartime tends to become a grievance, resented in peace-time. Yet actual power resided in the military commanders, not in the failing towns and vanished magnates; and Arthur's rule depended on the willingness of his captains to obey, and upon their ability to supply his needs. A few armed horsemen among unarmed civilians were in a position to enforce their orders; but they were not instruments for the restoration of justice, and a government that sought to restore ancient ways clearly had frequent cause to quarrel with the commanders upon whom it depended. The decisions of Arthur and his officers must heed both the temper of the *duces* and the protests of civilians, and must seek to reconcile the conflicts of one general and one area with another. Only years of quiet without conflict could renew the old habits of obedience and respect for government. But recurring conflict was built into the structure of postwar Britain, and quiet did not endure.

The victors of Badon faced an all but impossible task. They could act only according to their notions of their past, but they were subject to the pressures of their chaotic present. The most emphatic witness to the stature of the historical Arthur is that they succeeded for as long as they did. Gildas observed that evil tendencies had been growing for a long time, but dates the definitive collapse of good government ten years or so before he wrote. It had lasted well into the 520s, nearly thirty years after Badon, throughout Arthur's lifetime and some few years beyond. The twenty years allotted to the rule of Arthur after Badon are pictured as years of internal peace, the civil wars as an evil that followed them.

Camlann

A bald notice in the Cambrian Annals is the only record of Arthur's end:

> the Battle of Camlann, where Arthur and Medraut fell.

The entry is placed 21 years after Badon, and should indicate a date a year or two either side of 515. Later legend insists that Medraut was the enemy and not the ally of Arthur, but the earlier Welsh bardic tradition makes him a hero who served Arthur. The Annal could bear either meaning, and the only other record of a fifth or sixth century Medraut makes him the heir of a southern dynasty, and perhaps locates his son in Suffolk. Nothing else is known of the battle or its cause, or even of its whereabouts. Camlann means 'crooked glen', and the Roman fort at Birdoswald on Hadrian's Wall has that name. But so did other places; one in Merionethshire is still so called, and there are many crooked glens in England whose former British name has perished.

But whatever the place and cause of the battle, the result was catastrophe. With Arthur died the unity of Britain, and all hope of reviving it under British rule. In the next generation, Gildas denounced the anarchy that followed; but it did not occur to him that a strong central government could or should be established to check it. He admitted Roman law and magistrates; he endorsed the fourth-century criticism of the emperor Maximus, a rebel against a legitimate emperor; and he praised the government of his own youth, that Arthur had headed. The rule of Arthur had been an age of order, truth and justice, to be praised in retrospect; but Arthur was also the author and the patron of the *duces* whom Gildas denounced. When his empire fell, it could have been restored only by the predominance of the brutal Maelgwn, or of some other general, over his rivals, a tyranny that neither Gildas nor any other civilian could have welcomed. In retrospect the institution of the emperor was ranged on the side of the generals against the judges. No one wished its return; civilian and conservative opinion saw no future in the emergence of a supreme tyrant, and the local tyrants had no wish for a master. The emperor and his restored Roman government were dead and best forgotten, no longer practical politics.

Arthur dominates and unites the history of two centuries; his victory was the climax and consummation of the fifth-century struggles; and his undoing shaped the history of the sixth century, the mould wherein the future of the British Isles was formed. He was at once the last Roman emperor in the west, and the first medieval king of the country now called England. He left behind him the memory of a splendid failure. The story-tellers who sang of a strong, just and chivalrous king might have chosen for their hero Edwin of Northumbria, or Maximus, or Cormac of Ireland, or Theodoric of Ravenna or another famous name. They chose Arthur, and preserved his essential story. Yet even the barest outline of who he was and what he did must be inferred from dubious uncertain hints. There is just enough to show that Arthur existed, and was honoured in the next few generations as the greatest general and ruler of the recent past; just enough to show that in Britain he subdued the Germans who elsewhere mastered Europe, that the prestige of his victory and the force of his character maintained for two decades a strong government against impossible odds among the ruins of Roman Britain. He left a golden legend, and he rescued a corner of the Roman world from barbarian rule for a short space. Posterity may echo the judgement of the Norman historian William of Malmesbury,

> this is that Arthur of whom modern Welsh fancy raves. Yet he plainly deserves to be remembered in genuine history rather than in the oblivion of silly fairy tales; for he long preserved his dying country.

TABLE OF DATES

Capital letters denote Emperors, Popes and major rulers. (W. . West; E . . East).
Italics denote battles. Italic capitals denote Irish Kings.
The span of years shown indicates either the reign or the effective adult life of the
   individual concerned; birth dates are not given.

THE EMPIRE	THE CHURCH	BRITISH ISLES
350		
CONSTANS (W) 337–350	Hilary of Poitiers	*MUIREDACH* 325–355
CONSTANTIUS (E) 337–361	353–368	
MAGNENTIUS (W) 350–353		Paul the Notary 353
JULIAN (W) Caesar 355–361	Synod of Rimini 359	*EOCHAID* 356–365
360		
JULIAN 361–363	DAMASUS 366–384	Barbarian raids 360, 364, 367
JOVIAN 363–364	Ambrose of Milan	
VALENTINIAN I (W) 364–375	371–397	*CRIMTHANN* 365–378
VALENS (E) 364–378	Martin of Tours	Border dynasties founded c. 368
	372–c. 397	
370		
GRATIAN ((W) 375–383		*NIALL* 379–405
Adrianople 378		
VALENTINIAN II (W) 375–393		
THEODOSIUS I (E) 379–395		
380		
MAGNUS MAXIMUS (W) 383–388	Augustine of Hippo	First Migration to
	386–430	Brittany ?388
390		
Offa of Angel c. 390/420?	Victricius in Britain	
ARCADIUS (E) 395–408	c. 396	Saxon raid c. 397
HONORIUS (W) 395–421	St. Albans, Whithorn ?	
	founded	
400		
THEODOSIUS II (E) 408–450	Pelagius c. 400–418	*NATH – I* 405–428
CONSTANTINE III (W) 407–411		
410		
Goths take Rome 410	Sicilian Briton 411	Britain independent
	Fastidius 411	COEL HEN dux ? c. 410/420
Visigoth federates in Gaul	Amator, Auxerre -418	AMBROSIUS the Elder
418	Germanus of Auxerre	? c. 412/425
	418–448	Drust (Picts) 414–458
420		
Eomer of Angel c. 420/460?	Jerome died 420	*VORTIGERN* c. 425–c. 459
VALENTINIAN III (W) 423–455	CELESTINE 422–432	*LOEGAIRE* 428–463
Vandals take Africa c. 429	Germanus, Britain 429	HENGEST and Horsa land c. 428

ABROAD	THE CHURCH	BRITISH ISLES
430		
Aëtius supreme in the west c. 433–454	Patrick in Ireland 432–c. 459 SIXTUS III 432–440	Cunedda, and Cornovii, migrations c. 430? *Wallop* c. 437
440		
Aëtius consul III 446 CHILDERIC I (Franks) c. 440?–481	LEO I 440–461 Patrick's *Declaration* c. 440/443 Germanus in Britain	First Saxon revolt c. 441/2 *Aylesford, Crayford* c. 445/449
450		
MARCIAN (E) 450–457 AVITUS (W) 455–456 Aegidius in Gaul 455–464 LEO I (E) 457–474	Patrick's *Letter* c. 450 Northern Irish sees c. 459	*Richborough* c. 450 Coroticus, Clyde, c. 450 Massacre c. 458. Aelle, South Saxons Second Migration to Brittany c. 459
460		
Icel of Angel c. 460/480? Syagrius in Gaul 464–486 ANTHEMIUS (W) 467–472	HILARY 461–468 Faustus at Riez 462–c. 495 Ibar, Enda, Kebi in Rome c. 465	AMBROSIUS AURELIANUS c. 460–c. 475 *AILLEL MOLT* 464–482 *ANGUS* of Munster c. 465–492
470		
ZENO (E) 474–491 Odovacer ends western emperors 476	Sidonius of the Auvergne 470–479 Docco died c. 473	ARTHUR c. 475–c. 515
480		
CLOVIS (Franks) 481–511 *Soissons* 486	Illtud's school c. 480–c. 510 Brigit c. 480–524	*Portsmouth* c. 480 Cerdic c. 480–c. 495 Migration of Angel kings c. 480 *LUGAID* 482–505
490		
ANASTASIUS 491–518 THEODORIC in Italy 493–526	Abban and Ibar, Abingdon, c. 498	Irish attacks on Britain 495/510 *Badon* c. 495. Partition.
500		
Poitiers 507 Gaul becomes France End of main Elbe cemeteries	Benedict of Nursia c. 500–c. 542	Demetia recovered c. 500/510 Dal Riada Scots c. 500 Dyfnwal, Clyde, c. 500 *MAC ERCA* 505–532
510		
SONS OF CLOVIS 511–561★ JUSTIN I 518–527	Dubricius c. 510–c. 540	*Camlann*, Arthur killed, c. 515
520		
Beowulf c. 520/550 JUSTINIAN 527–565	Samson c. 525–c. 563	Vortipor c. 515–c. 540 MAELGWN c. 520–551
530		
Africa reconquered 533, Italy 533–544 THEUDEBERT (East Franks) 533–548	Finnian of Clonard c. 530–551 Gildas' book c. 538	Saxon migrations from Britain to Europe c. 530/550 *TUATHAL* 532–548
540		
Bubonic plague 543–547 THEUDEBALD (East Franks) 548–555	Kentigern exiled c. 540 Columba, Derry 544 Cadoc c. 545–c. 580 Brendan's voyages 545/560	Eliffer of York c. 540/560 Morcant, Clyde, c. 540/560 Gabran, Dal Riada, 541–560 *DIARMAIT* 548–564 Plague 547–551

ABROAD	THE CHURCH ABROAD	THE CHURCH IN THE BRITISH ISLES
550		
	Radegund at Poitiers 550–587	David c. 550–589
	PELAGIUS I 555–560	Comgall founded Irish Bangor 558
560		
CLOTHAIR killed Chramn and CONOMOR 560		Daniel at Bangor, Menai c. 560–584
BRUNHILD 566–613		Columba at Iona 563–597
JUSTIN II 565–578		Gildas in Ireland 565
Lombards in Italy 568		
570		
TIBERIUS 578–582	Gregory of Tours 573–594	Gildas died 570
	PELAGIUS II 578–590	Kentigern, Glasgow, c. 575–c. 603
580		
MAURICE 582–602		Aedan of Ferns c. 585–627
590		
	GREGORY the Great 590–604	Augustine Archbishop of Canterbury 597–604
	Columban in Gaul and Italy 595–615	
600		
PHOCAS 602–610		
610		
HERACLIUS 610–641		
620		
PEPIN I Mayor 624–639	HONORIUS I 625–640	Edwin baptised 625
630		
DAGOBERT I 630–638		Aedan of Lindisfarne 635–651
Arabs took Damascus 634, Jerusalem 637		
640		
Arabs in Egypt 640, Persia 642, Africa 647	Eligius bishop 640–659	Hilda of Whitby c. 640–680
GRIMOALD, Mayor, 642–656		

BRITAIN	IRELAND	THE ENGLISH
550		
RHUN of Gwynedd 551–580?		CYNRIC took Salisbury 552
BRIDEI, Picts, 554–584		AETHELBERT of Kent 555–616
560		
PEREDUR, York, c. 560–580	*AINMERE* 565–569	IDA, Bamburgh, c. 560–c. 570
RIDERCH, Clyde, c. 560–c. 600	*BAETAN* c. 569–588	*Wibbandun* 568; Ceawlin
CONALL, Dal Riada, 560–574		and Cutha beat Aethelbert
570		
URIEN of Reged c. 570–c. 590		*Bedcanford* 571
Arthuret 573		*Dyrham* 577
AEDAN, Dal Riada, 574–609		
580		
MOURIC, Glevissig,	*AED* m. Ainmere	ADDA, etc., Bernicia,
c. 580–c. 615	588–601	c. 570–588
Caer Greu 580. PEREDUR killed		AELLE occupied York?
Tintern c. 584		AETHELRIC 588–593
590		
Lindisfarne c. 590		CEAWLIN killed 593
OWAIN of Reged c. 590–c. 595		AETHELBERT supreme
Catraeth 598?		c. 593–616
		AETHELFERTH 593–617

	NORTHERN ENGLISH	SOUTHERN ENGLISH
600		
Degsastan 603	AETHELFERTH in York 604	
610		
Chester c. 613	EDWIN 617–633	CYNEGILS, West Saxons,
		611–643
620		
		PENDA 626–655
630		
Catwallaun killed Edwin 633	OSWALD	
	634–642	
640		
Penda and Welsh killed	OSWY 642–670	CENWALH, West Saxons,
Oswald 642		643–672

TABLE OF DATES

ABROAD	THE CHURCH ABROAD	THE CHURCH IN NORTHERN BRITAIN AND IRELAND
650 EBROIN, Mayor, 656–681	Fursey died 649	
660 Arabs took Syracuse 664		Synod of Whitby 664
670 Arabs besiege Constantinople 673–675	Killian of Wurzburg c. 670–689	Wearmouth founded 674 Caedmon died c. 678
680 PEPIN II, Mayor, 681–714		Bede at Jarrow c. 681–735 Adomnan, Iona, 686–704
690	Willibrord, Frisia, 695–739	
700 Arabs in Spain 710 CHARLES MARTEL 714–741 *Poitiers* 732 PEPIN III 741–768	Boniface of Mainz killed 755 Alcuin of York and Tours 766–804	
800 CHARLEMAGNE, 768–814		

*SONS OF CLOVIS
 THEODORIC I, East Franks, 511–533
 CHLODOMER, Orleans, 511–524
 CHILDEBERT, Paris, 511–558
 CLOTHAIR I, Soissons, 511–561
 Orleans, 524–561
 East Franks, 555–561
 Paris, 558–561

THE CHURCH IN SOUTHERN BRITAIN	THE NORTH	MERCIA AND THE SOUTH
650		
	Oswy killed Penda 655 OSWY supreme 655–658	WULFHERE 658–675
660		
Theodore Archbishop of Canterbury 669–690	Plague 664	Second *Badon*; Morcant killed 665
670		
Barking, Chertsey founded 675 Aldhelm c. 670–709	EGFERTH 670–685 *Trent* 679	West Saxon underkings 672–c. 682 AETHELRED 675–704
680		
	ALDFRITH 685–705 Ferchar, Dal Riada, 680–696	CEADWALLA 685–688 INE 688–726
690		
		WIHTRED, Kent, 691–725
700		
	Pict and Scot wars Northumbrian civil wars	Coenred 704–709 Ceolred 709–716 AETHELBALD 716–757 OFFA 757–796 First Scandinavian raid 789
800		
	KENNETH MacAlpine 830–860 united Picts and Scots	EGBERT, West Saxon, 802–839 RHODRI MAWR, Wales, 844–877 ALFRED 871–?900

SUMMARY OF EVENTS

350–400. The Imperial Government, under pressure on the Rhine and Danube, kept the garrison of Britain under strength. Britain prospered, in spite of occasional raids. Christianity prevailed by the end of the century.

400–450. The Rhine frontier broke, 406/407. The emperor Constantine III, a Briton, cleared the barbarians from Britain and Gaul, but was suppressed by the legitimate emperor, Honorius. The Goths took Rome, 410. Honorius told the British to govern and defend themselves, legitimising local emperors. The British repelled foreign enemies, but divided in civil war. Vortigern (c. 425–c. 458) employed Saxons, or English, to defeat the Picts, barbarians beyond the Forth; he neutralised mainland Ireland and reduced Irish colonists in western Britain. The British nobility, led by Ambrosius the elder, rebelled against Vortigern and the Saxons; Vortigern enlisted more Saxons, who rebelled against both parties, c. 441, and destroyed Roman British civilisation. After heavy fighting, the political leaders of the British were assassinated, and much of the surviving nobility emigrated to Gaul, c. 459.

450–500. A national resistance movement of the citizens (*Cymry*) was initiated by Ambrosius Aurelianus the younger, c. 460, and triumphed under Arthur at Badon, c. 495. The English remained in partitioned areas, chiefly in the east. The political forms of the Roman Empire were revived, but its economy had been destroyed.

500–550. The central government disintegrated with the death of Arthur (c. 515). Numerous generals became warlords of regions, Maelgwn of North Wales the most powerful among them, and provoked the resentment of civilians of all classes. A monastic reform movement on a mass scale freed the church from dependence upon the warlords; it spread to Ireland, and also prompted a massive migration to Brittany. Bubonic plague ravaged the mediterranean and also Britain and Ireland, 547–551.

550–600. The second Saxon, or English, revolt permanently mastered most of what is now England, destroying the remnants of the warlords. By 605, Aethelferth of Northumbria and Aethelbert of Kent were between them supreme over all the English. Kent was converted to Roman Christianity, 597. Columba of Iona established Irish monastic Christianity among the Picts, and among the Scot or Irish colonists of Argyle, 563–597.

600–650. The empire and Christianity of Kent collapsed, 616. Northumbrian supremacy, 617–642, was overthrown by Penda of the Mercians, with Welsh allies. The monastic impetus faded in Wales but renewed its vigour among the Irish.

650–800. The Mercian kings held empire over the southern English; the Northumbrian monarchy lost authority after 700. The Northumbrians and Mercians accepted monastic Christianity from the Irish, and the English and the Irish carried it to Europe north of the Alps. Its practices conflicted with those of Rome. Archbishop Theodore, from Tarsus (669–690), presided over the fusion of native monastic and Roman episcopal Christianity among the English; the Irish and the Welsh conformed later. Scandinavian raids began in 789, and sovereignty over the English passed from the Mercian to the West Saxon kings early in the 9th century.

ABBREVIATIONS
used in the Notes

Italic figures and letters give National Grid Map references:
  Two letters and four figures, as *TL 01 23*, refer to Great Britain.
  One letter and two figures, as *N 58*, refer to Ireland.
  One letter and one figure, as *H 2*, refer to Brittany.
The National Grid for Great Britain is explained on Ordnance Survey maps, in the
  Automobile Association Handbook, and elsewhere.
The Irish National Grid is shown on Maps 9 and 27, pp. 153 and 373 above.
The Grid devised for Brittany is shown on Map 14, p. 255 above, and explained in the
  notes thereto.

A single bold capital letter, as **A**, refers to the appropriate section of *Arthurian Sources*,
  cf. p. xi above, whose contents are

A	Annals	**H**	Honorius' Letter
B	Badon	**I**	Inscriptions
C	Charters	**J**	Jurisprudence, Law
D	Dedications	**K**	King Lists
E	Ecclesiastics	**L**	Localities, Geography
F	Foreign persons and places	**M**	Miscellaneous
G	Genealogies	**N**	Names of Places
GA	Armorican	**O**	Ogam Script
GB	British	**P**	Persons, laymen
GE	English	**Q**	Quotations from texts
GF	Foreign	**R**	Roman institutions
GI	Irish	**S**	Saxon Archaeology
followed by the initial letter(s) of the		**T**	Texts discussed
territory concerned			

ACR	Sir Cyril Fox *The Archaeology of the Cambridge Region* 1923, rev. 1948
Ant.	Antiquity 1927–
Ant.Jl.	Antiquaries Journal 1921–
Arch.	Archaeologia 1773–
Arch.Jl.	Archaeological Journal 1845–
ASE	Nils Aberg *The Anglo-Saxons in England* Uppsala 1926
BT	*The Text of the Book of Taliesin* Llanbedrog 1910
CIIC	*Corpus Inscriptionum Insularum Celticarum* ed. R.A.S. MacAlister, 2 vols. Dublin 1945–49
CPNS	W. J. Watson *The History of the Celtic Place-Names of Scotland* Edinburgh 1926
DAB	*Dark Age Britain* (Studies presented to E. T. Leeds) ed. D. B. Harden, London 1956
Dark Age Dates	*Dark Ages Dates* John Morris, see Jarrett and Dobson pp. 145 ff.
DEPN	*Dictionary of English Place-Names* ed. E. Ekwall, Oxford 1936; ed. 4, 1960

ABBREVIATIONS

DSB E. T. Leeds *The Distribution of Anglo-Saxon Saucer Brooches* in *Arch.* 63 1911/12, 159 ff.
ECMW *The Early Christian Monuments of Wales* ed. V. E. Nash-Williams, Cardiff 1950
EHR English Historical Review 1886–
EPNS *English Place-Names Society Survey* by counties, Cambridge 1924–
EWGT P. C. Bartrum *Early Welsh Genealogical Tracts* Cardiff 1960
Feil-Sgribhinn *Feil-Sgribhinn Eoin mhic Neill* (MacNeill Essays) Dublin 1940
FAB W. F. Skene *Four Ancient Books of Wales* 2 vols, Edinburgh 1868
HE *Historia Ecclesiastica*
HF *Historia Francorum*
ILS *Inscriptiones Latinae Selectae* ed. H. Dessau, Berlin 1902–15
JRS Journal of Roman Studies 1911–
HRSAI Journal of the Royal Society of Antiquaries of Ireland 1870–
JTS Journal of Theological Studies 1900–
LBS S. Baring-Gould and T. Fisher *The Lives of the British Saints* 4 vols., London, 1907–13
Jones A. H. M. Jones *The Later Roman Empire* Blackwell, Oxford 1964
Mansi J. D. Mansi *Sacrorum Conciliorum nova et amplissima Collectio* 1759; facsimile, Paris and Leipzig 1901
MA Medieval Archaeology 1957–
Meaney A. Meaney *Gazetteer of Early Anglo-Saxon Burial Sites* London 1964
Not.Dig. *Notitia Dignitatum* ed. O. Seeck, Berlin 1876, reprint Frankfurt-am-Main 1962
PL *Patrologia Latina* ed. J. Migne, Paris 1844–
PLECG N. K. Chadwick *Poetry and Letters in Early Christian Gaul* London 1955
Plettke A. Plettke *Ursprung und Ausbreitung der Angeln und Sachen* Hildesheim 1921
PLRE *The Prosopography of the Later Roman Empire* ed. A. H. M. Jones, J. R. Martindale, J. Morris, Cambridge, Vol. I 1971, Vols. II and III forthcoming
PNK *Place-Names: Kent* J. K. Wallenberg, Uppsala 1931, 1934
P and P Past and Present 1952–
RIB *The Roman Inscriptions of Britain* ed. R. G. Collingwood and R. P. Wright, Oxford 1965
SC *The Saxon Chronicle* Rolls, 23, 1861, ed. B. Thorpe; MHB 291; ed. J. Earle, Oxford 1865; rev. C. Plummer, 2 vols, 1892–99; D. Whitelock and others, text London 1952, translation 1961; translated G. N. Garmonsway, Everyman's Library 1953
SyAC Surrey Archaeological Collections 1854–
WHR Welsh History Review 1960–

NOTES

The notes aim to indicate the main sources relevant to each subject discussed. Space prevents discussion of many of the possible alternative interpretations that could be based upon them. The figures refer to the page and paragraph where the word noted is to be found.

Proper names are themselves references, since they are discussed and indexed in *Arthurian Sources;* whose relevant sources (*see* Abbreviations) are here cited for many of the more important persons, places and subjects. References are to the page and paragraph.

Introduction

xv.2   BIELER: *Irish Ecclesiastical Record* 1967, 2.

xv.3   GILDAS, NENNIUS, PATRICK: text and translation, ed. M.Winterbottom; J.Morris; A.B.E. Hood, Phillimore, forthcoming.

xv.3   ARTHURIAN SOURCES: Phillimore, forthcoming.

xvii.2   CHADWICK: *Growth of Literature* 1, xix.

1   Britain in 350 (pp. 1–9)

1.1   ARMED CONFLICT: see R.

2.1   CLAUDIAN: *de Laudibus Stilichonis* 3, 150–153.

2.3   CIVITAS, VICI, PAGI: see R.

3.3   INVASIONS, DEVASTATION, FRONTIERS: see R.

4.1   AUSONIUS: his estate, *de Herediolo* 29 ff.; his uncle, *Professores Burdigalenses* 17, cf. *Parentalia* 5; his father, *Parentalia* 3, *Epicedion*, etc.

4.3   PHILO: Ausonius *Ep.* 22.

5.1   IUGUM: the evidence is summarised by Jones LRE 62 ff.; the assessment varied from province to province, and was sometimes by area. In Syria, a *iugum* was reckoned at 40 *iugera* (about 25 acres) of average land, 20 of good land, 60 of poor land. The calculation of the British *iugum* is not known.

5.2   DIOCESE: see R.

5.2   MILITARY COMMANDERS: see R.

5.2   GARRISONS: see R.

5.3   GEOGRAPHY: see R, and Fox *Personality of Britain.*

6.2   PEASANTRY: see especially Jones LRE 774 ff.

8.1   BACAUDA: see especially E.A.Thompson in *P and P* 2, 1952, 11 ff.

9.3   AUSONIUS: *Mosella* 389 ff.

2   Ending of the Western Empire (pp. 10–28)

10.1   MAGNENTIUS: see PLRE 1.

10.1   ALAMANNI: Ammian 16, 12, 4; cf. Zosimus 2, 53.

10.1   MURSA: casualties rated at 54,000, Zonaras 13, 8.

10.2   CONSTANTIUS AT MURSA: Sulpicius Severus *Chron.* 2, 38, 5–7.

11.1   CONSTANTIUS' INQUISITION: Ammian 14, 5. 2–9.

12.1   TOIL AND SWEAT: Barnabas 10.

12.1   BARREN ELM: Hermas 3, 2.

12.1   IRENAEUS: *adversus Haereseos* 4, 46.

12.3   CHRISTIAN COMMUNITIES: see Duchesne *Fastes Épiscopaux* 1, 31–32; Lyon, Paris, Sens, Rouen, Reims, Metz, Bordeaux, Bourges and Toulouse, with Arles and Vienne in Provence, Trier and Cologne in the Rhineland, are the known pre-Constantinian bishoprics; cf. Greg. Tur. HF 10, 31, and p. 335 below.

13.2   ARIAN CONTROVERSY: the clearest concise account, here cited, is that of Sulpicius Severus *Chron.* 2, 38 ff.

14.1   AUGURIUS: see E.

15.2   RAIDS: in 360 and 364, Ammian 20, 1 and 26, 4, 5; in 367, Ammian 27, 8 and 28, 3, 7–8.

15.3   COUNTRY HOUSES: notably Park Street near St. Albans, and Norton Disney on the borders of Lincolnshire and Nottinghamshire, see R.

15.3   LONDON: see L.

16.2   NIALL: see G INA and p. 157 below.

16.3   AREANI: variant *Arcani*.

16.3   YORKSHIRE SIGNAL TOWERS: see p. 51.2 below.

16.3   ANTICIPATORS: *Not. Dig.* Occ. 40, 31 *Praefectus numeri Supervenientium*
17.2   *Petueriensium, Derventione.*

17.2   CRIMTHANN: see G IML, and p. 157 below.

17.2   BRITAIN, CHANNEL: see L Alba, Icht.

17.2   IRISH COLONIES: see L.

17.2   VALENTIA: see L.

17.3   PATROL UNITS: *Exploratores* at Risingham and High Rochester, *Raeti Gaesati* at Risingham and Cappuck, RIB 1235, 1243–4, 1262, 1270, 1217, 2117. Neither the forts nor troops of north-eastern Northumberland have yet been identified; see R.

17.4   NORTHERN LISTS: see G introduction, and BA, BN.

18.1   THEODOSIUS . . . AFRICA: Ammian 29, 5, 35.

18.1   AUGUSTINE: *Ep.* 199, 46: cf. Jones LRE 652 and note.

18.2   FRAOMAR: Ammian 29, 4, 7, *potestate tribuni Alamannorum praefecit numero.* He was doubtless *tribunus gentis Alamannorum*, analogous to the *tribunus gentis Marcomannorum* in Pannonia Prima, *Not. Dig.*, Occ. 34, 24. The *vir tribunitiae potestatis* whom Germanus met in 429 (Constantius ch. 15) was perhaps a similar *Tribunus gentis*.

18.3   DEMETIA: see G BD.

18.3   PATRICK: *Ep.*, 2.

19.2   SYMMACHUS: *Oratio* 4, 6.

20.2   GRATIAN: Rufinus HE 11, 13; Ausonius *Gratiarum Actio* 14. Ammian 31, 10, 18 compares him with Commodus.

20.2   MAXIMUS: see P, and PLRE 1 Maximus 39.

20.2   BRITTANY: see p. 250 below.

21.5   UNITS: Claudian *de bello Getico* 414 ff.

21.5   LEGION: the *Notitia Dignitatum* omits the 20th, but names the other legions of Britain.

23.2   JEROME: *Commentary on Ezekiel*, Prologue, and preface to book 3.

23.2   YOUNG BRITON: Sicilian Briton (see E and pp. 340 ff. below) *Ep.* 1, 1 (PL Sup. 1, 1687 ff.).

23.5   AMMIAN: 27, 3, 14.

24.3   EFFICIENT HEAD: e.g., Ambrose *Ep.* 11, 4 *totius orbis Romani caput Romana ecclesia.*

25.2   EUSEBIUS: Ambrose *Ep.* 63, 66.

25.3   MATTERS OF FINANCE: Ambrose *Ep.* 40, 27.

25.3   OLD TESTAMENT: Ambrose *Ep.* 20, 23.

25.3   MILAN: Ambrose *Ep.* 20, cf. 21 (*contra Auxentium*); Augustine *Confessio* 9, 7; Paulinus *vita Ambrosii* 13.

26.1   THESSALONICA: see especially Ambrose *Ep.* 51, 6 ff.

26.2   MARTIN: Sulpicius Severus; ELECTION *vita Martini* 9, cf. *Dialogi* 1, 26, 3; SCHOOL *vita* 10; AMATOR *Dialogi* 3, 1, 4; VICTRICIUS *Dial.* 3, 2, 4; CLERGY ALONE *Dial.* 1, 26, 3; VALENTINIAN *Dial.* 2, 5, 5; LAY JUDGE *Chron.* 2, 50, 5; BANQUET *vita* 20, 2; 20, 5–7.

27.3   SAME MOUTH: Gregory the Great *Ep.* 11, 34.

28 1   MARCELLINUS: *Chronicle* AD 454, on the assassination of Aëtius.

3 Independent Britain: The Evidence (pp.29–43)

29.1   HONORIUS' LETTER: Zosimus 6, 10; cf. **H**.

29.2   PROVINCIAL COUNCIL: see **H** and **R**.

30.5   COINS: see **R**.

31.5   ARCHAEOLOGY OF THE BRITISH: see **M**.

32.2   PAGAN ENGLISH: see also **S**.

32.2   PLETTKE: *Ursprung* 65 dates the migrations to Britain to some time before 441/442, citing L.Schmidt *Allgemeine Geschichte* 159 ff., who rightly based his conclusions on the Chronicle of 452 (p. 38 below). Plettke uses this date as a main criterion for the dating of German pottery and brooches; cf. e.g. pp. 44–45 where the latest forms of vessels of Type A 6 are prolonged 'perhaps into the early 5th century' because they are occasionally found in England, and type A 7 is centred on the early 5th century both because it derives from A 6 and because 'diese Form besonders haüfig in England gefunden ist und die Hauptüberwanderung der Angelsachsen doch wohl mit Sicherheit in die erste Hälfte des 5. Jahrhunderts zu setzen ist.' In general, Plettke's dating, and the reasoning behind it, remain the basis of modern German archaeological dates; so Tischler *Sachsenforschung* 41 'Unsere Chronologie . . . weicht letzten Endes nur wenig von der Anschauung Plettkes ab.' German estimates of Anglian and Saxon burial dates about the Elbe still ultimately derive from the Chronicler of 452; the notion that there exist independent 'German dates', which can be used to guide dates in Britain, is an illusion.

33.1   BROOCHES: see **S**

33.1   CRUCIFORM BROOCHES: cf. p. 269 below. The most useful study is still that of Åberg ASE 28 ff. The principal corrections are that Åberg's starting date is a generation too late; his groups III and IV are contemporary; and the border lines between groups need adjustment by closer attention to the foot of the brooch. The term 'cruciform' is restricted to the series of brooches that begin with Åberg's group I; it excludes the prototype brooches found at Dorchester, Beetgum and elsewhere, and also 'small long' brooches, sometimes miscalled cruciform.

33.1   SAUCER BROOCHES: see especially Åberg ASE 16 ff.; Leeds DSB; SYAC 56, 1959, 80 ff.; cf. p. 269 below, and **S**.

33.2   AFTER 400: until recently unnecessary uncertainty has bedevilled modern

English, but not German discussions of the date when the first pagan cemeteries came into use. Bede's date of '450' (p. 39 below) was long repeated without examination; an equally untenable date of about 360 has been advanced by Myres ASP 71 ff. The argument stresses some vessels that 'on the Continent are dated in the fourth or at latest the early years of the fifth century', i.e. about 400, not 360. Such relatively small numbers do not date cemeteries. Most migrating or conquering peoples bring with them a small proportion of objects that are at least a generation old; the Roman conquest of AD 43 brought with it a number of Arretine and other pots that were then 20 or 30 years old, but these vessels do not alter the date of the Roman invasion; and early English graves in Britain also contained a few brooches, as well as pots, that were fashionable in Germany about 400. A proportion of objects about 30 or 40 years old forms a necessary part of the furniture of cemeteries first used about 430. The extreme date of 360 appears to rest chiefly on a single vessel, typologically intermediate between one dated in continental English territory to the 3rd century and another of the early 5th century, and is for that reason placed halfway between, 'no later than the second half of the fourth century'. A vessel with so frail a date is not enough to alter the date of a national migration by two generations.

Equally important is the evidence of what is not found in Britain. Brooches that in Germany are normally dated to the later fourth century, notably the prototypes of the cruciform brooch, of the Beetgum or Dorchester-on-Thames pattern, and the latest Germanic 'crossbow' forms, have not yet been discovered in pagan Saxon cemeteries in England; and those that date to 'about 400', notably the 'equal arm, series 2' and the 'tutulus', are very rare; two of the former and one of the latter are known. The essence of the matter however is that the ultimate criterion that persuades German scholars to date a pot or brooch to the fourth century or to the early fifth is whether or not its parallel has been found in England. In general, the continental dates fit the rest of the evidence because they rest on the assumption that the pagan cemeteries of England began in the early fifth century; that assumption is securely grounded because it is based on the contemporary statement of the Chronicler of 452, reported by Schmidt, and adopted from him by Plettke. The dating based upon it has stood the test of time.

33.3   CHIP CARVED: or *Kerbschnitt*, cf. p. 51 below.

33.3   SCANDINAVIA ... DATING: the chief independent means of dating are gold bracteates (medallions) and coin hoards, from the late 5th century; but as yet they give few dates to other objects.

34.1   HALF A DOZEN PERIODS: based chiefly on cruciform brooches, the periods are A, 430/470: B, 460/500: C, 490/530: D, 510/590, subdivided into D 1, 510/540; D 2, 530/560; D 3, 550/590; E 570/610; F, 7th century. Maps 3, 6, 18, 21 and 22 (pp. 59, 107, 285, 297, 305) show the sites and areas where burials began in these periods. A number of sites on the margins of periods might alternatively be shown on the succeeding or preceding maps.

34.1   COINS: e.g. J.Werner *Münzdatierte Austrasische Grabfünde.*

34.1   WEAPONS: e.g. the axe termed 'francisca' is found in dated Frankish graves from the early 5th century, and might in theory be as early in Kent. Though it has not yet been reported in dated English graves before the later 6th century, it has sometimes been treated as though it were by itself evidence of a 5th century date in Britain. In general, dates assigned to weapons as yet inspire little confidence.

34.1   PURE TYPOLOGY: e.g. Harden's important study of glass vessels paid 'little

or no attention to the evidence of associated objects. The omission is deliberate'
(DAB 139). The neglect of evidence is in some particulars troublesome; the
largest class of vessels (Cone beakers III a i and Claw beakers II a) are
assigned by typology to the 5th and early 6th centuries, but have not yet been
found in dated graves earlier than the mid or late 6th century, cf. MA 2, 1958,
37; SyAC 59, 1959, 115.

34.1 ANIMAL ORNAMENT: the fundamental work is Salin *Tierornamentik*. Animals
clearly represented, mostly in the late 4th and earlier 5th centuries, present
fewer problems; abstract motifs, part animal and part otherwise, tread upon
uncertainties.

34.2 RECENT STUDIES: notably Meaney *Gazeteer*, that for the first time pulls
together all known sites, though the information, dates and grid reference
locations require close examination; Myres ASP is an important preliminary
to a full corpus of the pottery, though the starting date of c. 360 is not tenable
(p. 33.2 above). Hawkes and Dunning *Soldiers and Settlers* MA 5, 1961, 1 ff.
have made a new and important class of object available for study, though it is
still over easy for the unwary to treat late Roman metal as 'Germanic'.

35.2 BRITISH AUTHORS: especially Pelagius, Fastidius, the Sicilian Briton and his
colleagues, with Patrick and Faustus of Riez, see E, and JTS 16, 1965, 26 ff.
and pp. 338 ff. below.

35.5 GILDAS: see T and E.

36.2 ROMANS: Gildas 18, 1.

36.3 WHIPS: Gildas 7, 1.

37.1 ARMED FORCES: Gildas 14, 1.

37.2 NO EARLIER AGE: Gildas 21, 2 cf. p. 70 below.

37.2 COUNCILLORS: Gildas 23, 1.

37.2 AMBROSIUS: Gildas 25, 2 ff. cf. pp. 48 and 95 below.

37.3 NENNIUS: see T. The Kentish Chronicle, ch. 31, 36–38 and 43–46; the
Chronographer, ch. 66.

38.2 CHRONICLE OF 452: see T.

38.2 ANOTHER ... ALLUSION: in asserting his suzerainty over the Germanic peoples
of Europe, in 448, Attila the Hun claimed to rule the 'Ocean Islands', evidently
Britain, (Priscus, FHG 4, 90, Fragment 8); his claim implies that he then
regarded the island as under German control, cf. C.E. Stevens EHR 56,
1941, 263.

38.3 BRITISH VICTORIES: Zosimus 6, 5, cited p. 70 below; cf. H.

38.4 MIGRATION: Sidonius *Ep.* 3, 9; Jordanes *Getica* 45; Greg. Tur. HF 2, 18;
Mansi 7, 941; see E Mansuetus, and p. 90.5 below.

39.1 WHEN THEY DIED: Gildas 26, 3.

39.1 BADON: see B and p. 112 below.

39.2 AETIUS: Gildas 20, cf. F.

39.3 BEDE: see E.

40.1 BEDE ... AETIUS ... DATE: see T. Bede also corrected the error in the manuscripts of the Chronicle. He inserted the year date, '23rd year of Theodosius'
into the middle of the entry, though it is placed at about Theodosius' 10th
year. The correction was emphasised by the insertion of a correct date, the
'8th year of Theodosius' at the end of the preceding entry. Elsewhere in Bede's
Chronicle year dates are very rare, and are placed after the opening words of
the entry, and at the right place in the sequence of events. The evidence is
discussed in *Dark Age Dates* 152 ff., where however the date '443/4' on p. 154
is a misprint for 453/4; see also T.

40.2 SAXON CHRONICLE: see T.

41.2   BRITISH: some confusion arises from the use of 'Breton'. In English, its meaning is restricted to the British who have retained their national name in France, in Brittany. It is a valid modern geographical term, for the British of Brittany have long been sundered from Britain, save in their language. But when the word is applied to their 5th and 6th century ancestors, it implies a separation that had not yet occurred. The British who settled in Roman Armorica and gave it the modern name of Brittany were as fully British as their relatives at home; and were numerous elsewhere in northern France, not yet confined to Brittany.

41.2   COMBROGI, CYMRY: see p. 98, and L.

41.3   ANGLES, SAXONS: see L; cf. p. 311.

41.3   WEST SAXONS: Jutish and Saxon ornament is prominent in the early graves of the West and South Saxons, but not of the East Saxons. The earliest name of the West Saxons was however *Gewissae*, or Confederates, and the term Middle Saxons is not known before the late 7th century. The name did not arise from a belief that the southern English were descended from the Saxons of Germany rather than the 'Angles'; its use created that belief; cf. p. 294 below.

42.1   CONTINENTAL ORIGIN: cf. p. 269.

42.2   ANGLO-SAXON: see L; in 1865 Earle published *Two Saxon Chronicles Parallel*, not 'Anglo-Saxon', and Kemble published *The Saxons in England* in 1848. The titles were retained in revised editions in 1896 and 1876. The hybrid term was used earlier, but plain 'Saxon' lingered long.

42.3   SCOT: the origin of the Latin word is not known. It was not used in the Irish language.

42.3   PICT, CRUITHNI: see L and pp. 186 ff. below.

43.2   PERIODS: outlined in *Dark Age Dates* 1966; summarised Frere *Britannia* 1967, 381 ff.; cf. 'phases' Myres ASP 1969, 63 ff.

4   Independent Britain: Vortigern (pp. 44–70)

44.1   THE BRITISH: Zosimus 6, 5, probably citing Olympiodorus and other contemporaries, cf. H.

44.2   HORDES: Gildas 19, 1–4.

44.2   NATH – 1: Yellow Book of Lecan 192 b 25, cited Watson CPNS 192, cf. Book of Leinster 190ª 27 (4,836); cf. O'Curry 591. All that remains is the title of a lost tale.

45.1   IRISH SETTLEMENT: see L Dal Riada, Maps 7, p. 128; 25, p. 362; and p. 158 below.

45.2   HOMILY: *de vita Christiana*, PL 4, 1031 ff., ascribed to Fastidius in one MS; Augustine quotes a copy that had reached Sicily by 412, cf. JTS 16, 1965, 32 ff.; see T Fastidius.

45.2   FASTIDIUS: Gennadius *de Viris Inlustribus* 56; see E.

45.2   FASTIDIUS: *de Vita Christiana* 11 and 14.

48.2   PROCOPIUS: BV I, 2.

48.2   KINGS ANOINTED: Gildas 21, 4.

48.2   AMBROSIUS: see p. 95 below.

48.3   SICILIAN BRITON: *Ep. 2 opto te semper Deo vivere et perpetui consulatus honore gaudere*. For the imagery, cf. Prudentius *Peri Stephanon* 2, 559–560 *quem Roma caelestis sibi Legit perennem consulem*, on St. Lawrence. The Saint earned office in heaven by martyrdom; the unchristian British magistrate's only qualification was earthly office, that reformed conduct might perpetuate in heaven. The metaphor is pointless unless he were a consul.

48.3   CONSUL: the elder Ambrosius is also called *unus de consulibus Romanicae gentis* in the fable of the dragons on Snowdon, Nennius 42. The fable is older than medieval usage of the word, and the title therefore may derive from early tradition.

49.3   NOTITIA DIGNITATUM: see T.

49.4   COMMANDS: *Comes Britanniarum* listed in *Not. Dig.* Occ. 7, 154–156, 200–205; *Comes Litoris Saxonici* Occ. 28; *Dux Britanniarum* Occ. 40.

49.4   SAXON SHORE FORCES: The *Anderetiani*, listed in the *Notitia* in the field army of Gaul, on the Rhine, and at Paris (Occ. 7, 100; 41, 17; 42, 22), probably came from Anderida, Pevensey; the units of the three southern forts of Portchester, Pevensey and Richborough, *Exploratores, Abulci*, and *Secundani* also appear in the field army of Gaul (Occ. 7, 109; 110; 84; cf. 5, 241). The duplicate names, as elsewhere in the *Notitia*, suggest that detachments, and occasionally whole units, were posted from the coastal forts to Gaul by Constantine and earlier emperors, from Pevensey on two separate occasions.

50.2   VALENTIA: see L, and p. 17 above.

50.4   OUT OF DATE: S.S.Frere, *Britannia* 230 ff., 354 ff., discards earlier views that the Wall list was more than a hundred years out of date, but deems it 'inconceivable' that 'old regiments survived' after the raid of 367. The frontier was then reorganised and reconstructed. But reconstruction does not imply that any units other than those named by Ammian were annihilated, disbanded or replaced. Valentinian had no new troops to spare, and on other frontiers retained the remnants of similar old units of the lesser schedule who had survived worse disasters.

51.1   REBUILDING: e.g. the Commandant's House at Housesteads, *Arch. Ael.*[4] 39, 1961, 279 ff.; cf. 38, 1960, 61 ff.

51.1   BURIALS: e.g. Saxon, see S, Cumberland, Birdoswald; Durham, Hurbuck (Lanchester); Lancashire, Ribchester and Manchester; Northumberland, Benwell and Corbridge; Westmorland, Brough-under-Stainmore and perhaps Low Borrow Bridge. British, Chesterholm, Brigomaglus, RIB 1722 = CIIC 498, late 5th century (Jackson LHEB 192 note 2) or later, probably also Old Carlisle, Tancorix, RIB 908.

51.2   YORKSHIRE TOWERS: p. 16 above; see especially *Arch. Jl.* 89, 1932, 203 ff.

51.2   FARMING SITE: see S Yorkshire, Scarborough, Crossgates.

51.3   WALES: see R.

51.3   IRISH: see p. 158 below.

51.3   KERBSCHNITT: see S.

52.1   TWO UNITS: Fraomar, under Valentinian, probably *tribunus gentis Alamannorum*, cf. p. 18.2 above; *numerus Hnaudifridi*, 3rd or 4th century, at Housesteads, RIB 1576, cf. 1593–4; the commander of the mid third century *numerus Maurorum* at Burgh-by-Sands RIB 2042, cf. *Not. Dig.* Occ. 40, 47, was Roman; and so doubtless was the commander of the early third century *cuneus Frisiorum* at Housesteads RIB 1594, cf. 1593.

52.2   GENTILES: *Not. Dig.* Occ. 42, 33 ff.

52.2   COMMERCIAL POTTERIES: 'Romano-Saxon' ware, cf. J.N.L.Myres in DAB 16 ff. Though some of the vessels there discussed are now held to be earlier, the majority are not.

52.2   PAGAN ENGLISH GRAVES: a very few contain an occasional sherd of 'Romano-Saxon' ware, for surface Roman sherds of all kinds are not uncommon; unbroken Roman, and perhaps Romano-Saxon, vessels are found, but very rarely.

52.2　SERVICE WITH ROME: for example, Silvanus the Frank, impeached before Constantius, dared not seek refuge with the barbarian Franks, since they would certainly either kill him or sell him, Ammian 15, 5.

53.1　AEGIDIUS, SYAGRIUS: see especially Greg. Tur. HF 2, 11, 18, 27; cf. F.

53.1　DALMATIA: see F Marcellinus.

53.2　ROMAN EMPIRE: Eugippius *vita Severini* 20.

53.2　BATAVIANS: *Not. Dig.* Occ. 35, 24; the MS reads *novae* for *nonae*.

53.2　MAMERTINUS: Eugippius *vita Severini* 4.

53.2　BARBARIAN GARRISON: Eugippius *vita Severini* 2.

53.2　REFUGEES: Eugippius *vita Severini* 30.

53.3　EGYPT: papyri, cited Jones LRE 662–3, with note 128.

54.2　COEL HEN: see G BN and BEB.

54.4　THE ISLAND: Gildas 21, 2–3.

55.2　VORTIGERN: see P and G BV.

55.2　AMBROSIUS: see P.

56.2　THE FEATHERED FLIGHT: Gildas 22, 1–2.

56.2　TRANSMARINI: Gildas 14; coracles, *curucae*, modern Welsh *cwrwg*, Gildas 19, 1; booty carried *trans maria*, in the plural, by Picts, as well as Scots and Saxons, Gildas 17, 3.

57.2　NORFOLK: an inscribed Pictish knife-handle found on the surface at a Roman farming site at Weeting in Norfolk, near the Devil's Dyke (*Ant. Jl.* 32, 1952, 71; *Norfolk Archaeology* 31, 1955, 184; cf. R.R.Clarke *East Anglia* pl. 44) might have been lost by a Saxon or Roman who took it from a Pict; or by a raiding Pict. There is no evidence to show how early the Picts adapted Ogam script (see O) to wood and bone; see p. 191 below.

57.3　TIME DREW NIGH: Gildas 22–23; 'keels', *cyulae*.

57.3　THREE KEELS: *ciulae* Nennius 31.

60.3　EXCAVATED EVIDENCE: See S. There is no evidence for the settlement of federates in Gaul before 418, or in Britain before the 420s (cf. p. 33.2 above). *Gentiles* are attested by texts in Gaul and Italy, perhaps by pottery in Britain, but not by cemeteries. Cemeteries in Gaul that contained both German and Roman grave goods were probably used by newly raised barbarian units of the Roman army, perhaps *Auxilia Palatina*.

61.2　HENGEST: Nennius 38.

61.2　ORKNEYS: a Saxon urn in Edinburgh Museum, see S, said to have been 'found in Buchan', may be mislabelled; or may be a relic of this expedition, a freak counterpart to the Pictish knife in Norfolk, p. 57.2 above.

61.2　FRENESSICAN SEA: probably the Forth, see L.

61.3　CEMETERIES: see S.

62.1　DUMFRIES: Watson CPNS 422 demonstrated that the name means 'Fort of the Frisians' linguistically, but proposed a fanciful alternative, solely because he did not think that Frisians settled in Scotland; Glensaxon (CPNS 356) and similar names might concern English settlement at this, or any other date.

62.4　GERMANUS . . . ARMIES: Constantius *vita Germani* 17, cf. Bede HE 1, 20.

63.1　LLANGOLLEN: see p. 64 below. The traditional site, marked by an obelisk, north of Maes Garmon, at Rhual (*SJ 223 647*), near Mold in Flintshire, is probably no more than an antiquarian guess from the place name.

63.2　NENNIUS: 32–35, placed at the beginning of Vortigern's reign; the second visit, Nennius 47, is placed at the end of the reign.

63.2　CATEL: see G BP.

63.2　POWYS: see G BP.

63.2　ELISEG: ECMW 182, see G BP.

63.2   BRITTU: see **G** BP; it is possible that the names derive from a single individual, Catellius Brutus.

63.3   PAGENSES: Jackson LHEB 443, cf. 91.

63.3   CORNOVII: see **G** BC.

64.1   WELSH POEM: *Angar Kyvyndawt* BT 21, 14 (FAB 529–530; 134) '*py dydwc garthan Gereint ar Arman*', 'why Geraint committed (?) the camp to Germanus'; the work is a late hotch-potch of allusions to earlier, lost poems.

64.2   PICT SAXON . . . ALLIES: late Welsh legend called the Powys foreigners *Gwyddyl Ffichti*, 'Irish Picts'; the earliest reference is in the 13th century Jesus Genealogy 23 (see **G** BGG 480); the phrase may originate from a misunderstood 'Scotti (et) Picti' in a version of the Germanus tradition.

64.3   MOEL FENLI: *SJ 163 601*, see **L**.

64.3   MOEL-Y-GERAINT: *SJ 202 419*, otherwise called Barber's Hill, see **L**.

64.3   GERMANUS CHURCHES: see **E**.

64.4   UNWARY CRITIC: e.g. PLECG 259 ff., cf. **E** 'German mac Guill'.

64.5   PALLADIUS, PATRICK: see **E** and p. 345 below.

65.1   SAXON RAID: see **A** 434; the texts do not support the translation 'raid from Ireland'.

65.2   MARRIAGE: see **E** Foirtchern and **G** BV, of p. 166 below.

65.2   IRISHMEN . . . CHRISTIANITY: e.g. **E** Coelestius, Corcodemus, Michomerus.

66.2   NENNIUS: 62, reproducing the 7th century spelling, Cunedag, cf. LHEB 458; *atavus* means ancestor in general, not only great-grandfather.

66.2   GENEALOGIES: see **G** BGG.

66.2   KIDWELLY: Nennius 14.

66.2   FIGURE . . . CORRUPTED: see **G** BGG 430.

67.1   VOTADINI: Gododdin, see **L**.

67.1   TRAPRAIN LAW: in East Lothian, *NT 58 74*, see **L**.

67.1   YEAVERING BELL: *NT 928 924*, see **L**.

67.2   INSCRIPTIONS: see p. 124 below.

68.1   SPLENDID IN BATTLE: BT 69, 11–12; 24; 70, 5–6; 11–12; cf. FAB 257,200. Durham and Carlisle, *Kaer Weir a Chaer Liwelyd*; Caer Weir, Durham, did not exist before the Norse invasions, and is an anachronism, comparable with a modern statement that a Roman fort is 'in Yorkshire'.

68.2   OCTHA: see p. 61 above.

68.2   GERMANIANUS: see **G** BNM. The dynasty of Decianus (see **G** BA and p. 17 above), probably Lothian, may also have originated at this time, but is more likely to have been established somewhat earlier.

68.3   CORNWALL: Cornovia, etc. The name does not come into use in any form until after the English conquest of Devon; see **L** and **G** BC. It means the land of the Cornovian Welsh.

69.3   COHORS: *Not. Dig.* Occ. 40, 34.

69.3   FORTS IN WALES: see **R**.

69.3   IUVENTUS: see **R**.

70.1   THE BRITISH: Zosimus 6, 5, cf. p. 38 above.

70.1   AFFLUENT: Gildas 21, 1, cf. p. 37 above.

5   The Overthrow of Britain (pp. 71–86)

71.1   THE PICTS: Nennius 31.

71.1   AMBROSIUS: see **P**, and p. 95 below.

71.2   AUGUSTINE, PELAGIUS: see pp. 339 ff. below.

72.4	THE KING: Nennius 36.
73.1	RANSOMS: Alaric demanded 4000 lb. of gold in 407, rather more in 409; some senators are said to have received 4000 lb. of gold in rent annually; cf. texts cited in Jones LRE 185–6, 554.
73.4	CHRONOGRAPHER: Nennius 66.
73.4	VITALINUS: see G BV.
73.4	WALLOP: unduly ignored by Ekwall. Possibly *guoloppum* Jackson *Ant.* 13, 1939, 106; see L.
74.2	HENGEST: Nennius 37. Chartres MS 19 keels; other MSS 16, 17 or 18.
74.2	HENGEST'S DAUGHTER: Nennius 37.
74.4	HENGEST: Nennius 37.
75.1	CANTERBURY: see L.
75.2	OCTHA: see p. 61 above.
75.2	EBISSA: the name is perhaps Celtic, and, if so, implies a joint command by a Roman officer and a German Captain.
75.3	COMPLAINED: Gildas 23, 5.
75.4	BARBARIANS: Gildas 23–24.
75.4	GREATER TOWNS: *coloniae.*
76.1	CAISTOR-BY-NORWICH: JRS 21, 1931, 232 and plate xxi. The excavator's interpretation has been challenged, but without good reason.
76.1	COLCHESTER: Hull *Roman Colchester* 41. The north-east gate was twice stormed; the most likely occasions are the first and second Saxon revolts, about the 440s and the 570s.
76.1	LINCOLN: the burnt stones are preserved in place for public view.
76.4	CERAMIC INDUSTRY: see M.
77.2	SOEMIL: see G END.
77.3	SAXON CEMETERIES: see S.
78.1	AETIUS: Gildas 20, 1.
78.1	WATER TABLE: see M.
78.1	FIRE OF VENGEANCE: Gildas 24, 1.
78.1	WENT HOME: 25, 2.
78.1	THE EAST: Gildas 24, 1; cf. 23,3; cf. p. 57 above.
78.2	UNEXPECTED RAID: Eugippius *vita Severini* 4.
78.2	THE CITIZENS: Eugippius *vita Severini* 30.
79.2	VERULAMIUM OVEN: *Ant. Jl.* 40. 1960, 19–21; *Ant.* 38, 1964, 110–111; *Civitas Capitals* 97.
80.2	ELAFIUS: Constantius *vita Germani* 26–27. The name is Roman and needs no emendation, see P, and PLRE Aelafius.
80.3	SOUTHAMPTON: cf. the Gallic tradition that on one of his visits Germanus sailed from near Cherbourg, de Plinval *St. Germain* 46.
80.4	VORTIGERN'S SON: Nennius 43.
81.1	SECOND ACCOUNT: Nennius 44 assigns four battles to Vortimer, but names only three. If the figure 4 is not a scribal error, it may derive from a tradition that included the battle of the mid 450s (SC 473, cf. p. 86 below).
81.1	ARCH: *Excavations at Richborough* 5, 1968, 40 ff.; cf. RIB 46 ff.
81.2	HORSA: see G EK.
82.1	STRATEGY: cf. Map 3, p. 59.
82.5	VORTIMER'S PROPHECY: Nennius 44.
83.2	BARBARIANS RETURNED: Nennius 45.
83.2	BARBARIANS SENT ENVOYS: Nennius 45.
84.2	HENGEST ... TOLD HIS MEN: Nennius 46. Most MSS read *Eu Saxones, eniminit saxas,* with minor variants; two read *nimed Eure* (or *hlore*) *saxes.*

84.3 FAUSTUS OF RIEZ: see **E** and p. 338 below.

84.3 VORTIGERN HATED: Nennius 48.

85.1 WRETCHED SURVIVORS: Gildas 25, 1.

86.1 FOUGHT AGAINST THE WELSH: SC 473.

6 The War (pp. 87–115)

88.1 WESTERN EMPIRE: cf. p. 28 above.

90.3 NORTH OF THE LOIRE: Sidonius *Ep.* 1, 7, 5 *supra Ligerim*; cf. p. 91 below; to Sidonius in the Auvergne 'beyond the Loire' meant to the north (and east) of the river.

90.3 BRETTEVILLE: *Annales de Normandie* 10, 1960, 312, based on M.H.Chanteux in *Recueil . . . Clovis Brunel*, 248 ff. A large number of churches and places named in honour of 6th century British monks, extending eastward into Belgium, also suggest a substantial British element in the population; see Map 4 and notes thereto, and **D**. The place name Breteuil, near Evreux, 40 miles south of Rouen, and near Beauvais, 60 miles south of Amiens, probably has the same origin, as have other places scattered throughout France, J.Vendryes *Feil-Sgribhinn* 163 ff.

90.4 RIOTHAMUS: Sidonius *Ep.* 3, 9; see **G** AC.

90.5 NEW LANDS: Mansuetus (see **E**) is termed 'Bishop of the British' in 461, Mansi 7, 941, cf. p. 38 above. His name is also inserted, at much the same date, in the episcopal lists (cf. p. 123 above) of Toul, on the borders of Burgundian territory, and of Meaux and Senlis, in Syagrius' dominions; both Senlis and Toul list subsequent bishops with British names, cf. **E** Amon and Conotigernus. The reason may be that substantial numbers of Mansuetus' British congregation settled in these towns. The place names and dedications of these regions have not yet been examined in the manner of those of Normandy.

90.5 BACAUDAE: cf. p. 8.

91.1 FREQUENT CHANGES: Jordanes *Getica* 45.

91.1 PREFECT: Sidonius *Ep.* 1, 7, 5.

91.2 LOWER LOIRE: Greg. Tur. HF 2, 18; see **T**.

91.2 ODOVACER: see **P** and p. 93 below.

92.3 FRISIANS: *vita Meloris* 1, cf. **E**.

92.3 JOHN REITH: see **G** AC.

92.3 GRADLON: see **G** AC, Wrdestan *vita Winwaloe* (cf. **E**) 2, 15.

93.1 GOTHIC ADMIRAL: Sidonius *Ep.* 8, 6, 13–15.

93.2 SOUTH COAST HARBOURS: Sidonius' words *de continenti in patriam vela laxantes* imply that their home was not on the European mainland; and was therefore in Britain.

93.2 ALAMANNI: see **G** AC Daniel, Budic, and p. 130 below.

94.1 AELLE: SC 477 (= c. 456); see **P**.

94.2 ARUN: cf. Map 6, p. 107.

94.3 ESSEX: see **S**; the sites by Tilbury appear to belong to the first settlement of the 420s, and are exceptional, remote from inland Essex.

95.1 SEALS: PSA 22, 1863, 235 cf. 87; cf. *Arch. Jl.* 16, 38; the objects, probably seals, contain about 75% tin and 25% lead.

95.2 SURVIVORS: Gildas 25–26.

95.2 LAST DEFEAT: Gildas 2 *postrema patriae victoria*; cf. 26, 1 *novissimaeque ferme de furciferis non minimae stragis*.

95.2 NENNIUS: 43, conclusion of the first account, after Vortimer's victories, cf. 56.

95.3 AMBROSIUS: see **P**.

95.3   ARTHUR: see **P**.

95.3   COMMANDER: *tunc Arthur pugnabat . . . cum regibus Brittonum, sed ipse dux erat bellorum* Nennius 56.

96.2   WELSH POEMS: see **T**.

96.2   GERMAN CAVALRY: see E.A.Thompson *The Early Germans*, especially pp. 127–130, with texts there cited; cf. *P and P* 14, 1958, 2 ff.

96.2   ENGLISH . . . HORSES: Procopius BG 8, 20, 28.

96.3   ARMORICAN CAVALRY: see **G** AC 520 Budic, 550 Conomorus, and p. 258 below.

96.3   ONE POEM: *Marwnad Gereint,* cited p. 104 below.

96.3   ECDICIUS: Sidonius *Ep.* 3, 3, 3–8. Sidonius was Ecidicius' brother-in-law, and was therefore well-informed. The story is reproduced by Greg. Tur. HF 2, 24, where the words *et octo* have fallen from the text. See PLRE 2; for the date, cf. C.E.Stevens *Sidonius Apollinaris* 202.

98.2   COMBROGI: not *Combroges* Jackson WHR Special Number 1963, 85; cf. p. 41 above.

98.2   COMBERTON: see **N**.

99.2   CADBURY CASTLE: see **L**, and p. 137 below.

100.2   AMBROSIUS . . . NAME: see **P** and **N**. Discordant explanations advanced by various editors of older EPNS volumes include several types of plants and birds and the alleged personal name of an 'archaic Vandal'.

102.1   EXCAVATION . . . GROUPS: see **S**, and Map 5.

102.1   DUNSTABLE: *Beds. Arch. Jl.* 1, 1962, 40, C.L.Matthews *Ancient Dunstable* 71.

103.2   PEVENSEY: SC 491 (=c. 470).

103.3   WEST SAXON ENTRIES: see **G** EW; **T**, SC; cf. p. 323 below.

104.3   PORT: SC 501 (=c. 480).

104.4   GERAINT: BBC 71–72 (folios xxxvi a–b), RBH 1042 ff., cf. FAB 1, 266 ff.; 2, 37 and 274; translated WBT 43.

106.3   OESC: see **G** EK and **B**.

106.3   THE SAXONS: Nennius 56.

106.3   THE KINGS: cf. p. 272 below.

106.3   ANGEL EMPTY: Bede HE 1, 15; Nennius 38.

109.1   SURREY: see **S**.

109.3   DYKES: cf. Fox ACR ed. 1948 Appendix iv, p. 123.

110.1   HASLINGFIELD: EPNS Cambridgeshire 77, where the inferred name **Haesela* is a variant of Esla. Other Eslingas settled at Essendon near Hertford (EPNS 233) and at Eslington near Alnwick, in Bernicia, (DEPN 169), both probably in or after the late 6th century. See **S**, and **N**.

111.5   NENNIUS . . . POEM: Nennius 56, see **T**. The sites are 1, the river Glen; 2–5, the river Douglas in Lindsey; 6, the river Bassas; 7, Celidon Forest; 8, Fort Guinnion; 9, the City of the Legion; 10, the river Tribruit; 11, Agned Hill, or Bregion; 12, Badon Hill.

112.5   BADON: see **B**.

114.3   RICH GOTH: Theodoric the Great, cited in *Anonymus Valesianus* 61 (12).

7   The Peace of Arthur (pp. 116–141)

116.1   ARTHUR: see **P**.

116.2   POET: Aneirin *Gododdin* 1241–2.

116.2   HEIRS OF . . . ARTHUR: cf. p. 242 below.

116.2   NAME OF ARTHUR: the name of Arthur was given to their sons by Aedan of Dal Riada and his son Conang; Peter of Demetia; Pabo of the Pennines

(G IDR; BD; BN); by Coscrach of Leinster (CGH 78 R 125 a 41); and by Bicoir the Briton, probably of the Clyde, Annals 626. All these children were born and named in the mid or late 6th century; no other child is known to have been named Arthur for 500 years, until after the diffusion of the Norman romances.

The name of Arthur, father of Ascelin, whose land at Caen William the Conqueror appropriated about 1070 (Ordericus Vitalis 7, 13), suggests that tales were told of Arthur in Normandy at least a hundred years before the composition of the oldest known Norman romances of the Arthurian Cycle. There are also three or four Arthurs in DB.

The letters ARTR, inscribed on ECMW 287, probably about 700 AD, Jackson LHEB 668 note 1, are however not likely to represent the name Arthur.

117.2   RULERS: Gildas 26, 2.

117.3   ARTHUR LEGEND: see **P**.

118.1   PEREDUR: see **G** BN 560.

118.1   TRISTAN: see **G** AC 550 Conomorus, Drustanus; cf. *P and P* 11, 1957, 15–16.

118.2   PRINCE CONSORT: Tennyson *Idylls of the King*, dedication.

119.2   GREAT JEOPARDY: Malory *Morte d'Arthur* 1, 5.

119.2   IN THIS REALM: Malory *Morte d'Arthur* 20, 17.

119.2   SIR BORS: Tennyson *Holy Grail* 702 ff.

119.2   ARTHUR'S KINGDOM: R.L.Green *King Arthur* p. 11.

120.2   CERTAIN TYRANT: *vita Paterni* 21.

120.2   BUT LO: *vita Cadoc*, prologue. The hill 'Bochriu Carn' is Fochriw *SO 10 05*, cf. Map 7, p. 128 and notes thereto.

120.3   GREAT GENERAL: *vita Cadoc* 22. The place is named 'Tref Redinauc', now Tredunnock, *ST 37 94*, cf. Map 7, p. 128 and notes thereto.

121.2   CATO AND ARTHUR: *vita prima Carantoci* 4.

121.2   CUILL: *vita Gildas* (Caradoc) 5, Hueil; cf. *vita Gildas* (Rhuys) 2, Cuillus; cf. **G** BAB. Linguistically, Cwyl evolves from Coel.

121.2   ILLTUD: *vita Iltuti* 2.

122.3   GILDAS . . . SIXTH CENTURY SPELLING: *Beatus Gildas Arecluta . . . oriundus, patre Cauuo* (misread as *Cauno* MGH) vita Gildas (Rhuys) 1; the names are 'clearly . . . sixth century . . . from contemporary manuscripts' LHEB 42, cf. 306, 307.

123.3   DUMNONIAN POEM: see p. 104 above.

123.3   NENNIUS POEM: Nennius 56, see **T** and p. 111.

123.4   DYFNWAL: see **G** BA and BNM.

124.2   MARIANUS: see **G** BGM.

124.2   INSCRIPTIONS: see **P** Cauuus. The relevant stones are

    1 ECMW 282 Llanfor *SH 94 36*, near the Roman fort of Caer Gai. CIIC 417.

       Cavo[s] Seniargii [filius] (hic iacit)

    Possible variant readings *Cavoseni Argii* or *Cavos Eniargii*

    Date: 5th to early 6th ECMW; early to mid 6th LHEB 521. The stone is extant.

    2 ECMW 283 Caer Gai *SH 87 31*. CIIC 418.

    Hic iacet Salvianus Burgo Cavi, filius Cupetian[i]

    Possible variant readings: *hec* for *hic*; *Burso* for *Burgo*.

    Date: 5th to early 6th ECMW; not noticed LHEB. The stone is lost; the reading derives from a 17th-century copy.

    3 ECMW 284 Llan-y-mawddwy *SH 90 19*, seven miles south of Caer Gai. CIIC 419.

    Filiae Salvia[n]- hic iacit Ve . . . maie uxsor Tigirnici et filie eius Onerat- [uxsor ia]cit Rigohene [mater? . . .]ocet- [et? . . .]ac-

Possible variant readings: *Verimate, Vetti[a] Maie*; [*hic iac*]*it Rigohene*.

Date: 6th century ECMW; not noticed LHEB. The stone is lost; 18th century reading reproduced ECMW.

4 ECMW 285 Tomen-y-mur *SH 70 38*, the next Roman fort on the road from Caer Gai to Caernarvon. CIIC p. 397.

D M Barrect- Carantei

Date: 5th ECMW, apparently solely on the basis of the formula DM; not noticed LHEB. The stone is lost; the reading is 19th century.

5 CIIC 514 Liddel Water, Roxburgh, between Newcastleton *NY 48 87* and Hawick *NY 56 96*. PSAS 70, 1935–6, 33.

Hic iacit Caranti fili Cupitiani

Date: late 5th to early 6th LHEB 290. The stone is extant.

6 CIIC 510 Kirkliston *NT 12 74*, 8 miles west of Edinburgh.

In [h]oc tumulo iacit Vett[i]a f[ilia] Victr[ici?]

Possible variant readings: *Vettr; Vict[o]r[is]*.

Date: early 6th LHEB 407. The stone is extant; it was found in a long cist cemetery.

Notes

1 and 2. *Burgo Cavi*, placed between the name of Salvianus and of his father, is not a personal name; it should indicate the place to which he belonged. *Burgus* is the normal late western Latin for a small fort, in this case 'the fort of Cavos'. Since Cavos is buried nearby, he is likely to have been the person who named the fort.

2 and 5; 4 and 5. The personal names Carant(e)us and Cupetianus are both otherwise unrecorded in these centuries in Britain; it is therefore improbable that two pairs of different people bore the names in the same context.

3 and 6. Vettius is a Roman family, not otherwise known in Britain in these centuries; the restoration is uncertain, but if it was inscribed on both stones, it suggests the likelihood that the persons were related.

The Persons

If the three pairs of people who have the same name were identical, as seems probable, the relations between them are

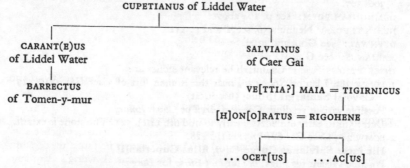

All dates suggested for British inscriptions of the 5th and following centuries rest upon somewhat fragile assumptions; but those advanced for these stones are consistent with the relationships that the stones report, except for the date given to the lost Barrectus stone, on the basis of a formula not otherwise known. The deaths of both sons of Cupetianus are placed '5th to early 6th'; Salvianus' descendants are allotted to the 6th century. Cupetianus' lifetime should therefore be mid to late 5th century. The stones suggest that Salvianus moved from his father's homeland, on the borders of the Selgovae and the Votadini, to central Wales, about the end of the fifth century; and that his nephew accompanied or followed him, while his daughter may have used the same family name as a native of the Edinburgh region.

Salvianus was an approximate, perhaps a younger contemporary of Cavos, who named the fort where he lived and died in Merioneth. A text in 6th-century spelling names a Cauuus, father of Gildas; his home was north of the Clyde, but his son was in Wales, in infancy, by about the year 500 (see p. 205.3). A late, but quite independent genealogical tradition lists half a dozen relatives of Gildas, two of them in or near Roman forts within ten miles of Caer Gai, the rest elsewhere in mid Wales, at Caersws, Clyro and near Abergavenny (G BAB).

Each separate strand of evidence bristles with uncertainties. They combine to suggest a migration from the lands of the Votadini and their neighbours to Merioneth and mid Wales at about the time when Cunedda's nephew Marianus is said to have moved from Votadinian territory to name Merioneth; and at a time when the lands by and south of Forth and Clyde are said to have obeyed Dyfnwal, apparently a firm ally of Arthur. The context suggests that the movement was Arthur's answer to renewed Irish attacks, matching the Demetian campaign in the south (p. 126).

124.3   FERGUS: see **G** IDR and p. 180 below.

125.1   CUNORIX, EBICATOS: see **P** and p. 137 below; for the dates, see **O** and **P**.

125.1   SILCHESTER: Ebicatos may have had a neighbour or successor, noteworthy in his own day. Berkshire is the shire of Barruc or Berroc, and until the 12th century the woodland in the south-east of the county, north of Hungerford and including the early English area about East Shefford, bore the same name; Asser (ch. 1) in the 9th century supposed that the county was named from the woodland. 'Barruc' is a pre-English regional name, and is commonly derived from British *barr* (top), with locative suffix -*aco*-. But, since elsewhere in Britain 'Barrock' names normally refer to single hilltops, and since British regional names that are not of Roman origin often derive from 5th- or 6th-century rulers, an alternative possibility is that Barruc was the personal name of a local lord, either of Silchester or of a small territory on its north-eastern border. If so, the name is probably Irish, cf. **L**.

125.1   CYNRIC: see **G** EW and p. 225 below.

125.2   CATWALLAUN: see **G** BGG and p. 168 below.

125.2   ILLAN: see **G** ILD and p. 168 below.

125.3   KIDWELLY: see Nennius 14, cf. p. 158 below.

125.3   DEMETIA: the dynasty were of the Ui Liathain, not of the Dessi, see **G** BD and p. 158 below.

126.2   BRYCHAN: See **G** BB and texts in VSBG and EWGT.

126.4   THEODORIC: see **P**. The significance of the name is easily overlooked because the Welsh form, Tewdrig, superficially resembles Tewdwr, which transliterates Theodore and is Englished as Tudor. There is no direct relationship between Germanic Theude-ric and Greek Theo-dorus. Tewdrig's Germanic ancestry is confirmed by the name of his father, Theudebald, transcribed in the Brychan documents as 'Teithfallt', or in similar spellings.

127.1   NAMED PLACES: see note to Map 7, p. 128. The distances are Brecon (Llan Maes) to Lan Semin 24 miles; thence to Methrum 28 miles; thence to Caer Farchell 31 miles (to Porth Mawr 35 miles).

127.1   LLAN MARCHELL: the name should normally denote the monastery of a monk named Marcellus, but might mean a monastery established at a place already named after Marcellus. In North Wales a Marcellus or Marcella named Llanmarchell, the old name of Denbigh; Ystrad Marchell near Welshpool; and Capel Marchell in Llanrwst, LBS 3, 438, but there is no trace of a monastic Marcellus in South Wales.

129.1   BOIA: see **P** and **E** David.

130.2   TRIGG: see **G** BB.

130.2   BROCAGNUS: CIIC 478 cf. **G** BB.

130.2   FINGAR: see **E** Fingar, Guiner and **P** Theodoric.

130.2   CORNISH PARISHES: see Map 25, p. 362.

130.3   BUDIC ... MAXENTIUS: see **G** AC and p. 93.

132.3   RECTORES: Gildas 1, 14; for *speculator* in the meaning of bishop, not here relevant, see AB 76, 1958, 379.

133.2   MASUNA: Dessau ILS 859.

133.2   ARMORICA: Greg. Tur. HF 4, 4, cf. p. 251.3 below.

133.3   AMERAUDUR: e.g. BBC 72, 9 cited p. 104 above.

133.3   VORTIPOR: see **G** BD.

133.4   IUDICES: see p. 201 below.

133.4   MAGISTRATUS: ECMW 103.

135.2   RECTORES: Gildas 1, 14; cf. p. 132 above.

136.1   DIVORTIO: Gildas 10, 2.

136.1   KEMPSTON: see **S** and Map 18, p. 285. These sites will be better understood when 'small long' brooches have been more closely studied.

137.1   CITIES: Gildas 26, 2 *sed ne nunc quidem, ut antea, civitates patriae inhabitantur; sed desertae dirutaeque hactenus squalent*; cf. **T**.

137.1   JEROME: *Ep.* 1, 3; the city of Vercellae in northern Italy was in 370 *raro habitatore semiruta*; but its decay did not prevent a consular governor from holding his court in the city.

137.1   WROXETER: *Ant. Jl.* 48, 1968, 296, cf. **P** Cunorix, cf. p. 125 above.

137.1   SILCHESTER: CIIC 496 cf. **P** Ebicatos, cf. p. 125 above. Local tradition also named a former supposed ruler whose name may possibly have been British. Camden's *Britannia* 1, 222 (Gough) reported that local people gave the name 'Onion's pennies' to Silchester Roman coins, 'fancying this Onion a great giant who formerly lived in this city'. I am grateful to Mr K.R.Davies, who drew my attention to this statement and to the possibility that 'Onion' might derive from the Welsh name En(n)iaun.

137.2   VERULAMIUM, MAGIOVINIUM: unpublished, see **L**.

137.2   LATE CEMETERIES: see **M**.

137.2   COLCHESTER, YORK, LONDON see **L**.

137.3   CADBURY CASTLE: *ST 62 26* in South Cadbury parish, to be distinguished from nearby North Cadbury, and also from Cadbury, near Congresbury, *ST 43 64*, south-west of Bristol. The site has been dubbed 'Camelot' by antiquarians from the 16th century to the 20th; though not Camelot, it was an important fortress of the Arthurian period, cf. *Ant. Jl.* 47, 1967, 70; 48, 1968, 6; 49, 1969, 30; 50, 1970, 14; 51, 1971, 1; *Ant.* 41, 1967, 50; 42, 1968, 47; 43, 1969, 52; 44, 1970, 46.

139.2   WALES ... TRIBUTE: see p. 220.3.

139.2   NO NEW EMPEROR: later traditions name two sons of Arthur, but do not regard either of them as rulers of any territory, cf. **P** Arthur.

140.3   CAMLANN: ACm 537 cf. **A**.

140.3   MEDRAUT: see **G** BLS, and **P**. The only other record of the name Medraut is BYS 51, Dyfnauc Sant m. Medraut; Dyfnauc (Domnoc) is a common name, but the only 6th or 7th century Domnoc known in Britain named Dunwich in Suffolk, Bede HE 2, 15.

141.2   WILLIAM OF MALMESBURY: *de Gestis Regum* 1, 8.

INDEX

Italic figures refer to the notes.

An asterisk (*) indicates a note on the name or word concerned.

The letters f (*filius*) and m (*mac* or *map*) mean 'son of'; f. means 'following'.

Modern conventions on the spelling of names vary, and are often arbitrary; thus, Aethelbert or Ethelbert are nowadays equally familiar, Athelbert unfamiliar, but Athelstan prevails over Ethelstan or Aethelstan. The most recognisable form is normally used. Irish names are normally given in plain English spelling.